READERS' GUIDES TO ESSENTIAL CRITICISM SERI

CONSULTANT EDITOR: NICOLAS TREDELL

Elmer Kennedy-Andrews	The Poetry of Seamus Heaney
Daniel Lea	George Orwell: *Animal Farm/Nineteen Eighty-Four*
Rachel Lister	Alice Walker: *The Color Purple*
Sara Lodge	Charlotte Brontë: *Jane Eyre*
Philippa Lyon	Twentieth-Century War Poetry
Merja Makinen	The Novels of Jeanette Winterson
Stephen Marino	Arthur Miller: *Death of a Salesman/The Crucible*
Britta Martens	The Poetry of Robert Browning
Matt McGuire	Contemporary Scottish Literature
Timothy Milnes	Wordsworth: *The Prelude*
Jago Morrison	The Fiction of Chinua Achebe
Merritt Moseley	The Fiction of Pat Barker
Pat Pinsent	Children's Literature
Carl Plasa	Toni Morrison: *Beloved*
Carl Plasa	Jean Rhys: *Wide Sargasso Sea*
Nicholas Potter	Shakespeare: *Antony and Cleopatra*
Nicholas Potter	Shakespeare: *Othello*
Nicholas Potter	Shakespeare's Late Plays: *Pericles/Cymbeline/ The Winter's Tale/The Tempest*
Steven Price	The Plays, Screenplays and Films of David Mamet
Berthold Schoene-Harwood	Mary Shelley: *Frankenstein*
Nicholas Seager	The Rise of the Novel
Nick Selby	T. S. Eliot: *The Waste Land*
Nick Selby	Herman Melville: *Moby Dick*
Nick Selby	The Poetry of Walt Whitman
David Smale	Salman Rushdie: *Midnight's Children/The Satanic Verses*
Enit Steiner	Jane Austen: *Northanger Abbey/Persuasion*
Patsy Stoneman	Emily Brontë: *Wuthering Heights*
Susie Thomas	Hanif Kureishi
Nicolas Tredell	Joseph Conrad: *Heart of Darkness*
Nicolas Tredell	Charles Dickens: *Great Expectations*
Nicolas Tredell	William Faulkner: *The Sound and the Fury/As I Lay Dying*
Nicolas Tredell	F. Scott Fitzgerald: *The Great Gatsby*
Nicolas Tredell	Shakespeare: *A Midsummer Night's Dream*
Nicolas Tredell	Shakespeare: *Macbeth*
Nicolas Tredell	Shakespeare: The Tragedies
Nicolas Tredell	The Fiction of Martin Amis
David Wheatley	Contemporary British Poetry
Martin Willis	Literature and Science
Matthew Woodcock	Shakespeare: *Henry V*
Gillian Woods	Shakespeare: *Romeo and Juliet*
Angela Wright	Gothic Fiction
Michael Whitworth	Virginia Woolf: *Mrs Dalloway*
Andrew Wyllie and Catherine Rees	The Plays of Harold Pinter
Forthcoming	
Dana Aspinall	Shakespeare: As You Like It

Readers' Guides to Essential Criticism
Series Standing Order ISBN 978–1–4039–0108–8
(outside North America only)

You can receive future titles in this series as they are published by placing a standing order. Please contact your bookseller or, in the case of difficulty, write to us at the address below with your name and address, the title of the series and the ISBN quoted above. Customer Services Department, Macmillan Distribution Ltd, Houndmills, Basingstoke, Hampshire, RG21 6XS, UK

Brian Friel

SCOTT BOLTWOOD

Consultant Editor: Nicolas Tredell

 macmillan international HIGHER EDUCATION

 palgrave

First published 2018 by
Palgrave

Palgrave in the UK is an imprint of Macmillan Publishers Limited, registered in England, company number 785998, of 4 Crinan Street, London N1 9XW.

Palgrave® and Macmillan® are registered trademarks in the United States, the United Kingdom, Europe and other countries.

ISBN 978–1–137–52305–1 hardback
ISBN 978–1–137–52304–4 paperback

A catalogue record for this book is available from the British Library.

A catalog record for this book is available from the Library of Congress.

For Saul and Ananda

CONTENTS

Surveys the background, context, and influences behind Friel's first international success. It then reviews the interpretations of the play's ground-breaking splitting of the main character into two characters as a way to dramatize inner thoughts. Finally, it looks at discussions of memory, music, emigration, and oedipal struggle in a play that is seen as having given voice to a new generation of playwrights.

Explores a group of plays sharing a focus on love and memory. Although Friel experiments with unexpected settings and character motivations, the chapter focuses on the playwright's dramaturgical maturation, leading to his first overtly political play.

Explores how in these plays Friel sought to infuse his fascination with memory and family drama with such national issues as history and the country's rapid modernization. It also focuses on how these plays portray the violence and culture of violence associated with The Troubles.

Examines two plays that mark a turning point in Friel's career, where he develops a more pronounced ability to construct Chekhovian family dynamics. It focuses on the first of Friel's three great plays of 1979–1980, *Aristocrats*, where he skilfully explores the burdens of family, history, class, and ambition.

Surveys the many and diverse critical responses to the play that many have identified as Friel's masterpiece. It reviews the proposed sources and development of the play, and the work's exploration of memory, artistic inspiration, ritual, and love.

Considers the play that redefined Friel's career, establishing him as the decade's preeminent playwright. It looks at how the play's overt incorporation of theories of language create a multi-layered exploration of two cultures in conflict, each seeking to translate the other. It also surveys the debates that arose over Friel's representation of history, his adaption of historical sources, and the play's view of Irish nationalism.

Looks at the plays written for Field Day, a Northern Irish theatre company that Friel established in 1980. In the wake of the critical controversies created by *Translations*, these works allowed Friel to explore more fully his views of how the confluence of language, history, and politics structure daily lives.

Explores Friel's most loved and most staged work. It considers how Friel mines the lives of his mother and aunts to explore the social disruptions that beset Ireland as it became a newly independent state. It examines the conflicts between desire and social *mores*, religion and spirituality, and memory and history. Finally, it surveys the many discussions of the play's diverse use of dance as an expression of these tensions.

Presents the diverse responses to this decade's plays, united only by their setting in contemporary Ireland. It explores Friel's critique of contemporary Ireland as a nation whose unprecedented economic success has materially enriched the country yet engendered existential crisis among its citizens.

Considers Friel's plays written amid declining health and the search for a defining artistic statement. It considers his unexpected decision to set plays in Central Europe and Russia, as he explores the intersection between artistic inspiration and personality. Finally, it looks at his last play, set in Ireland, and its treatment of class, art, oedipal conflict, and the scientific justification of colonialism.

Considers the playwright's legacy following his death in 2015. It also considers how and why the critical focus might change in the years to follow.

INTRODUCTION

As of this writing, the Palgrave series of *Readers' Guides to Essential Criticism* includes two other guides on contemporary playwrights: one on the works of Tom Stoppard (2003) and the other on the works of David Mamet (2008). With the inclusion of this volume on Brian Friel, we should recognize some important commonalities. For example, each of these playwrights emerged in the second half of the twentieth century as the dominant dramatist of his nation: Ireland, the United Kingdom, and the United States. Although all three have written many innovative works, each of them has had numerous plays that have become popular throughout the entire English-speaking world. Such plays as Friel's *Dancing at Lughnasa* (1990), Stoppard's *Arcadia* (1993), and Mamet's *Glengarry Glen Ross* (1983) are all frequently staged and are part of school curricula throughout the English-speaking world, from Australia and South Africa to the United States and the British Isles. Similarly, this selection of one Irishman, one Englishman, and one American recognizes the dominant role each has played in the theatre trends of his nation, even though each country can be characterized as rich in playwrights representing a diverse spectrum of ethnicities, gender positions, religions, and backgrounds.

Moreover, the two elder playwrights—Friel and Stoppard—similarly enjoyed worldwide success in the mid-1960s with plays that combined radically innovative staging practices and nearly unprecedented box-office success: Friel's *Philadelphia, Here I Come!* (1964) and Stoppard's *Rosencrantz and Guildenstern are Dead* (1966). While Mamet's career has expanded to include novels, poetry, screenplays, and film directing, Friel and Stoppard are still primarily thought of as playwrights, and they have repeatedly reinvented their careers with important theatrical works in the 1970s, 1980s, 1990s, and 2000s. In Friel's case, aside from short fiction early in his career and theatre direction late, his reputation as a world dramatist rests upon several plays. Such works as *Philadelphia, Here I Come!* (1964), *Faith Healer* (1979), *Translations* (1980), and *Dancing at Lughnasa* (1990) have been used to represent the best of contemporary drama in surveys of English literature or world drama; similarly, they continue to be widely staged both by repertory companies and the most important commercial theatres in Dublin, London, and New York. Within Ireland, Friel is now recognized as the unrivalled playwright of the second half of the twentieth century, and his emergence in the early 1960s is universally treated as a turning point for Irish drama. Indeed, when considering Friel's very early stated hope that he could someday write 'the great Irish play', most critics would argue only over whether he fulfilled his ambition three or four times.

Friel's career spanned fifty years, from his two radio plays of 1958 to his last stage drama in 2008, and he wrote more than thirty works overall: twenty full-length, original plays, six translations or adaptions, seven one-act plays ranging from fifteen minutes to more than an hour, three screenplays, and two radio plays. In addition, this book will briefly survey his important fiction of the late 1950s and early 1960s: more than 100 essay/stories for newspapers and thirty conventional short stories. This large body of literature has been the subject of critical analysis for more than forty years; not only has his work been discussed in well over 200 articles and book chapters published in Ireland, England, and the United States (not to mention Japan, Taiwan, Brazil, France, and Hungary), but there are well over twenty monographs and essay collections devoted solely to his career.[1]

While the reader of this Guide will certainly recognize the importance of several themes that various critics have identified as important to an understanding of Friel's work (such as his explorations of Love, History, Language, Politics, Oedipal Relationships, or Sororal narratives), I have opted for a chronological survey of Friel's career instead of a thematic one as creating the most comprehensive and coherent view of each play's critical history. Moreover, when confronting such an innovative and, at times, controversial playwright and the immense body of criticism that has quickly emerged, some areas will remain beyond the scope of this work. First, since Friel's fame rests upon his drama, I will necessarily only briefly survey the critical responses to his prose. While I will point my reader to the criticism and, in subsequent chapters, recognize the relationships of some plays to earlier stories, my treatment of his stories will explicate the criticism only of two that are most relevant to his career as playwright. Second, except in rare circumstances where the theatre reviews are of particular importance to a play's critical history, this book will ignore the many reviews of premieres, transfers, or notable revivals published in Belfast, Dublin, London, and New York newspapers. However, I frequently point the reader to the valuable summaries of reviews that can be found in the books of such critics as Ulf Dantanus, Anthony Roche, and Maria Szasz.

CHAPTER ONE

Early Journalism and Stories

Journalism, 1957–1963

Although Friel became a theatre sensation in 1964 with *Philadelphia, Here I Come!*, he spent the latter half of the 1950s and early 1960s becoming increasingly well known as a writer of newspaper articles and short fiction. His very first story, 'The Child,' appeared in the Irish literary journal *The Bell* in 1952, but he was not published again until he began writing for two Dublin-based newspapers: *The Irish Times*, for which he wrote seventy-six pieces between September 1957 and May 1962, and the *Irish Press*, for which he wrote fifty-nine between April 1962 and August 1963. This body of 135 articles, amounting to approximately 150,000 words, represents an immense corpus from the writer's early career; however, since newspaper pieces were never republished in book form, listed in bibliographies, or included in the Friel Papers (the archive housed in the National Library of Ireland), this material escaped scholarly attention until 1999.

In surveying the *Irish Press* pieces in 'Meet Brian Friel', the first article on them (1999), George O'Brien recognizes that these works are important to understanding Friel's ideological evolution largely because they provide a rare view of the writer's personal opinions and experiences:

■ These articles reveal a different Friel from the dispassionate, unobtrusive narrator of the short stories and the invisible orchestrator—everywhere present and nowhere seen—of the plays. Friel is typically at the centre of whatever event a particular column depicts, a Friel of outspoken opinions, a Friel who readily divulges biographical information. (31) □

However, in O'Brien's opinion, the bulk of his *Irish Press* columns 'do not significantly alter' our view of Friel's early career and should serve only to help us better chart his emergence as a playwright.

Conversely, in two critical treatments of the newspaper pieces—a chapter in my 2009 book and my 2014 article in the *Irish University Review*—I argue that these works cause us 'to alter the accepted view of Friel's career' ('Mildly Eccentric', 306). In my analysis of the seventy-six *Irish Times* pieces, I seek to redefine how the critical community should view Friel's newspaper work. Rather than referring to them as 'articles', I argue that these pieces should be viewed as early examples of 'flash fiction' that have broad similarities to Jorge Luis Borges' 'essay/stories' of the same period, works that blur the traditional distinctions between 'reliable reportage' and 'blatant fiction' (311). Indeed, I explore how creating a *sui generis* writing style between fiction and journalism allowed Friel the freedom to lampoon police intimidation, electoral gerrymandering, and the pressures for social conformity in Northern Ireland.

By looking at such *Irish Times* essays as 'After the Catastrophe', 'Stalked by the Police', and 'Now about these rats...' in my book, I delineate Friel's 'psychological traumas of citizenship ... on the wrong side of the border in the north of Ireland, an area where he feels at once both native and alien' (*Brian Friel*, 17). Exploring Friel's alienation from both Northern Ireland and the southern Republic of Ireland, an area he frequently visits, I use these articles to argue for a crisis in the young writer's political identity and his disillusionment with both Irish states.

Finally, in both book chapter and article, I consider the relevance of this journalism to Friel's identity as playwright. For example, in the newspaper article 'It's a Long Way to Dublin', Friel 'recounts the long trip from Derry to Dublin with his family, a journey taxing both emotionally and physically', yet he fails to inform his audience that the trip was undertaken to see the premiere of his play *The Enemy Within* at the Abbey Theatre (*Brian Friel*, 15). More significantly, though the *Irish Press* publishes ten instalments of Friel's 'American Diary' from April through June 1963, in none of these does he even mention in passing that he is in America solely to learn the craft of theatre with the renowned Northern Irish director Tyrone Guthrie, who had invited Friel to observe the rehearsals for the inaugural season of Tyrone Guthrie's theatre in Minneapolis, Minnesota (15–16, 34–38).

While most of the newspaper stories force the reader to expand and redefine the nature of the mid-century Irish story, twelve of the *Irish Times* pieces and five of those in the *Irish Press* are written as conventional short fictions. For example, 'Conversation in a Bus' (*Irish Times*, 7 March 1961) presents the debate between two uneducated, working-class Irishmen, arguing about whether the new state hospital is safe for Irish nationalists. 'Marching with the Nation by Howard B. Hedges, Junior' (*Irish Press*, 19 January 1963) tells the story of an American Midwesterner who discovers 'Moral Rearmament or something, and all ... those Commies and guys, and the rest of us standing up against them'. In short, Friel's career as a story writer emerged through his journalism.

Story Stories, 1959–65

Friel first became known internationally as a writer of stories for the *New Yorker*, which published twelve of his stories between 1959 and 1965. Eventually, he collected thirty-one of his stories, published in the *New Yorker* and other journals such as *House Wife* and *U.S. Catholic*, into two volumes, *The Saucer of Larks* (1962) and *The Gold in the Sea* (1966). In 1979, he selected ten as a core corpus under the title *Selected Stories* published in 1979 with an introduction by Seamus Deane. While the perceived significance of his stories has never rivalled that of his plays, the stories have nonetheless continued to interest both scholars and general readers alike. In his survey essay in *The Irish Short Story* (1984), Robert Hogan describes 'Ginger Hero' and 'The Death of a Scientific Humanist' as 'among the finest of postwar stories' from Ireland (187). Richard Rankin Russell has pointed out (2012, 323) that Friel is represented in such recent anthologies as *The Penguin Book of Irish Fiction* (1999), which includes 'Foundry House', and *The Oxford Book of Irish Short Stories* (2010), which includes 'The Diviner'.

Many of the critics who have written books about Friel's drama have started their studies discussing the short stories and the young writer's transition from fiction to drama. The first book-length treatment of Friel, written by D.E.S. Maxwell in 1973, devotes its first third to a survey of eleven stories. Maxwell wrote his book in the tense early days of the Troubles as the Civil Rights Movement in Northern Ireland of the 1960s was overtaken by the sectarian strife remembered in the Battle of the Bogside (August 1969), Bloody Sunday (January 1972), and many other outrages in the 1970s and 1980s. Thus, he carefully sought to shield the Northern Irish playwright from any association with political sectarianism. He repeatedly asserts that Friel's stories are 'social…not narrowly political', 'not out…to incite political action' (17, 30).

Maxwell's survey of eleven stories is second in scope only to Elmer Andrews' analysis of eighteen in his 1995 book. Andrews supplely seeks to explore the many facets of 'the tension between the ideal and the real' in these works (35), and his extensive analysis allows him to categorize and discuss Friel's numerous stories about animals, fathers and sons, and encounters with the 'Other' in its various forms. Ultimately, though much has been published on Friel's stories, the work of Maxwell and Andrews still largely defines the general terms of discussion of the stories' themes and characteristics.

In his *Brian Friel* (1990), George O'Brien's analysis of ten stories offers one of the most thorough treatments. In such statements as 'Friel speaks for a culture, not a polity', O'Brien echoes Maxwell's general attempt to shield the author from the politics of the Troubles, and he more carefully dissects Friel's attempt to 'studiously avoid the Border' in his stories which take place in both the Republic's County Donegal and Northern Ireland's counties Derry/Londonderry and Tyrone (7). Indeed, for O'Brien the Border in Friel's fiction does not reflect a division separating two political orders; rather, it reflects longstanding differences between cultures within Ireland:

■ The divisions are between different areas of life. One area is the world of work, duty, and the discipline of family structure, and has the general label Tyrone. The other is a world of play and the relaxation of family constraints—an asocial world. This is generally known as Donegal. (8) □

Richard Rankin Russell's 2012 article 'Brian Friel's Short Fiction: Place, Community, and Modernity' emphasizes that an exploration of 'Friel's theory of place' is still both a relevant and rich topic of analysis (302). While attentive to the conventional thematic division between the rural and urban in these stories, Russell is particularly interested in exploring these fictional communities as in states of 'flux', culturally evolving because of 'modernity's encroachment into that region' (306).

Maxwell is also the first to situate Friel's stories in relation to those by Frank O'Connor (1903–66), the dominant Irish short story writer of the mid-twentieth century, though he recognizes that Friel's regional concerns would be distinct from those of O'Connor's Cork. Nonetheless, in Friel's understated language, psychological characterizations, and general subject matter, many writers have seen O'Connor as both a model and an inhibiting influence on the young writer. In his survey, 'The Contemporary Irish Short Story', Robert Hogan describes Friel as 'something of a rural, Northern O'Connor' (Hogan 1984, 187), while Richard Pine claims that Friel eventually abandoned the story because he 'owed too much to the influence of a master like Frank O'Connor' and could never break free of his influence (Pine 1999, 92). In his book's detailed treatment of the stories, Elmer Andrews carefully explores Friel as the stylistic heir of both mid-century story writers Frank O'Connor and Sean O'Faolain, one of O'Connor's most influential contemporaries (8–10). As recently as 2011, Anthony Roche claims that Friel himself '[concluded] that he would never produce anything beyond what Frank O'Connor had achieved' and thus abandoned fiction for drama (3). In most discussions, O'Connor's influence is assumed rather than demonstrated; however, Andrews is somewhat of an exception. His comprehensive exploration of the stories is introduced by an attempt to align Friel's thematic concerns with principles articulated by O'Connor in his 1962 study of the short story *The Lonely Voice* (8–9).

With almost three dozen stories in the two collections and another dozen stories only published in magazines, it is not within the purview of this survey to summarize the criticism of every story.[1] The scholarship over the last four decades has tended to concentrate on a handful of tales; indeed, most of the criticism and all the most detailed analyses focus on only four stories: 'Among the Ruins', The Diviner', 'Foundry House', and 'The Saucer of Larks'.

Not surprisingly, these are among the ten stories that Friel himself selected for inclusion in *Selected Stories* (1979), the only collection of his stories currently in print.[2]

'The Diviner', from the 1966 collection *The Gold in the Sea*, has attracted some of the most sustained interest and along with 'Foundry House' will serve as this book's examples for the critical treatment of the stories. Like 'Mr Sing My Heart's Delight' and 'The Illusionist', 'The Diviner', a story in which a water diviner finds the body of a drowned man when all others fail, focuses on the powerful emotions unleashed when an outsider enters one of Friel's isolated communities. In his introduction to *Selected Stories*, Seamus Deane seeks to describe the various aspects of the tension between the individual and society that provide the story with its complexity:

> ■ Vertically imposed upon the horizontals of class is the system of authority officially represented by the priest and unofficially by the diviner. It is a form of authority which does not derive from class although it operates within and has effects upon the class system. After science (the divers from the British naval base), and religion (Father Curran with his rosaries) and society (the organised efforts of the professional classes) have all failed, the diviner's magic takes over. (13) □

This idea of the diviner's magic, his 'mysterious gift...capable of putting the people in touch with what lies hidden' (Andrews 1995, 19) has increasingly attracted critical attention to this story. In *The Diviner* (1999), his study of the author, Richard Pine claims that throughout his career Friel himself has acted 'in the persona of the diviner' (38), just as Elmer Andrews had likened the diviner to 'the artist' in his 1995 study (19).

'Foundry House' has attracted a considerable amount of scholarship largely for two reasons: first, of all Friel's stories, it most carefully explores the tradition of the Irish Big House; second, it can be seen as an initial exploration of the themes later developed in one of his plays, *Aristocrats* (1979). As a literary theme, the Big House—a term usually referring to the cultural influence of the ruling Protestant Ascendancy in colonial Ireland—has fascinated authors from Maria Edgeworth's *Castle Rackrent* (1800) through Elizabeth Bowen's nostalgic *The Last September* (1929) to such recent works as William Trevor's *The Silence in the Garden* (1988). Critics have variously discussed how Friel uses this story to explore the nostalgic hold that the Hogans, the once-powerful local landholding family, exert on their tenant Joe Brennan. Andrews broadly establishes how 'individual speech patterns swiftly, vividly, establish character' before moving on to the specifics of how Joe's 'own sense of identity' relies upon the Hogans' past greatness (39). Likewise, Deane claims that Joe 'needs to believe' in the Hogans' continued local importance, 'and, thus the actual decrepitude of the Hogans cannot be admitted or articulated by him' (14).

'Foundry House' has also proven attractive to such recent scholars as Richard Rankin Russell and Chu He, both of whom have sought to move beyond explications of Friel's fascination with an individual's 'necessary delusion' (Russell 2012, 316). For his part, Russell seeks to explore the manner that the story takes place in the liminal space between city and the natural world. But of greater importance to Russell is the way in which the character Joe, 'a radio-and-television mechanic' who visits the Hogans to help them with the technological demands of their tape recorder, awkwardly witnesses this Big House's debilitating confrontation with Modernity (315–17). In her 'Brian Friel's Short Stories', He attempts to shift the cultural context of the story by exploring the story's reception by the American audience, which would have first encountered it in the 18 November 1961 issue of the *New Yorker*. By comparing 'Foundry House' to 'The Visitation', which was also published in 1961, He argues that 'the Irish characters are actually the mouthpiece of the Americans' who have themselves begun to romanticize Ireland in the wake of John F. Kennedy's election to the United States presidency in 1960 (51).

However, for every discussion of the story since the premiere of Friel's *Aristocrats* in 1979, the relationship of the story to the later play has been the primary subject. Both story and play focus on the rare example of a Catholic Big House and the unexpected impact of a recently received tape recording from the family's daughter, who has served as a nun in Africa for many years. Seamus Deane, in his introduction to Friel's short story collection, focuses on its relationship to the play (14–15), and in 'Donging the Tower' (1993) John Cronin gives special attention to

■ the essential distinction...between the short story's necessarily sharp focus on a single character, the subservient Joe Brennan, and the greater freedom granted by dramatic form for the searching exploration of numerous figures and many issues. (9) □

In *Brian Friel: Theatre and Politics* (2011), Anthony Roche explores how Joe, the momentary interloper into the Hogans' world, is 'split into two ... working-class outsiders from the town' in the play: Willie and Eamon (77–78). In contrast to Joe, both Willie and Eamon are intimate friends of the family, yet even they are enthralled by its past grandeur.[3]

The widespread interest in the narrative debt of *Aristocrats* to 'Foundry House' reveals the broader question that critics frequently ask: why did the young writer, who had enjoyed considerable success with his short fiction, completely abandon the art-form? Or, as Richard Rankin Russell put it in 2012:

■ In 1965, Irish playwright Brian Friel emphatically told Graham Morrison, 'I don't concentrate on the theatre at all. I live on short stories.... the short story is the basis of all the work I do.' By 1968, however, Friel had virtually stopped writing stories. To date, no critic has sufficiently explained why Friel moved from writing short fiction and drama to solely writing drama. (451) □

While recognizing the 'obvious financial reasons for Friel's attraction to writing plays', Andrews suggests that 'the move from short story to drama may be seen to represent Friel's desire to withdraw his own ego, his own voice, and to foreground, exploit and celebrate the dialogic or polyphonic nature of language' (45). Repeating assertions by Dantanus and Cronin that Friel himself felt that his stories were too dependent upon Frank O'Connor's influence (Dantanus 1988, 21; Cronin, 3), Richard Pine suggests that Friel was also wary 'of being too easily seduced by the demands of the American market' for Irish stories (92–93).[4] However, many critics merely rely upon the assumption that this period from his first published story in 1952 through the early 1960s was mere 'prentice work by a writer who had yet to discover his true medium' (Cronin, 3).

Ultimately, as in the case of 'Foundry House', the stories are frequently examined for insights into the creative processes that produced the later plays. Thus, O'Brien and McGrath discuss the debt of the 1967 play 'Losers', one of two short plays united under the title *Lovers*, to the story 'The Highwayman and the Saint' (O'Brien 1990, 25; McGrath 1999, 61). Similarly, Andrews points to 'Aunt Maggie, the Strong One' as a source for *The Loves of Cass McGuire* (35). More recently, Tony Corbett and Christopher Murray have commented on the roots of the 1990 *Dancing at Lughnasa* in 'A Man's World', a story in the collection *The Saucer of Larks* (1963). Despite his success as a writer of short fiction, Friel was increasingly drawn to writing for the theatre, and the fledgling radio plays and stage drama of the period from 1958 to 1963 are the subject of the next chapter.

CHAPTER TWO

Early and 'Withdrawn' Plays

By virtue of his success as a story writer, Friel could have been considered a promising young writer of fiction. However, Friel himself frequently stated that he 'always felt the stories were overshadowed by [Frank] O'Connor' and he 'was never satisfied' with them.[1] Thus, beginning in the late 1950s, he started to explore whether he could apply his skills elsewhere, and he looked to the theatre. However, the young Friel had no experience in theatre; the Derry of his youth had no theatre company, and in his writings or interviews Friel has never referred to any experience in amateur dramatics. Indeed, in one of his few autobiographical sketches, 'Self-Portrait' of 1972, he says,

> ■ I found myself at thirty years of age embarked on a theatrical career and almost totally ignorant of the mechanics of play-writing and play-production apart from an intuitive knowledge.[2] □

Not surprisingly, Friel's short stories initially provided him the avenue to explore drama. He had read a few of his earliest stories himself on the radio; for example, 'Pearls before Swine' was broadcast on Radio Éireann on 21 May 1956, and 'A Red, Red Rose' was broadcast on the BBC Northern Ireland Home Service on 5 April 1957. Given this familiarity with the medium, his two first plays, *A Sort of Freedom* and *To This Hard House*, were also written for the radio. While several of Friel's plays of the 1960s would later be adapted for the radio, these earliest plays were solely radio works and never staged. Writing for radio also provided him an introduction to some of the major figures of Belfast theatre: the actors in the BBC production of his first radio drama included Harold Gold-blatt, Doreen Hepburn, and Colin Blakely, who were all established stage actors with the Ulster Group Theatre, which at the time was Belfast's most successful professional theatre. In fact, the Friel Papers, the archive housed in Dublin's National Library of Ireland, contains a letter dated 5 June 1958 from Ronald Mason, who produced his plays for the BBC, stating that he had passed Friel's first stage play on to James Ellis, the Group Theatre's Artistic Director.[3]

A Sort of Freedom (1958)

In accordance with the conventions of the Northern Ireland Home Service, *A Sort of Freedom* was a 55-minute play, starting at 7pm on Thursday, 16 January 1958. The play focused on the somewhat parallel dilemmas faced by Jack Frazer, the owner of an established haulage company, and Joe Reddin, his oldest and most loyal employee. The domestic tragedy arises from both men's intransigence in the face of the pressure to conform to their era's social norms. Without offering a more compelling explanation beyond the fact that 'it doesn't seem right to me to force anyone to do a thing...against their conscience', Jack Frazer seeks to evade the health department's requirement that his newly adopted baby son be inoculated against tuberculosis.[4] After a conversation with Jack, Joe Reddin adopts his employer's devotion to the 'principle' of freedom as the basis for his opposition: 'Jack Frazer is making a stand against what he thinks is wrong for his child just as I'm making a stand against what I think is wrong for me.'[5] Eventually, despite the attempts of their friends and especially their wives, each man suffers for his truculence: Joe loses his job, because of the pressure the union places on Jack's company, and the Frazer baby dies, accidentally suffocated among his blankets.

Discussions of *A Sort of Freedom* have been limited to the books on Friel, and the early ones for that matter: as Friel's career developed and the number of his plays increased, critics found his stage plays of far greater relevance to understanding his career. The first nuanced analysis of the play did not appear until Ulf Dantanus considered it in his 1988 study, *Brain Friel*. While he finds it occasionally 'overcharged and overstated', Dantanus argues that 'the subject of individual right versus communal and societal pressures' connects it with Friel's plays of the 1980s (55). However, despite his recognition of the stylistic weaknesses that will stand out to later critics, Dantanus also admires the delicacy of the final scenes in which each couple assesses their losses. He is especially conscious of Friel's ability to juxtapose Jack's sense of personal loss with his wife's empathy for the Reddin family and her 'wider and deeper sense of loss' regarding their marriage (57). Elmer Andrews largely follows Dantanus's lead in his later study, *The Art of Brian Friel* (1995), seeing the play as a cautionary drama about inflexible personal freedom. However, Andrews' strength is in his concise alignment of the play's two wives, Rita Frazer and Mary Reddin, who effectively embody a calm practicality opposed to the 'pig-headed, irrational, self-destructive refusal to compromise' seen in the men (47).

Writing two years after Dantanus, George O'Brien in his *Brian Friel* more assertively establishes the parallels between the narratives concerning Jack Frazer and Joe Reddin, though he convincingly demonstrates that Jack manipulates the much more innocent Joe, describing him as 'a plaything of Frazer' (33). More than any other writer before or since, O'Brien also anchors the play in the world of Friel's stories, where characters fail to adapt to change and become victims of their 'capacity for self-delusion' (34). O'Brien associates the play's Joe Reddin with Joe Brennan in Friel's important story 'Foundry House', both of whom suffer because of their overly developed and idealized devotion to their social betters.

In his 2011 study, Anthony Roche briefly recognizes these established issues only to better allow his reading to dwell on the atmosphere of the play, which links it both to Sean O'Casey earlier *Juno and the Paycock* (1926) and Friel's own later *Translations* (1980). For Roche, *A Sort of Freedom* has a debt to O'Casey's consciousness of the great and ultimately foolish personal sacrifices that people make in the name of 'principle' (18). In his analysis, this foolishness is seen most not in Jack's refusal to inoculate his baby boy, because the baby's death is reported as unrelated to inoculation or otherwise, but in Joe's refusal to join the union, because his family's economic suffering at the play's end directly results from his stance against the union. Similarly, Roche quite skilfully associates offstage infant death both in *A Sort of Freedom* and *Translations* with creating the socio-political mood that defines each play.

To This Hard House (1958)

Although it was broadcast over the Northern Ireland Home Service barely three months after *A Sort of Freedom*, *To This Hard House* has very little in common with Friel's first radio drama. This play presents a much more claustrophobic story of a small family in the fictional mid-Ulster village of Meenbanid. The main conflict is between Daniel Stone and his two grown children, Fiona and Walter. Fiona is thirty-four, unhappily lives at home, and during the course of the play attempts to elope with her long-time boyfriend, though she soon returns home when he fails to show up for their rendezvous. By contrast, the play chronicles Walter's rise to professional prominence when he is appointed principal of the region's large and very modern school. Yet Daniel cannot be proud of his son, because his own one-room school is on the verge of closure as the modern schools have lured his students away. Thus, the play ends with Daniel forced into retirement, resentful of his children, and poised to accept home Fiona, who has sheepishly returned after her failed elopement.

Desmond Maxwell (1973) sees this play as a study of 'various degrees of compromise with disappointment' common to such stories as 'The Flowers of Kiltymore' and 'The Gold in the Sea', and he is especially interested in the play's examination of the definitive shift in 'a family struggle of wills where authority and judgment are deserting the father' (50). Conversely, Dantanus presents a considerably more nuanced reading of the play as a sociological portrait of a family caught in the grips of a fundamentally changing society:

■ Behind the seemingly simple question of the number of children attending his small Meenbanid school lies one of the most fundamental developments of modern Irish history, the depopulation of the countryside. In urbanization, and emigration, its causes and effects, Friel has found one of his most potent and powerful themes. (60) □

Against the general background of families moving from Meenbanid to find work in Newtonabbey, Dantanus presents the Stone children as emblematic of the era, with Walter moving to Enniskillen and then on to wherever his employment dictates. Similarly, Fiona briefly follows her sister, Rita, to London, and during the course of the play Rita announces that she will move on to Canada. However, for Dantanus, such depth cannot mask the play's flaws, which are those of an inexperienced playwright: heavy-handed exposition, predictable plot development, 'irony heavy and overwritten', convenient coincidence, and 'in much of the second half of the play, melodrama completely unbalances the action' (63–64).

When George O'Brien turns to the play in his study, he slightly expands the focus on family to emphasize the pervasive frustration of hopes that affects all the major characters. Of course, Daniel Stone ends the play in physical decline as well as unwanted retirement, and Fiona endures the humiliation of returning home rejected by her supposed fiancé, but even Walter's professional rise is not without its disadvantages (34). As O'Brien points out, the school inspector's first visit to Clareford focuses on the exposure of Walter's poor management and previously unreported waste (35). Finally, rather than viewing *Hard House* as inferior to *A Sort of Freedom*, as in Dantanus's analysis, O'Brien argues for an assessment that balances the play's heavy-handed narrative with its greater awareness of language, especially as it is used by David and Walter Stone (35).

Subsequent critics, such as Elmer Andrews and Martine Pelletier, spend little time on this second radio play, and generally their treatments are limited to narrative summaries, since these plays have never been published and the manuscripts are accessible only in the National Library of Ireland.[6] However, when Anthony Roche turns to the play in his 2011 book, *Brian Friel*, he provides the single most useful assessment of this otherwise ignored work. Roche finds the importance of *Hard House* not in the play itself but in how the play anticipates diverse themes in Friel's later plays. Roche introduces his discussion by identifying the clear link between *Hard House* and the ground-breaking *Philadelphia, Here I Come!* 'in that they focus on a family conflict between the generations, most centrally between a father and son' (12). Indeed, while the play reveals Daniel Stone as an overbearing father, Roche recognizes that the professional tensions and competition between Walter and his father focus our attention on the importance of the father–son relationship. Roche also connects this professional competition in a rapidly modernizing educational system with a similar dynamic in *Translations*, which was written more than two decades later but set in 1833; in the latter case Manus refuses to compete against his father for the position of principal in the new national, English-language school that is to open in Baile Beag (13). Finally, Roche concludes his argument by drawing one final connection within Friel's oeuvre, identifying a common element that links *Hard House* with *The Gentle Island* (1971): the 'geographic displacements that would become a signature of Friel's drama' (14). Whereas *The Gentle Island* focuses on the last family on Inishkeen, a deeply troubled family that remains on its western island after all the other families have abandoned it, 'the Meenbanid citizens are being lured up the road by the promise of the availability of television'.

A Doubtful Paradise (1960)

As an aspiring playwright from Northern Ireland seeking to learn the trade, Friel would have found a very different hierarchy of Irish theatres from today's. The Abbey Theatre, which today is venerated as the birthplace of an Irish national theatre, 'burned to the ground with the loss of all scenery, props, many costumes, play scripts, records, and so on' on the night of 18 July 1951.[7] It took over fifteen years for the Abbey to be rebuilt, and in his history of the Abbey Theatre Robert Welch describes this era, from 1951 through 1966, as characterized by 'shoddy and often poorly written formulaic plays', produced by a 'demoralized' company (161–62). Throughout the 1950s, as the Abbey declined, the reputation of Belfast's Ulster Group Theatre climbed. The Group had been formed in 1940 when the dramatic actor/manager Harold Goldblatt, the comedian R.H. MacCandless, and the director J.R. Mageean created a repertory company to perform in the Ulster Minor Hall in Belfast. Over its twenty years, the company premiered plays by such titans of mid-century Irish theatre as George Shiels, St. John Ervine, and Joseph Tomelty; it also premiered Friel's first play, *A Doubtful Paradise*. While the direct relationship between Friel and the Group Theatre is limited to this single play, in my article 'More real for Northern Catholics', I explore the diverse ways that his plays from *A Sort of Freedom* to *The Blind Mice* are indebted to the themes and commonplaces of Ulster drama in the 1950s (4–15).

A Doubtful Paradise opened on 27 August 1960, running for two weeks. It presents the Logue family of Derry City: the father Willie, who is obsessed with French culture; his wife Maggie, a patient home-maker; and their three children, Una, a nurse, who settled in London four years prior to the play, Chris, their younger daughter, who shares her father's temperament, and Kevin, a struggling lawyer in Belfast. The very brief treatment in Maxwell's book aligns *Paradise* with the concerns and structure of *To This Hard House*, for both plays centre upon a father of three adult children; both feature an adult daughter who lives in London and who fails in her attempt to elope, and a son who is struggling to advance in his professional career (51). Dantanus more broadly aligns the play with Sean O'Casey's *Juno and the Paycock*, declaring that Maggie Logue 'reminds us of Mrs Boyle' and Willie, 'too, is a "peacock"' (66–67). Indeed, for Dantanus, the play highlights Willie's disastrous meddling in his children's lives by foisting his own social ambitions upon his son and his cultural pretensions on his daughter.

However, the treatments of *Doubtful Paradise* in Maxwell and Dantanus are largely perfunctory, and only Elmer Andrews and Anthony Roche consider the play worth careful examination. While these two discussions have distinct differences of focus, both are aware of the relevance of Arthur Miller's *Death of a Salesman* (1949), with its main character Willie Loman, to Friel's comedy, with its Willie Logue. As Roche points out in his *Brian Friel,*

■ Both Willies are dreamers, and have infected their children with aspirations; but they have failed to supply them with the practical skills to attain them. The 'children' are now in their mid-thirties and more unsettled than ever. (24) □

In an analysis that predates Roche's, Andrews develops the similarity between the two Willies, which leads Andrews to consider the relation of Friel's first stage play to his later satires of 'fake culture' in *The Communication Cord* (1982) and *The London Vertigo* (1990), his adaption of Charles Macklin's *The True Born Irishman* of 1761 (51). Moreover, more than Maxwell or Dantanus, Andrews shows particular interest in exploring the richness of both Willie's and Maggie's characters. Indeed, in his discussion of Maggie's crafted diction, 'self-awareness', and 'realistic approach to life', Andrews displays his attentive reading of this otherwise unavailable play.

Ultimately, though, Roche delves into this play to a degree unsurpassed by any other critic; indeed, he clearly sees the play as important politically for its harsh portrayal of the class barriers facing Northern Catholics, especially Kevin, whose suspension from the bar seems, to Roche, like a punishment for this Catholic Derryman's presumption to enter a field dominated by Belfast Protestants (2011, 20). Similarly, he identifies and explores the multiple ways that Willie's daughters Una and Fiona 'mirror' Daniel Stone's daughters in *To This Hard House*. These elder children have married, moved to London, and broken off all contact with their fathers, while the younger Fiona Stone and Chris Logue are both charmed by male suitors who abandon them. Roche claims, however, that *A Doubtful Paradise* is more satisfactory because 'Chris's father [Willie] has colluded in what befalls his daughter' (21).

The Enemy Within (1962)

The Enemy Within (1962) is the first play of Friel's sanctioned corpus; though he had three plays staged before *Philadelphia, Here I Come!*, *The Enemy Within* is the only one of these three that he allowed to be published during his lifetime. Nonetheless, it was a play about which he remained equivocal:

> ■ It's not good, but it was a commendable sort of play. I wouldn't put it any stronger than that. There's nothing very wrong with it and there's certainly nothing very good about it.[8] □

The Abbey Theatre staged it for nine performances over four weeks as part of a summer festival of new plays. While its initial run was even shorter than the two weeks enjoyed by *Doubtful Paradise*, it proved itself a moderately popular work: it was revived at Belfast's Lyric Theatre the following September, and subsequently it was adapted for radio broadcast by Radio Éireann (April 1963), BBC Northern Ireland Home Service (June 1963), and even BBC Television (March 1965).

The play's popularity in part rests on its focus on Ireland's Saint Columba (c. 521–97 CE), who founded the famous monastery on the island of Iona that did much to spread Christianity into Scotland. Set in the fall of 587, Friel's play focuses on the spiritual trials the saint endured when he allowed his brother Eoghan to entice him back into the secular world of war and politics. Returning to Iona after riding beside his brother in raids intended to protect the power of his family dynasty and defeat religious schism, Columba discovers that his spiritual mentor Caornan has died in circumstances that abruptly make him realize that he has compromised his spiritual integrity for worldly acclaim.

Although the play would seem to have a claim for prominence as the earliest play that Friel did not repudiate, its stature among critics has declined from being considered a relatively interesting play to an overlooked one; indeed, in the four books published after 2010, only one discusses it. In his 1973 study, Maxwell defines the play as exploring 'exile, loss, home, and the endless quest of the spirit', and this idea that *The Enemy Within* is defined by Columba's self-imposed exile from the worldly temptations of family and home dominates much of the criticism (57).[9] Later critics have sought to burrow more deeply into Columba's temptations; for example, Elmer Andrews seeks to identify as Columba's 'enemy within' the 'submerged, 'private', forces in personality…which threaten the established order' (78). In this reading of the play, Columba is tempted to intervene in Ireland's political and religious feuds because of his 'irrepressible "life-force" itself, the love of adventure and risk' that resist the regulation of monastic discipline and spirituality (82). Moreover, Andrews, and McGrath following him, view this as not unrelated to 'the dilemma of the artist…torn between his God and his *patria* (as Joyce dubbed the combined temptation of family and country)' (82).

Later readings of the play expand Columba's nostalgia for his idyllic homeland into more politicized readings. In *Theatre and the State* (2001), Lionel Pilkington argues that the prominence given in the play to the English novice
Oswald marks a movement 'towards England in order to embrace the reju-
venating power of international capitalism' (161). In my *Brian Friel, Ireland,
and the North* (2007), pursuing a postcolonial reading that takes its cue from
Aijaz Ahmed and Homi Bhabha, I discuss the play as exploring the historical
moment when Ireland was poised to become the colonizer of Britain through
Columba, a religious leader who maintained his grip on his dynasty's political
authority as well (42–52). Roche's 2011 book develops a compatible reading of
the play in which this view of an ancient Ireland destabilized by internal strife
becomes a stage upon which to explore contemporary Ireland, where differences between Irish and Pict, Christian and pagan, resonate with 'Catholic
native and Protestant planter' (27).

The Blind Mice (1963)

Although written before *The Enemy Within*, *The Blind Mice* is Friel's last play to
be withdrawn after its premiere, and he has never allowed its publication. It
focuses on the return of Father Chris Carroll to his Northern Irish hometown
after five years of imprisonment in China. His time in solitary confinement has
left him physically degraded and mentally fragile, and the celebratory atmosphere of the return of the 'hero of Thian-hee' has been shaken by rumours that
the young priest earned his release through renunciation of his faith. The play
thus takes its audience through the communal outbursts of anger beyond the
walls of the house and the clerical examinations of the young man within the
house that sadly culminate in Chris's psychological collapse at the play's end.

In *The Diviner* (1999), Richard Pine makes the most prescient comment when
he states that 'perhaps the significance of *The Blind Mice* ... is the fact that, like the
story "The Child", he wishes to suppress it' (106). Indeed, in the earliest full treatment of the play, Ulf Dantanus (1988) argues that it 'represents, in some respects,
an important step forward': there is 'more control of theme and technique', 'far
less overwriting', 'a more varied approach to dialogue, expressing character better', and in general many 'fine scenes' (69).[10] Dantanus also most bluntly states
what has become the general assumption that the play was withdrawn for reasons that were more 'emotional and personal than critical'; that the play 'was an
attempt by Friel to de-church himself', reflecting his decision in 1947 to abandon
his plans to enter the priesthood and withdraw from the seminary in Maynooth.

After 1990, few of the monographs consider the play, with the works by Elmer
Andrews and Anthony Roche the primary exceptions. Although brief, Andrews'

assessment remains one of the most perceptive. While he almost entirely refrains from summarizing the play, he skilfully encapsulates its most important traits: diagnosing the play's awareness of the media's point of view, its complex construction of multiple priests and their motivations, and the portrayal of Father Chris's mother who is both suspicious of outsiders and insightful regarding her son's strengths and weaknesses (54–55). On the other hand, Roche provides one of the fullest summaries of this otherwise unavailable play and one that also argues for its importance to our understanding of such subsequent plays as *Philadelphia, Here I Come!* (1964), *Living Quarters* (1977), and *Dancing at Lughnasa* (1990). Finally, my 2009 article 'More real for Northern Irish Catholics' similarly argues that this play marks a significant development in Friel's skill in dialogue timing and staged action when compared to his previous plays (11–12). Moreover, I argue that such scenes in *Blind Mice* as the family's evening meal reveal 'the young playwright's ability to write a naturalistic ensemble scene', the type of which will elicit comparisons to Chekhov in such later plays as *Aristocrats* (12–13).

The first five plays of Friel's career reveal a rapid evolution in the young playwright's ability to construct character and plot, with *The Enemy Within* and *The Blind Mice* achieving limited success throughout Ireland. However, these plays fail to suggest a talent capable of producing *Philadelphia, Here I Come!*, an *avant-garde* play that enjoyed immediate international acclaim, and the subject of the next chapter.

CHAPTER THREE

Philadelphia, Here I Come! (1964)[1]

Ballybeg

Philadelphia, Here I Come! was Friel's first theatrical success, and it is also the first of his thirteen Ballybeg plays. Whereas only *Philadelphia* actually takes place in the imagined locality's town centre, *Crystal and Fox* (1968), *Living Quarters* (1977), *Translations* (1980), and *Molly Sweeney* (1994) all depict events that take place more or less in its immediate environs. *Aristocrats* (1979), *Give me Your Answer, Do!* (1997), and *The Home Place* (2005) are set in different manor houses located in or overlooking Ballybeg, while the tragic murder of Frank Hardy in *Faith Healer* (1980) occurs on the night the characters arrive at the town after many years of wandering. Finally, several other plays are set close enough to Ballybeg for it to be identified as the nearest town. The characters in *Dancing at Lughnasa* (1990) are easily able to walk there; *The Communication Cord* (1982) and *Wonderful Tennessee* (1992) are set in the 'townland of Ballybeg'; and though the events depicted in *The Gentle Island* (1971) take place on Inishkeen island, at the play's end, the character Shane is rushed to Ballybeg Hospital on the mainland.

Although Ballybeg is clearly located in County Donegal, in Ireland's extreme northwest, Tony Corbett (2002) has documented our inability to establish its exact location with any specificity:

> ■ In *Faith Healer*, it is described as 'not far from Donegal town'. In *Translations*, it is clear that Ballybeg is on or near the coast, and 23 miles from Glenties . . . . . Other places mentioned as significant—Buncrana, Greencastle, and Burnfoot—are on the Inishown peninsula. *Wonderful Tennessee* again places it in 'north-west Donegal', while in *Aristocrats* the border is 20 miles away, and Letterkenny is the main telephone exchange. (72) □

Thus, Corbett declares that 'Ballybeg is an emblem of all Irish towns'. Martine Pelletier (1997) has helpfully described Ballybeg as 'une source d'authenticité sans les constraints du réel', as the paradigmatic small Irish town that is neither the impoverished countryside nor the industrialised city (129).[2] More poetically, in *Spelling It Out* (2009), his tribute to his old friend, Seamus Heaney described it as 'the hub of [Friel's] imagined world...a crystal into which this playwright gazes to discover his vision of reality'. However others, most notably Richard Pine, have argued that Ballybeg is modelled upon the Glenties, north of Donegal town, where the young Friel would visit his mother's relatives.[3] Indeed, Pine discusses Friel's early travelogue 'A Fine Day at Glenties' (1963) as a place where we can find 'all the visionaries and sceptics and domestic exiles of Friel's plays' (49). Considering the Ballybeg plays of the mid and late 1990s, my book (2009) observes how drastically Friel's fictional town changes between the first play set in 1964 and the last 'contemporary' play set in 1997:

■ Not only has Ballybeg entered the service culture of late twentieth-century consumerism with tourism and its own health club...but with its array of Indian anaesthetists and Chinese restaurants, [*Give Me Your Answer, Do!*] provides its audience a glimpse of a town radically changed from the desolate hinterland that thirty years earlier Gar O'Donnell repudiated. (187–88) □

Finally, one would not be able to resolve the location of Ballybeg by means of the films based on Friel's plays. While Friel himself served as screenwriter for John Quested's 1975 film of *Philadelphia, Here I Come!*, the credits only state that it was 'filmed on location in Southern Ireland'. Conversely, though Joan FitzPatrick Dean (2003) identifies the Kilruddery Estate as the location for the Ballybeg in Pat O'Connor's 1998 film of *Dancing at Lughnasa*, she emphasizes that this location was chosen to avoid '*per diem* and other expenses for cast and crew' (28). Moreover, Dean notes how generally unsuited the film's 'deeply romanticized' setting is; unlike the play the set shows 'no hint of human habitation: no demarcated or cultivated fields, no houses, vehicles, structures, walls, or even livestock' (28–29).

Tyrone Guthrie and the Guthrie Theatre, Minneapolis

Throughout his career, Friel has expressed increasingly dismissive views of the director's role. In interviews beginning in the late 1960s, he advised actors to approach the script as musicians, whose job is to 'play...the score' as written and 'the director interprets to the best of his ability what the author intends, and only this' (55).[4] By 1991, however, in an interview with Mel Gussow, he dismisses directing as 'almost a bogus career', because 'a director should be "obedient" to the play'.[5]

Nonetheless, the impact of the influential director Tyrone Guthrie (1900–71) on the young playwright has been seen as 'crucial' throughout the criticism;

in his *Brian Friel* (1988), Ulf Dantanus claims that Friel's brief apprenticeship at the Guthrie Theatre in Minneapolis 'may have determined Friel's future in a way similar to that whereby Yeats directed Synge to the Aran Islands' (50). Guthrie had gained an international reputation in the 1940s as the director of the Old Vic, and his later career was noted for his ground-breaking productions at the Edinburgh Festival and Stratford, Ontario. In his *Companion to Post-War British Theatre* (1986), Philip Barnes describes Guthrie as having been 'extremely influential' from the 1930s through the 1960s (102). Known especially for his 'provocatively experimental' Old Vic Shakespeare productions and his role as one of the founders of the Stratford, Ontario, Shakespeare festival, Guthrie returned to Belfast for the summer of 1957 to direct the Ulster Group Theatre production of Gerard McLarnon's *Bonefire*. In his analysis of the political controversy caused by this staging of sectarian violence in *Theatre and the State in Twentieth-Century Ireland* (2001), Lionel Pilkington describes Guthrie's deft and very public manipulation of both the Northern Irish politicians and journalists to thwart their attempts to first ban and later rewrite the play (176–77).

During April, May, and early June of 1963, Friel was hosted by Guthrie in Minneapolis, Minnesota, where the young writer observed rehearsals for *Hamlet* and *Three Sisters* for the opening of Guthrie's new theatre. As early as 1964, Friel himself described the importance of Guthrie's influence on him in a brief essay entitled 'The Giant of Monaghan'; similarly, in one of his last essays, 'Seven Notes for a Festival Programme' (1999), he identifies Guthrie as one of the very few modern directors who hadn't 'bamboozled' audiences.[6]

In his essay 'Friel and Performance History' (2006), Patrick Burke asserts the importance of the young playwright's short apprenticeship with Guthrie because it provided him with the practical stage experience that he had otherwise lacked (119). In *The Theatre of Brian Friel* (2014), Christopher Murray seeks to diagnose a broader importance that this 'strange internship ... as "observer"' had upon the emerging playwright (14). Harking back to Friel's assertion in a 1965 interview that Guthrie had revealed to him the ritualistic foundation of theatre, Murray is especially interested in exploring the impact of Guthrian ritual on *Philadelphia* itself, which Murray sees in such episodes as Gar saying the rosary with his father and Gar's memories of his courtship of Kate Doogan. Admittedly one must 'regard Friel's use of ritual as subversive' in the play, but in Murray's opinion, none the less emotionally powerful (19–22).

However, by far the most probing and comprehensive explorations of the relationship of Guthrie to Friel's career are offered by Anthony Roche and Maria Szasz. In his 2011 chapter on Friel's relationship with three directors (Tyrone Guthrie, Hilton Edwards, and Joe Dowling), Roche provides the first detailed analysis of the relationship between Friel and Guthrie. Roche provides considerable detail on Guthrie's interest in the fellow Northern Irishman as his career emerged in the early 1960s (34–36), but in exploring Friel's experience in Minneapolis, he makes very good use of Friel's diaries and an article by Herbert Whitaker, 'Tyrone Guthrie at Work', recounting Whitaker's observations on Guthrie when he 'sat in on those very same *Hamlet* rehearsals Friel attended' (36). Roche focuses on Guthrie's 'attention to actors' and the 'democracy of Guthrie's approach to directing', and Friel's own accounts of watching Guthrie at work (36–37). In connecting Guthrie directly to the play's content, Roche forcibly argues that Private Gar 'resembles nothing so much as Tyrone Guthrie in rehearsal with his actors' (40). While Roche provides valuable insight on Guthrie's supportive response to the draft of *Philadelphia*, he also convincingly argues that both Friel and Guthrie himself had reasons to oppose the choice of Guthrie to direct the play's premiere (40–42).

In the chapter 'Tyrone Guthrie as Mentor' in her *Brian Friel and America* (2013), Szasz valuably charts the impact of Guthrie on Friel's entire career. Her research uncovers many of the details that led up to Friel's introduction to Guthrie and his probable day-to-day activities as 'an observer' in Minneapolis (11–17). She is equally skilful in culling Friel's many references to Guthrie from diverse interviews, essays, and even letters. However, her work is most valuable in proposing the four 'lessons' that he learned from Guthrie: first, 'not to be afraid of criticizing Irish life' (18–19); second, the importance of ritual and the pervasive forms that ritual has taken in Friel's oeuvre (19–20); third, a 'willingness to experiment with dramatic form' (20); fourth, Friel's new understanding of Ireland itself, by virtue of his sojourn in America (20–22). Like Roche, Szasz also charts the role that Guthrie played in the development of *Philadelphia* itself, from commenting on the first draft of the play to sending Friel his reflections on the play's premiere (22–26). However, Szasz significantly downplays Guthrie's concerns over the play's most radical feature: splitting the main character into two actors.

Philadelphia, Here I Come!

Philadelphia, Here I Come!, which opened on 28 September 1964 as part of the Dublin Theatre Festival, is universally viewed as 'a watershed in Friel's career as a dramatist' (Dantanus, 50), the moment when this successful writer of short stories became recognized as one of the 'Big Five' young Irish playwrights, according to a 1965 *Ulster Week* article by Jonathan North, theatre critic for the *Belfast Telegraph*.[7] Moreover, *Philadelphia* has consistently been considered firmly on the short list of Friel's best plays throughout his career, and when *The Irish Times* published 'Brian Friel: Seven Key Plays' upon the playwright's death, *Philadelphia* was there among his other great works.[8]

Philadelphia quickly travelled to Broadway for the 1965–66 season and toured the United States the following year. But what makes *Philadelphia* truly exceptional was its international appeal: in the ten years following the play's premiere it was staged in Sweden (1967), England (1967), Germany (1968), the Netherlands (1968), Australia (1969), and Romania (1973). Significantly, it was the first of Friel's plays to be adapted as a film, with Friel himself authoring the screenplay for John Quested's 1975 adaption. More recently, it has also been translated and staged in Finland (1983), Japan (1986), and Malaysia (1998), with productions in—among other places—Brazil, Greece, Latvia, and Turkey in the new century.

While Friel's play joined the ranks of the 1960s most important English-language plays, alongside such works as Tom Stoppard's *Rosencrantz and Guildenstern Are Dead* (1966), *Philadelphia* had an even more profound impact upon Irish theatre. As early as 1991, when the play marked its twenty-fifth anniversary, Richard Pine claimed in a *Colby Quarterly* article that the impact of *Philadelphia* on subsequent Irish drama qualified Friel to be recognized as 'the father of contemporary Irish drama' (190). Similarly, in his survey of Irish drama from Dion Boucicault (1820–1890) to Friel, Nicholas Grene (1999) marks the premiere of the play as 'a new beginning in Irish theatre' (194), and among others Mary Trotter, in *Modern Irish Theatre* (2008), has similarly commented that many theatre scholars have the habit of 'skipping from [Sean] O'Casey's Dublin trilogy to Brian Friel's *Philadelphia, Here I Come!*' (65).[9]

Sources and Influences

Unlike today's critical practice which often considers recent plays by emerging playwrights, the critical landscape of the 1960s was much more conservative, focused on such established playwrights as J.M. Synge (1871–1909), Sean O'Casey (1880–1964), and George Bernard Shaw (1856–1950), with very occasional articles on the plays of Brendan Behan (1923–64). In other words, it would have been highly unusual for such journals as *Modern Drama* or *PMLA* (*Publications of the Modern Language Association*) to accept articles on such a young writer. Moreover, such Irish Studies journals as *Eire-Ireland* (founded in 1966), *Irish University Review* (founded in 1970), and *Études Irlandaises* (founded in 1975), which would have been more willing to publish articles on such writers, largely did not exist.

Although the 1960s did not yet have the scholarly milieu that encouraged the academic study of new works by emerging writers, *Philadelphia* caught the attention of various critics early on. Shortly after its premiere, the play was discussed by Robert Hogan, one of the mid-twentieth century's most influential critics of Irish Studies, who began writing on Irish drama at the end of the 1950s. His *After the Irish Renaissance* (1967) surveys Irish theatre between 1925 and 1965, and he gives brief attention to Friel's then-new play, calling *Philadelphia* 'a brilliant and beautiful study of isolation and its inevitably accompanying anguish' (197).

However, the first articles were not published until the 1970s, with James Coakley's 'Chekov [sic] in Ireland' (1973) the first to focus on *Philadelphia*. While Hogan had noted the innovative use of two actors to portray Gar O'Donnell, the play's putative hero, Coakley, is the first to attempt to analyse the function and significance of the play. He argues that, while splitting the main character seems to be a radical staging innovation, it actually achieves the most traditional ends:

■ the device obviously enhances the possibilities for character delineation of Gar, as intricate strands of experience buried with the private self are released and dramatized. Unseen and unheard by the other characters, often berating, cajoling, or goading his public counterpart, the private self is both omniscient narrator and confidant, a guide to the past, an alter ego who forces Gar to examine what he is about to leave. (196) □

Moreover, Coakley claims that the banter between the two Gars reinvigorates 'the old-fashioned Chekovian monologue'. In arguing his Chekhovian reading of *Philadelphia*, he asserts that 'as in Chekov' action 'concerns itself not so much with *events* in the characters' lives as with the *effects* of those events upon them' (194). In recognizing a Chekhovian essence to the play's reliance on 'memory', the article reveals the way the play balances 'humor with pathos' (195). However, Coakley's reading also distorts the play by resting its interpretation on Friel's use of 'realism': 'a realism neither photographic or reportorial....A realism no doubt better organized than life....To make us see things as they really are' (193).

In his brief discussion of Friel's emerging career in his 1972 book *The Theatre in Ulster*, Sam Hanna Bell also describes him as Chekhovian; however, Bell identifies the playwright's trait in his development of such minor characters as Master Boyle and Madge the housekeeper, who 'reveal their own tragedies as they approach and recede from the main conflict' (106). As Friel's career develops, a critical consensus emerges that affirms such a Chekhovian nature in his dramatic outlook and settings. However, as later chapters will demonstrate, it is the more realistic plays such as *Aristocrats* and *The Home Place* that most reveal Friel's debt to Chekhov.

A more compelling comparison has been made by Ulf Dantanus between *Philadelphia* and Eugene O'Neill's *Days without End* (1933), though Dantanus never claims that Friel knew the American play. O'Neill also split his main character John Loving into two characters. Dantanus judges *Days* the inferior play because 'the other characters, John's wife and his uncle, for instance, can hear the *alter ego*, i.e. Loving, speak' (92). Moreover, this alter ego dies at the play's end, restoring John Loving to a type of unitary identity (91).

Public Gar and Private Gar

The powerful theatrical impact of dividing the main character between two actors—Public Gar and Private Gar—has been a focal point for the criticism as well. Essentially everyone writing about the play until very recently feels compelled to reflect on the aetiology, teleology, or psychology of the splitting of Gar. Ulf Dantanus associates the play's alternation 'between the comic and the sad' directly with the interplay between the two Gars (96). Indeed, in this reading the two Gars become the poles for interpreting the play, with Private Gar ready for exile from Ireland and without sentimentality, while Public Gar is too ready to stay and fall under the charms of his memories, whether those memories be of his father at Lough na Cloc Cor, his aunt Lizzie, or his former girlfriend Katie Doogan (95–98).

While Dantanus argues that the relationship between the two Gars is a relatively straightforward bifurcation of a single personality, Anthony Roche's discussion of the play in *Contemporary Irish Drama from Beckett to McGuinness* (1994) sees Private Gar less as a complement to Public Gar and more as the instigator of Public's thoughts and actions. For example, Private provides the commentaries for Public's physical antics, which motivates him to be a footballer or concert violinist (87). More significantly, Private Gar is more concerned with recovering his mother's story and is the one who initiates the attempt to reconstruct her history: 'Like Oedipus, he is both the detective determined to expose what has been covered up and the guilty target of his own inquiry, his birth having been "responsible" for killing his mother' (93). In short, Roche sees Private Gar's 'most important dramatic function [being] to goad Public into remembering' his most emotionally vexatious memories, whether they concern his mother, Kate Doogan, or his decision to live with his aunt and uncle in Philadelphia (94).

Understanding the role of Private Gar is also the goal of Elmer Andrews' 1995 analysis of the play. He considers Private as representing all that culture represses. Indeed, Andrews sees Private less as a voice opposing sexual repression than the oppression of 'the small-town, highly conventionalized social order of Ballybeg' (85). To bolster such a view, he notes the preponderance of the play's 'representatives of the Law': 'a Senator, a Master, a Canon and a County Councillor'. Andrews' reading positions the play as the first of Friel's many plays— such as *Freedom of the City* (1973), *Aristocrats* (1979), and *The Communication Cord* (1982)—that in some way expose the deterioration of Ireland's political order.

While such interpretations all construct various literary Freudian readings of Gar's psyche, in her 'Schizophrenia and the Politics of Irish Experience' (1996), Maureen Hawkins is the first to propose a more clinical diagnosis of Gar's division as indicative of his 'schizoid condition' (466). Whereas, on the surface, such an interpretation may seem to threaten an over-reading of the relationship of Private to Public, the strength of Hawkins' argument relies upon her broader reading of Irish society, both as portrayed in the play and in sociological studies.

Noting that the Irish 'have the world's highest rate of hospitalization for schizo-phrenia', Hawkins relies upon the work of the psychiatrist R.D. Laing to under-stand how Ballybeg encouraged the emergence of Gar's two selves. Laing's *The Politics of Experience* (1967) explores the way that negative interactions with one's family and friends can '"disconfirm" one's experience—and so reject the validity of one's self-recognized identity—by denying that experience' (466). Hawkins employs this concept of a social nexus around Gar to reveal how

> ■ one by one, others implicitly deny it, often by refusing to acknowledge even that he is leaving; thus, they deny him the confirmation of saying or showing that they will miss him, though it is apparent to the audience that each denial is a result of their fears of acknowledging how much they do love him…because they fear that Gar will deny their experience of their relationships to him. Everyone is caught in a schizophrenogenic 'double-bind' situation. (467) □

In Hawkins' reading of the play, it is not merely Gar's father S.B. who ignores his imminent departure; in clearly identifiable ways each person who visits Gar minimizes or trivializes their relationship, thus undermining his psychologi-cal validity. While such a reading easily explains the father-son relationship, Hawkins describes its pertinence to understanding Gar's relationships to Mas-ter Boyle, the 'boys', Kate Doogan, and even aunt Lizzie (467–69). Indeed, Hawkins is able to show how even Gar's surrogate mother, Madge, feigns indifference to his departure and 'implicitly [rejects] him by confirming his fear that it is her niece's children whom she regards as her surrogate children, not him' (469). In short, Hawkins describes all of Ballybeg as a place where everyone 'habitually' denies the emotional needs of friends and family, thus becoming a model of Ireland's schizoid condition.

Memory

As early as Coakley's 1973 article, Friel criticism has identified the thematic importance of Gar's memories to the play. Indeed, Coakley calls *Philadelphia* 'a memory play set in the country of a young man's mind' (191). The play fluctu-ates between the present and Gar's recollection of key events in his life as the people he has known come to wish him a safe journey: his passionate courtship of Katie Doogan, his disastrous attempt to ask her father for her hand in mar-riage, the visit of his aunt and uncle from America, and his tantalizing uncertain memory of a fishing trip with his father at Lough na Cloc Cor. Coakley sees the role of memory, whether it is enacted or discussed, as most pervasively associat-ing the work with Chekhov. However, Coakley finds it difficult to move beyond the play's atmospherics in his attempt to associate the play's reliance on memory with what he refers to as Chekhovian ritual and 'human understanding' (192).

While the importance of memory is frequently a point of contact in the criticism, Elmer Andrews is the first to rigorously dissect its forms and function in the play. Andrews posits that for Friel 'memory ... is a creative faculty' (87), and we see this most in Gar's ability to focus on the creation of future memories from which he intentionally separates the 'coarseness' to preserve the 'precious, precious gold' (87). Yet Andrews distinguishes between the memories that are staged before the audience and those that ultimately cannot be confirmed, the lost memories regarding his mother and father (91–94).

Looking back on over forty years of scholarship concerning the playwright, in his *Theatre of Brian Friel* Christopher Murray observes that 'in Friel memory is usually related to music' (37). However, Andrews was the first to closely associate music and memory; looking forward to *Dancing at Lughnasa* (1990) from the perspective of *Philadelphia*, Andrews notes that Friel uses music to link especially powerful emotions with memories. In Gar's case, he explores the way Friel employs Mendelssohn's violin concerto to heighten the 'pathos and intensity' of Gar's language (92). Similarly, Andrews points out how Gar's crucial memory of an afternoon spent with his father at Logh na Cloc Cor seems even to be elicited by the music that Gar hears (92). In his 1999 article 'Brian Friel and the Condition of Music', Harry White also explores the manner in which Friel uses Mendelssohn's violin concerto 'as explicit resource and structural model in *Philadelphia*' (10), which 'reifies and ennobles' Gar's emotions as he thinks about his mother (8). Similarly, though with less refinement than Andrews, Tony Corbett discusses the modulation of Gar's emotions depending on whether the first, second, or third movement of Mendelssohn's work is heard (38).

Lough na Cloc Cor

The earliest criticism of *Philadelphia* is concerned with mapping out the more expansive themes of the play: Gar's emotionality, the father-son relationship, or the phenomenology of the two Gars. Thus, some of the dramatic nodes, such as Gar's repetition of a passage from Burke or the importance of his memory of a childhood fishing trip, were only slowly recognized by the criticism. Dantanus was the first to consider the role of Gar's memory of a childhood expedition with his father to Lough na Cloc Cor. In passing, he pairs it with S.B.'s memory of a boyhood Gar in a sailor suit to illustrate the wisdom of Madge's observation on the similarity of father to son (97–98). The year following Dantanus' book, Michael Etherton considers this pairing of memories as well, in his *Contemporary Irish Dramatists* (1989). Whereas Etherton also juxtaposes the possibly faulty memories of father and son to elevate Madge to the position of choric commentator on the two, he chides the play for raising but not answering the question 'what ultimate reality is there?' (158).

In his 1994 book, Anthony Roche sees the scene in which Gar asks S.B. whether he shares the memory as the play's crucial moment. Roche claims that throughout Episode Three, Private speaks considerably less, and Public approaches the possibility of 'full psychic integration' (100). In fact, in Roche's reading, this moment when Public speaks to his father rather than to Private about Lough na Cloc Cor threatens Private with 'extinction'. S.B. having failed to confirm Gar's memory, Roche notes that the two fail to speak to each other again in the play, and he compares the event to the chapel scene in *Hamlet*, where Hamlet leaves before he can hear a similarly crucial admission from Claudius (101). Thus, hearing both Gar and S.B., the audience privately understands the play's arc, but 'this does nothing to resolve matters at the formal or public level'.

Andrews' analysis of Gar's memory of this fishing expedition in his 1995 book profoundly reoriented the critical view its significance. Claiming that 'fictionalising memory…can play a valid and vital part in the construction of "truth" and identity', Andrews provides a lengthy quote from Friel's 1972 'Self-Portrait' in which he recounts a very similar and almost certainly false memory about his own father (93–94). Friel recalls an episode in the Glenties when he was nine; he and his father walked home from fishing, joyously singing, and in great spirits. He recounts this memory only to reveal its impossibility, yet he upholds its 'peculiar veracity' nonetheless (94). Likewise, Andrews argues that Gar and S.B.'s paired memories, though unreliable, affirm an important truth in the play: 'the love that each has for the other' (94). Borrowing from this use of 'Self-Portrait' shortly after Andrews published his book, F.C. McGrath (1999) argues that the two characters' irreconcilable memories are indicative not of their mutual love but 'the lack they represent: Gar's desire for a father he never had and S.B.'s desire for a son he never had' (70). Indeed, McGrath opines that the two fail to construct the beneficial relationship that each wants precisely because Gar resembles his father so much.

Writing in the wake of Andrews' analysis, both Tony Corbett, in his 2002 book, and Geraldine Higgins, in hers of 2010, seek to expand this reading by shifting from Public's attempt to share the memory with his father in Part Two of Episode Three to Private's pained announcement of the memory in Part One. Both Corbett and Higgins pair Private's outburst with S.B.'s memory of Gar in his sailor suit, and both similarly quote Friel's 'Self-Portrait'. However, Corbett concludes his analysis by emphasizing the difference between Friel's embrace of his unstable memory and the play's demand for certain, shared ones (39–40). By contrast, Higgins more carefully delineates the evidence that, as the night progresses, S.B. reveals subtle signs of his love for Gar, from 'reading the newspaper upside down' to the moment that he 'touches Gar's coat' (14). In her

reading, the moment when Gar and S.B. fail to affirm the memory is less significant than their inability throughout the play to 'read the other signals of love'.

By the time he publishes his 2011 book on Friel, Roche refers to this scene
as 'the celebrated "blue boat" episode'. He avoids the, by now traditional, interpretation of this scene by placing the emphasis on the dynamic between Public
and Private. In this reading, Gar's issue is less the possibility that his father will
share his memory than how S.B.'s reaction promises to reveal to Gar whether
or not his memory is a fantasy, whether 'the memory is historically accurate or
a narrative constructed out of his desire' as Gar himself fears (67). Roche then
asserts that Private's mocking laughter following S.B.'s inability to recall the
event reveals his celebration that father and son will not now be reconciled.

Finally, as if to show that the critical fascination with Lough na Cloc Cor
has far from exhausted itself, in his 2014 book, Richard Rankin Russell offers
the most detailed and comprehensive study of the trope yet to appear (58–61).
More faithfully than in the other discussions, Russell probes the play's three
scenes in which Gar, Public or Private, returns to the memory. Thus, he frequently notes details of importance; for example, he observes that

■ This memory is crucially set in spring and is full of potential for Gar and his
father's relationship, unlike the significant, immediately past events of the play
set during harvest—Kate's wedding and the visit by Gar's aunt and uncle. (60) □

While Russell is able to articulate the emotional content of Gar's memory
('a father's loving protection of his son'), he too struggles with the central
truth of the combined message of Gar and S.B.'s different memories and their
staged presentation.

S.B. O'Donnell and the father/son dynamic

Gar's father, S.B. O'Donnell, is central to Gar's memory at Lough na Cloc Cor,
and understanding Gar's relationship to his father is equally central to much of
the criticism. In his 1973 study of Friel, Maxwell states that 'the father/son relationship dominates Episode I' of the play because, more than in later scenes of
the play, the audience sees the wide and often contradictory feelings that Gar has
for his father (66). As if to reiterate this assertion, when Maxwell again writes
about *Philadelphia* a decade later in *A Critical History of Modern Irish Drama 1891–
1980* (1985), he more forcefully claims that S.B. is 'at the centre' of all of Gar's
relationships (204).

A fuller reading quickly followed, offered by Marilyn Throne in 'The Disintegration of Authority' (1988). By that time, the broad outlines of Friel's career

arc had become clear, allowing Throne to recognize the absence of mothers from the stage plays and that 'in all of the plays the children are presented as actually or psychologically crippled by their fathers' (163). Although the scope of her work extends beyond *Translations*, Throne treats *Philadelphia* as foundational for her argument. In her reading of the play, the very division of Gar's character into Private and Public is symptomatic of his 'psychological crippling' by his father's silence (163). However, such emotional damage can only be caused by 'the intensity of the love' that unites Gar to S.B., demonstrated most powerfully in the importance Gar places on his father's warmth long ago at Cloc Cor (168). In his monograph published the same year, Dantanus similarly argues that *Philadelphia* exploits the audience's desire for a moment of mutual recognition and understanding between father and son that might, in part, reconcile them and reconcile Gar to remaining home (96–98).

In his 1989 article 'Insubstantial Father and Consubstantial Sons', Thomas B. O'Grady minimizes any idea of a sentimental affection between Gar and his father, arguing for a more Freudian view. Indeed, as the title implies, O'Grady argues that Public Gar is the heir of Ireland's two preeminent Oedipal sons: Christy Mahon of J.M. Synge's *Playboy of the Western World* (1907) and Stephen Dedalus of James Joyce's *Portrait of the Artist as a Young Man* (1916) and *Ulysses* (1922). However, in this reading, the Freudian stakes for Public Gar are much diminished: instead of gaining Christy's dominance over or Stephen's independence from his father, the best that Gar can achieve is 'a patrimony of impotence and subservience' even should he free himself of his father's control (73).

Yet, for O'Grady, the play stages Private Gar's 'patricidal urge' to free Public Gar from his father's influence, 'to erect an insurmountable barrier between father and son rather than the precarious bridge which would satisfy Public Gar' (73). This reading of the play more strenuously separates Private and Public into disintegrated agents than in the readings of the Public/Private relationships offered by Dantanus, Andrews, or even Hawkins. For example, O'Grady argues not only that Public seeks to offer Private 'a series of alternative self-images' to engender in Public greater self confidence but also that Private 'knows from the outset' the psychological challenges that Public must overcome before his departure; he says, for example,

■ Public Gar, however, must proceed through a series of traumatizing reminiscences and confrontations before he can succumb to the instinctive wisdom of Private Gar and accept the painful necessity of his imminent departure for America. (74) □

For O'Grady, S.B.'s failure to share Gar's memory of fishing at Lough na Cloc Cor forces Private to accept 'the necessity of the patricidal impulse Private Gar has been inculcating throughout the play' (76). Thus, Public is able to achieve 'the final death of the heart' that may allow him to endure his future sojourn with his Aunt Lizzy in Philadelphia.

In a decidedly Žižekian amplification of this Freudian reading, Anthony Roche's *Brian Friel* explores the character of S.B. as 'the disciplinary father...the embodiment of the Law' who 'wields power over his son as victim' (65). Roche recognizes that, in his official role as county councillor, Gar's father is part of the local political structure and his close friendship with Canon O'Byrne further integrates him into 'the hegemonic exercise of power in the society' (65). However, in Roche's reading of the Lough na Cloc Cor dialogue between father and son, Public does not gain his psychological freedom from his father; rather, 'the underlying phantasmic frame giving consistency to his desires will remain unaltered and untransformed, as the stuttering final line of the play acknowledges' (68).

Edmund Burke's *Reflections on the Revolution in France*

Throughout *Philadelphia*, Gar will occasionally recite a passage from *Reflections on the Revolution in France* (1790) by Edmund Burke (1729–97). An important statement of British conservatism, Burke's book-length letter to 'a gentleman in Paris' constitutes a detailed and passionate defence of tradition and the monarchy, and Gar repeatedly quotes Burke's recollection of Marie Antoinette:

> ■ It is now sixteen or seventeen years since I saw the queen of France, then the dauphiness, at Versailles; and surely never lighted on this orb, which she hardly seemed to touch, a more delightful vision. (Burke 89)[10] □

In his introduction to Friel's *Selected Plays*, Seamus Deane is the first to direct our attention to Gar's reliance on Burke's description of the French queen. Earlier in this piece, Deane remarks that 'politics is an ever-present force' in Friel's plays (12) and that his art is 'profoundly political' (13); thus, it is not surprising that, for Deane, Gar's use of this passage encapsulates his attitude towards the social politics of Ballybeg. In this reading, Ballybeg is like pre-revolutionary France, the 'past civilization' that Gar is endeavouring to escape, and, 'however vulgar it may seem' in some ways, Philadelphia represents the modern, uncertain world where Gar's future lies (14).

Finding a way to develop Deane's assertion into a broader reading of the play has not been at all straightforward, and in 1988 Dantanus sought to argue that Gar expresses a pronounced desire to romanticize Ballybeg in spite of all his reasons to leave it. On the one hand, the play exposes 'the less attractive aspects of west-of-Ireland village life' (98), yet Gar

■ knows that the past holds strong attractions, that any memory of Ballybeg will be 'distilled of all its coarseness; and what's left is going to be precious, precious gold...' (99) □

Thus, for Dantanus, the refrain from Burke's *Reflections* serves to interrupt the sentimental memories of mother or romance that may tempt Gar to remain in Ireland by softening his rejection of the town.

Writing the following year, Michael Etherton also seeks to develop this socio-political interpretation of Gar's use of Burke in his chapter on Friel. He sees the quote from Burke as indicative of Gar's broader rejection of 'conservative rural Ireland' and its narrow brand of Christianity. However, Etherton's argument reveals the difficulty of proposing such a reading, leaving him to opine that 'perhaps Gar is being ironical over his own "rebellion" against conservative Ireland' (158); similarly, later commenting on Private's excoriation of the Canon, Etherton remarks that 'this little scene is as illogical as Gar quoting Burke, but within the overall theatrical inventiveness of the play this works for an audience' (159). The enduring attractiveness of Deane's argument is evidenced in John Harrington's 1997 analysis of the play, where he points out that Master Boyle, Gar's former history teacher, associates America with a rejection of the past and 'Public Gar attempts to adopt just that alleged American disregard for the past' later in the play (155).

In his 1993 article 'The Penalties of Retrospect', Neil Corcoran maps out an alternative context for Gar's subconscious use of Burke. The broad strategy of the middle section of Corcoran's article is to shift critical attention away from an analysis of father-son relationships to the issue of 'the absent mother' in diverse plays (18). Corcoran posits that in several plays of Friel's career up to *Faith Healer* (1979), the absent mother 'represents the lost value of a fundamental alternative to the repressive (and repressively weak) patriarchy' (20). In this sense, Gar's references to Burke are not about France's *ancien régime* but its queen Marie Antoinette, not about the Irish political context but a Freudian personal one. Thus, when Gar recites Burke, we see how a 'fetishised past dominates the present', how Gar's fascination with a dead parent prevents him from developing a relationship with a living one (19).

It is important to note that these early attempts to explain Friel's use of Burke were all short discussions, sometimes only a paragraph or two, serving larger arguments. While this begins to change with Corcoran, Anthony Roche offers the first nuanced readings of particular passages. Indeed, while Roche focuses on the early instances where Gar recites his passage, he is the first critic to actually recognize that there are ten separate places in which Gar quotes Burke, while earlier writers merely mention 'several' examples. As did Corcoran before him, Roche recognizes that Burke's passage suggests a fetishistic association for Gar with his dead mother, but Roche usefully explores the powerful instance when Public finds that Burke cannot soothe his emotions, leaving him to interrupt his recitation by shouting

'Shut up! Shut up!' (98). Roche employs several examples to argue that Gar's use of Burke constitutes 'the closest text for a language of the affections that Gar has', and with it Gar awkwardly attempts to negotiate his new relationship to his aunt Lizzie (97–98) and to bridge with S.B. the loss of his mother (100).

Music

Deane's interest in the repetition of Burke's description of Marie Antoinette, which pointed the way to future interpretations, invited others to similarly expand their discussion of *Philadelphia*. In his 1994 book *Contemporary Irish Drama* Anthony Roche turned his attention to another phrase repeated in various forms throughout the play: 'Philadelphia, here I come, right back where I started from'. Indeed, according to Roche's reading, the line is 'much more than just the declarative title of the play':

■ 'Philadelphia, here I come/ Right back where I started from' is repeated much more than would be naturalistically possible. It becomes, appropriately, a leitmotif that underscores a process of inevitability. (88) □

In considering Friel's selection of this song, Roche discusses the extent to which in the Irish cultural imagination America has become Ireland's Other, where open sexuality, jazz, and infinite possibility oppose Irish restraint, silence, and diminished possibility. However, Roche also points out that these two lines are in themselves 'deeply antithetical', because Philadelphia is not the city Gar started from. Albeit hesitantly, in 'Philadelphia' Gar expresses his desire for transformation, and Roche associates this song with Gar's many fantasies of future wealth, adventure, romance, and independence (88–89).

The following year, Elmer Andrews expands this limited analysis into a broader theory of Friel's use of classical music in his plays. In *The Art of Brian Friel* published in 1995, midway through Friel's long career, Andrews posits that *Philadelphia* begins 'a long experiment (culminating in *Dancing at Lughnasa* [1990]) with the possibility of expressing the deep rhythms of personality through music and/or musical language' (91). He instances Friel's use of Mendelssohn's violin concerto as background to, and perhaps trigger for, both Gar's reflections on his mother in her youth and likewise the 'unrealised or latent possibility' of his past happiness with his father (92). In both associations to Gar's lost relationships with his parents, Andrews claims that the play deploys music to chart Gar's 'irrational, fictionalizing memory' (93).

Writing not long after Andrews first sought to look beyond Friel's parody of the song first sung by Al Jolson, Martine Pelletier sought to account for the play's employment of diverse genres of music, most notably American song, Irish traditional, and European classical. While she also comments on the genuine or forced emotional buoyancy anticipating his American sojourn associated with Gar's singing of 'Philadelphia', she is more concerned with charting the play's deployment of such traditional Irish songs as 'All around My Hat' and 'She Moved through the Fair' (89). Pelletier observes that these moments are often equally filled with emotion, loss, and past failures (90). Nevertheless, she also finds Friel's use of classical music of greatest significance, because 'l'association musique classique et image de la mère' alerts readers to an important link between *Philadelphia* and the later *Aristocrats* (1979), where Chopin's music conveys the family's 'fidélité au souvenir de [leur] mère' (90).

Harry White's essay 'Brian Friel and the Condition of Music' (1999) presents a brief, yet surprisingly comprehensive argument for the play's modulation from the brash 'Philadelphia, Here I Come' to Mendelssohn's violin concerto, which introduces a more introspective, elegiac tone to the play. However, White sees the concerto structure as crucial to understanding the logic of the entire play: not only is Gar the 'conductor and soloist both structurally and metaphorically' but 'the play is his concerto' and the concerto model defines the play's linear development (10). Tony Corbett similarly asserts that 'it is not unusual to find [Friel] structuring sections of his drama after musical forms' (16), and he is especially intrigued by the shift in dramatic tone in *Philadelphia* signalled when Gar moves from playing the second movement of Mendelssohn's concerto to the third movement later in the play. For Corbett, this marks a shift from 'a feeling of irrecoverable loss', when Gar contemplates his dead mother, to the 'manic high spirits' later in the play as Gar contemplates his father while he is playing chess against the Canon (38–39).

Emigration and America

Despite the play's title, content, and associations with a song from America's Broadway theatre, few explore the play as one about emigration or the influence of American culture on the Irish. Indeed, it was not until 1997, in *The Irish Play on the New York Stage* by John Harrington, that anyone sought to delineate the play's American context. Rather than chronicling the many American productions of his various plays, Harrington's chapter 'Brian Friel: Erin on Broadway' focuses on *Philadelphia*: the promotional context for the 1966 David Merrick production (148–54), the other Irish plays that had been staged in the 1960s that influenced the reception of *Philadelphia* (155–56), and the success of this play, which influenced future productions of Friel's works (157–60).

Not only does Harrington explore *Philadelphia* as a play about emigration, he also asserts that Friel turns the expectations of the genre on its head. Whereas the emigrant is usually seen as a bold risk taker, while those who remain in the homeland are seen as dull and lacking ambition, Harrington argues that

■ The unpleasantness of Gar's prospects are underscored because... Katie Doogan is marrying some other, more successful, local boy. The logic on this occasion suggests that the quality stays in Ireland and the weak characters, like Gar, emigrate. (151) □

Harrington sees Friel's portrayal of America as complementary to Gar's temperamental weakness as well; American culture, he claims, is consistently imagined as 'vulgar' and 'gross' (146). Gar's stereotypes of America are confirmed in his Aunt Lizzy and Uncle Con, who embody 'the loud, brassy' culture of America (146). However, Harrington points out that Gar is generally excited, rather than offended, by America's perceived coarseness: 'However gross, the image of America is accepted by Private Gar as opportunity' (146).

Writing just a few years later, Nicolas Grene in *The Politics of Irish Drama* considers emigration as the primary subject of *Philadelphia*, seeing the play as concerned not so much with the attractions that America offers Gar as with 'the economic, cultural, and spiritual poverty of the Irish small-town experience' (199). Comparing the play to Tom Murphy's *A Crucial Week in the Life of a Grocer's Assistant* (1969), Grene maps out surprisingly extensive similarities between these two plays that explore the social conservatism, economic deprivation, and sexual frustration of 1960s Ireland (202). In short, Grene argues, '*Philadelphia* is ostensibly all about what makes Ballybeg an impossible place to live in, what forces the likes of Gar to emigrate' (205).

In his *Theatre and the State* (2001), Lionel Pilkington also sees *Philadelphia* as an emigration play but, unlike Grene, he sees it as one that resists the generic expectations for plot development. Rather than imagining Gar as a typical youth from the West of Ireland who has 'been left behind in the modernization programme ... for social and economic reasons', Pilkington points out that Gar is rather well placed. He has some university education, a secure job, and a father with some political stature; however, Gar's self-perception of his failure, leading him to emigrate, originates in his 'personal ineptitude', 'the most important' source of which is 'his frustrated sexual desire' (162). Thus, Gar's decision to live with his uncle and aunt in Philadelphia represents a 'hapless and fateful succumbing', but not to the economic privations of Co. Donegal; rather, it is a sign of his emotional infantilization, for he accepts his aunt as a substitute for his dead mother (162).

Maria Szasz presents the most comprehensive survey of the play's American background in her *Brian Friel and America* (2013), cataloguing such topics as

Irish emigration statistics for the early twentieth century, Friel's use of American slang, and the American popular culture references employed throughout the play. However, her work is most useful in her exploration of Friel's American and Irish-American characters. Szasz's treatment of Gar's Aunt Lizzy, who had herself emigrated to America twenty-five years earlier, is especially perceptive in recognizing her as a precursor to Cass McGuire, the main character of Friel's next play (37). Both women, she argues, return to Ireland having internalized American materialism and coarseness to their detriment. Szasz also offers a sustained consideration of Ben Burton, the first of Friel's 'seven American male characters' (38). She finds Burton juxtaposed to Lizzy in three important ways: unlike her, he is characterized by a generosity that expects no recompense; while everyone else is Catholic, he presents a positive image of Protestantism; and he fails to recognize much difference between Ireland and the United States (38–39). Finally, she astutely notes that though Gar has met and spent time with this 'laidback, mild-mannered' American, Burton has had 'no impact on the young Irishman's outrageous fantasies about America' (39).

In his chapter on the play, Richard Rankin Russell furthers this focus on the impact of American culture by looking at Gar himself. Whereas the earlier analyses tended to focus on broad cultural examples, Russell initiates his treatment by considering Gar's ideological relation to America; he notes that

■ Friel's Gar O'Donnell, 25 years old during the play, clearly comes of age as an adolescent during the 1950s and is caught up in the general movement of Irish culture toward America in that decade. While Irish culture had been greatly influenced by European culture in the 1930s and 1940s, [Brian] Fallon argues that, by the 1950s, '[i]ncreasingly, Irish culture faced westward rather than toward the Continent...' (37) □

This Americanization of Irish culture in a broad sense manifests itself most clearly in 'Gar's persistent adaptation of the American cowboy accent' (Russell, 39). Moreover, Russell attributes this and other such stereotypes of American heroism adopted by Gar to the widespread influence of American film, in particular, throughout Ireland (41–43). Indeed, whether Gar sees himself as cowboy, spy, pilot, or film maker, Russell seeks to trace the imprint of America wherever it may emerge in the play.

Ultimately, *Philadelphia, Here I Come!* was a watershed in the young writer's career, transforming Friel from a struggling Irish writer to the most successful playwright of his generation. The four plays that followed, premiered from 1966 through 1969, reveal an artist of growing confidence and ambition, one willing to experiment with form and explore unpopular subjects. Hence, the plays discussed in the next chapter failed to achieve *Philadelphia's* unqualified success.

CHAPTER FOUR

Plays of the Later 1960s

The Plays of Love

In the introduction to my 2007 study of Friel's plays, I discuss 'the symbiotic etiquette' that developed between the playwright and a core of critics who defer to his explanations of his plays (6 7). Unlike many late twentieth-century writers who frequently delivered public lectures or published essays, Friel stopped writing literary essays very early in his career in 1967 and gave few interviews.[1] Indeed, during the last fifteen years of his life Friel famously earned the reputation of being a recluse: not only did such Irish critics as Richard Pine and Fintan O'Toole sometimes substitute for him in interviews that were traditionally done with an author, but he conspicuously refrained from even speaking when featured in *Brian Friel* (2001), the documentary about him directed by Sinead O'Brien.[2]

Because his public statements were rare, his reported comments on the intention of his work sometimes exerted considerable influence on the critical views of his plays. As early as his 1970 interview with the Belfast playwright John Boyd for BBC Radio Four Northern Ireland, Friel claims that he wrote an 'accidental quartet' of plays on the theme of love:

> ■ Well, it began in the play about St. Columba. I followed through with *Philadelphia, Here I Come!* (which is a kind of love story), *The Loves of Cass McGuire*, *Lovers*, and the final play in this kind of accidental quartet was *Crystal and Fox*.[3] □

He similarly repeated this assertion that his plays from *Philadelphia* through *Crystal and Fox* 'were all attempts at analysing different kinds of love' in a 1972 interview with Des Hickey and Gus Smith.[4]

Thus, the idea that Friel's plays from 1964 through 1967 constituted a series exploring different types of love became a commonplace in the criticism, a truism that served as a jumping-off place for the later criticism. In his 1973 study of

Friel's writing, Maxwell identifies *The Enemy Within* (1962) as the first in a 'tetralogy on the theme of love and family' (55), which George O'Brien reiterates in his book's introductory remarks to his chapter on Friel's plays of the 1960s (53). Conversely, others like Ulf Dantanus chose to focus on a core trio of love plays, excluding *The Enemy Within* (104), which embody a Chekhovian 'sad awareness of the precariousness of individual life and love' (104–05). Dantanus's general approach is followed in two 1999 books: the first by F.C. McGrath (68) and the second by Nicholas Grene (212); while in her 1997 monograph, Martine Pelletier also recognizes that many later plays, especially those premiered between 1977 and 1980, share traits and themes with the core plays of the 1960s (50–51).

The Loves of Cass McGuire (1966)

Cass McGuire is the first of three plays that are universally recognized as companions to an important and successful work that directly preceded it.[5] *Cass McGuire* immediately follows *Philadelphia, Here I Come!*—indeed, it premiered in New York City while *Philadelphia* was still playing on Broadway—and it has been interpreted as a work that responds to and comments on the themes and setting of Friel's earlier success. By the time George O'Brien's *Brian Friel* appeared in 1990, he could nonchalantly comment that it was accepted as the 'sister play' to *Philadelphia* (55).

In his *Brian Friel*, Anthony Roche has argued that the period between April 1965 and October 1966 is vital to our understanding of the play's poor initial reception and fundamental to the evolution of Friel's relationship to subsequent directors of his work. According to Roche's research, the American producer David Merrick convinced both Friel and Hilton Edwards, despite their preference for a Dublin premiere, that it should open at the Helen Hayes Theatre in New York City, while *Philadelphia* was enjoying its successful Broadway run nearby at the Plymouth. However, this decision meant that the cast would have to be 'almost entirely American' because of established Actors' Equity employment agreements. Thus, Edwards found himself forced to work with American actors, whom he did not consider ideal for their parts (Roche, 49). Indeed, though the successful Broadway actress Ruth Gordon (1896–1985) was cast for the title role, Roche points out that 'neither playwright nor director were entirely persuaded of her suitability for the role' (49).

While poor casting may have in part contributed to the play's initial failure with New York audiences, Roche argues that Friel's dispute with Edwards and Merrick over the text had a formative effect on his relationship to the directors of his plays. Taking his cue from Patrick Burke's article 'Friel and Performance History', where he briefly mentions that 'the powerful Merrick organization was playing fast and loose' with the script in rehearsals (118), Roche explains the circumstances that led Friel to fly from Ireland to America accompanied by a lawyer to demand the restoration of his script (49). Roche concludes that this conflict over the arrangement and length of speeches led Friel to the conviction that his plays were never to be altered.

Cass McGuire closed in New York after barely two weeks, and John Harrington attributes the play's failure to Broadway's 'increasingly rigid expectations of what constituted an Irish play', as evidenced by the tepid reviews the premiere received in the press (157).[6] In his 2014 survey of Friel's career, Christopher Murray returns to Roche's assertion that the primary fault lay with Ruth Gordon, specifically because she could not grasp Cass's complexities as a character 'split between the Bowery and small-town Ireland', a character who is always 'partly phoney' because she uncontrollably vacillates between 'an outrageously rough American' and a ruined Mother Ireland (35). Murray usefully juxtaposes Edwards' premiere production to the successful revival the following year directed by Tomás Mac Anna at the Abbey Theatre, with iconic Irish actor Siobhán McKenna (1922–86) in the title role, who achieved what Gordon could not: a coarse heroine for whom the audience felt empathy.[7]

In his book's treatment of the play, Anthony Roche also outlines the cultural significance of casting McKenna as Cass; McKenna had played such iconic nationalist heroines as Cathleen ni Houlihan and Pegeen Mike, and Roche asserts that the play forms a pointed critique of Irish nationalism in 1966, the fiftieth anniversary of the Easter Uprising (74–75). Similarly, in my treatment of the play in *Brian Friel, Ireland and the North*, I consider Cass and Gar's father, S.B. O'Donnell, as representatives of Ireland's revolutionary generation who came of age in the years between the Easter Uprising (1916) and the end of the Irish Civil War (1923). Ultimately, despite the manifest differences between Cass and O'Donnell, Friel portrays a generation that must be seen as unsuccessful in its attempt to create a new nation (55–58).

As the sister play to *Philadelphia*, *Cass McGuire* comments on many of the themes that dominate the earlier play. Whereas Gar departs Ireland in the mid-1960s with hopes and dreams as a young man, Cass returns in the mid-1960s viewed as a failed émigré, to face the consequences of her earlier decision to emigrate to America. As with *Philadelphia*, much of the early criticism focuses on the role of Memory in the play. However, whereas Gar struggles to faithfully recover memories, almost every character in *Cass McGuire* seeks comfort in unreliable ones. Michael Etherton's discussion of the play in his 1989 survey *Contemporary Irish Dramatists* focuses on such 'deliberate mythologizing of the past' that allows characters to create comforting versions of their lives (164). While Etherton anatomizes how Cass, her fellow inmates Trilbe and Ingram, and even her brother and sister-in-law transform their pasts into '(remembered) idealism', both Dantanus and O'Brien, in their separate analyses, give greater attention to Friel's reliance on Wagner's *Tristan und Isolde* and his use of leitmotifs to structure the 'rhapsodies' that transform a character's past into illusory memory.[8]

While many subsequent critics, such as Tony Corbett and Geraldine Higgins, are content to rely upon the established interpretive models, Elmer Andrews and F.C. McGrath present the most exhaustive expositions of these ideas. For Andrews, 'the fluid, dream-like world of the play operates on several levels of reality simultaneously', and he uses this observation to carefully explore the play's initial scenes, both before Cass arrives and afterwards, when she openly challenges her brother for control of the play (96–98). Andrews then proceeds to explain how Wagner's theories of 'music drama' and 'total artwork' provide Friel with a method to create the world of his play. He explores how Trilbe's association with Wagner's 'Venusberg' from *Tannhäuser*, Ingram's with 'Magic Fire' from *The Valkyrie*, and Cass's with the 'Liebestod' from *Tristan und Isolde* create thematic associations with each character's story (99–102).[9] However, Andrews recognizes the inherent threat of such an aestheticizing transformation of the past:

■ The play, however, need not be seen simply as an endorsement of illusion. Trilbe and Ingram, for all their fantasizing, still pass most of their day in complete boredom.…As [Cass] becomes absorbed in her 'rhapsody', her language is sanitized, her vibrant humour disappears.…She has surrendered her own rebellious will and defiant individualism and assimilated Harry's values. (102–3) □

Writing twenty years later, Anthony Roche adds that Cass's association with the 'Liebestod' is 'imposed on her' over the course of the play, and it displaces her personal and emotional affection for the Irish melody by Thomas Moore 'Oft in the stilly night' (71).

For McGrath, while *Philadelphia* 'is perhaps Friel's most overrated play' (69), *Cass* presents the playwright's 'most profound and ambitious exploration of the social and psychological functions of illusion' (78). While likewise devoting attention to the play's debt to the experimentalism of Luigi Pirandello and its Wagnerian rhapsodies, McGrath's 1999 treatment breaks new ground in his analysis of Cass's relationship to her parents (81–82) and the extent to which even the brief appearances of minor figures (86–88) contribute to the play's thematic refinement. Moreover, McGrath ends his lengthy treatment by arguing that the play should also be read as an exposition of the struggle between Ireland's colonial and postcolonial elements. In this reading, Cass's brother Harry represents 'the new nationalist hegemony' that replaced the former colonial powers, while Cass embodies the new nation's disempowered minorities: the women, émigrés, and Northern nationalists (92–93).

Lovers: 'Winners' and 'Losers' (1967)

For the reader new to Friel, *Lovers* would seem to be clearly one of the most minor of his plays. However, this would not have been the view through the 1970s. Andrews introduces his book's treatment of the play, briefly citing the rapidity with which the play travelled from its opening at Dublin's Gate Theatre, under the direction of Hilton Edwards (1967), to its American production at the Vivian Beaumont Theatre (1968), to London's Fortune Theatre (1969). In his history of Friel's reception on the New York stage, John Harrington mentions that the play was 'very well received' and prompted the *New York Post* critic Richard Watts to opine that 'Brian Friel is the new top man in Irish dramatic writing and may well restore the theater of Ireland to the days of glory of Synge, Yeats, and O'Casey' (157). Even a cursory review of the play's initial production history suggests its popularity: the New York production enjoyed a national tour from February through June 1969, and in its first ten years the play was professionally staged a dozen times, in such countries as New Zealand, Switzerland, and Argentina.

Despite its early popularity, *Lovers* attracted neither sustained nor complex criticism, and the early strategies for reading the play have defined how it continues to be interpreted. Moreover, since the late 1990s, many of the book length discussions of Friel's career, including those by F.C. McGrath and Anthony Roche, dispense with the play in a paragraph or two. What comes out most in the criticism is the uneven pairing of the two short plays 'Winners' and 'Losers' that combine to form *Lovers*. The first stages the winners, Joe and Mag, teenage lovers who spend the day on a hilltop studying for their leaving exams; they look forward to their marriage in the near future, ignorant that they both will die later that day. In 'Losers', Andy narrates for the audience the story of his courtship and eventual marriage to Hanna. Unlike the previous pair, Andy and Hanna are much older, and their story is defined by their compromises and surrenders rather than the younger couple's dreams.

Writing barely five years after the play's premiere, Maxwell's book presents one of the longest treatments of the play and seeks to identify how the two short plays form a unified analysis of love as it accommodates the exigencies of quotidian life (78–84). However, he ultimately recognizes that 'Winners' and 'Losers' hardly propose a readily identifiable single story; indeed, he notes that the first play's sombre 'tissue of ironies' (81) sits awkwardly against the latter's 'robust, broadly satirical [comedy], drawing on farce' (84). Ultimately, Maxwell's basic argument that the two fated to die young are the 'winners because death forestalls a corruption of love' characterizes the subsequent critical orientation (80).

Dantanus follows the critical shift to an emphasis on 'Winners', and, in his reading, he argues for the importance of the metatheatrical Commentators who sit on the edge of the stage and read to the audience from their bound manuscripts, providing various personal and social contexts for Joe and Mag's story (110–12). Dantanus forcibly argues that the Commentators alienate the audience from any possible emotional tie to the young couple and encourage a 'more philosophical' attitude to their mysterious deaths. Maria Szasz broadens this reading of the Commentators' choric role by comparing them to the Stage Manager in Thornton Wilder's *Our Town* (1938), all of which contextualize tragic death within the broader continuity of a small town's survival (65–66).

O'Brien also recognizes that 'Winners' constitutes an '[exposé] of small-town mores', both the morality imposed upon the characters by their Catholic education and the class biases that occasionally erupt between the reasonably well-to-do Mag and the working-class Joe (60). Writing not long after O'Brien, Andrews also suggests that Mag and Joe are winners not only because an early death saves them from their future 'slow, miserable death-in-life' of unrealized aspirations (112), but also because it equally saves them from their class-based prejudices that seem poised to destroy their romance (113). Indeed, so strong is this interpretation based on class difference that it is echoed in the later, brief treatments offered by Nicolas Grene in 1999 in *The Politics of Irish Drama* (208) and Geraldine Higgins in *Brian Friel* (19–20).

My reading of 'Winners' in *Brian Friel* seeks to shift our interpretive context to the summer of 1966, which forms the play's setting. June, the month that Mag and Joe die, started a summer 'during which the UVF had formally declared war against the IRA … and carried out numerous attacks that terrorized, wounded, and killed' (67). Similarly, Co. Tyrone, where the action is set, is far from peaceful during the summer of 1966:

■ Throughout 1966 the peace of County Tyrone was disrupted repeatedly by Catholic protests against the injustices perpetrated by local Loyalist governments in such cities as Dungannon. (67) □

Thus, I argue that the play, written in the year when Friel resolved to move from Northern Ireland to the Irish Republic, embodies the hopelessness and pervasive fatalism that had come to define Northern Ireland for Friel (66–67).

Briefly, the scholarship on 'Losers', the companion to 'Winners', is considerably more uniform. Dantanus first identifies that the play relies upon a story 'The Highwayman and the Saint', which first appeared in the 1966 collection *The Gold in the Sea*: 'In a first-person narrative Andy tells more or less exactly the same story' (114). In both story and play, the romance between the middle-aged couple blossoms in secret opposition to the constraining pietistic attitudes of Hanna's household, but once the couple marry and they live with Hanna's mother, they surrender to their town's sexual prudery. O'Brien pursues a more detailed comparison of the two plays than Dantanus, though he adds that the failure of Andy's romance with Hanna results from the interference by 'the play's three institutions: Church, family, and marriage' (63). For Andrews as well, Andy and Hanna are the play's 'losers' because they are too weak to resist Catholicism's social and sexual norms: 'an old, repressive, life-denying order' (118).

Crystal and Fox (1968)

In 'Surviving the 1960s', his overview of Friel's early career, the playwright Frank McGuinness mentions that *Crystal and Fox* is one of Friel's least produced plays and attributes this thin staging history to the play's large cast (25). A similar observation could be made about the play's critical profile as well: this is a work that has attracted little engaged or original criticism. Moreover, many of the play's treatments situate it as primarily a Memory play; however, it is a Memory play in which the vague 'good thing' in the past that Fox struggles to recover leads him to torment those around him.[10]

George O'Brien offers the first nuanced attempt to assess the play in his 1990 book; for example, he rightly recognizes that this play is 'a culmination of sorts in Friel's career', the last of Friel's plays that relies on a simple plot structure focused on a single dominant character (65). This main character, Fox, spends the play alienating or betraying everyone associated with him until at the drama's end he is literally alone at a crossroads. Discerning the motive behind Fox's destructive behaviour has been one of Friel criticism's primary concerns, and O'Brien attributes it to Fox's 'set of compulsions' for gaining control of time and chance (66).

In his later treatment of the play in his book, Andrews refers to Fox as a 'tortured romantic hero ... the exponent of a deadly kind of idealism', while the specific nature of Fox's 'dream' remains elusive (108). Whereas, in his book, O'Brien argues that Fox attempts to return to an idealized past with his wife Crystal (67), Andrews seeks to articulate a more complex and vexed character who seeks 'to step out of the world of flux and change' to grasp a 'timeless' past perfection (107). In his 2014 study of Friel, Murray offers the reading of *Crystal and Fox* that most intentionally aligns the play with Friel's series of Love plays, and he finds a note in the Friel Papers at the National Library of Ireland to confirm the thematic importance of Fox's love for Crystal, his wife (43). But Murray recognizes that it is a distorted and destructive love that finds its most apt comparison to that of Shakespeare's Iago (44).

Conversely, Roche in his *Brian Friel* (2011) offers perhaps the most expansive reading of *Crystal and Fox* by looking to John Osborne's *The Entertainer* (1957) to find the play's artistic and cultural touchstone. Both plays consider the dying out of popular working-class theatre and the impresarios who struggle against social change and personal bitterness (85–90).

The Mundy Scheme (1969)

The Mundy Scheme, Friel's farcical depiction of the Irish government in crisis, is unusual among his many plays. Along with *The Communication Cord* (1982), it is the very rare example of a Frielian comedy; however, it is truly unique for it occupies the space between the author's fully acknowledged oeuvre and the plays officially withdrawn. Once he had disowned such plays as *The Blind Mice*, Friel never allowed their performance or publication. However, while he has never allowed its publication by Gallery Press or Faber, which have published almost every one of his plays, it was published by Farrar, Straus, and Giroux in 1970. Similarly, while he has never allowed its performance since 1969, he did allow its staged reading at the Peacock Theatre during the Friel Festival in 1999 held to commemorate his seventieth birthday, where it was one of nine plays representing the playwright's career.

The earliest scholarship on the play makes observations about Friel's intention to expose the 'shoneenism, xenophobia, [and] time-serving religion' of the Irish political class (Maxwell, 87), and the subsequent discussions of the play are dominated by this line of analysis.[11] In my 2007 treatment of Friel's plays, I interpret the play's view of politics through the lens of Frantz Fanon's analysis of a postcolonial state's inept and corrupt governing politics as described in his 'Pitfalls of National Consciousness' (in *The Wretched of the Earth* [*Les damnés de la terre*], 1961). In particular, I read the play with attention to Fanon's exploration of such a postcolonial government's reliance on corrupt land policies, and I compare the development of necro-tourism in the play to the more traditional types of tourism developed in other postcolonial nations (89–92).

Maria Szasz also departs from the conventional reading of *Mundy* by focusing on the play's characterization of Americans and American influence: '*The Mundy Scheme* presented by far Friel's most interesting, as well as most disturbing image of America' (148). Szasz looks at the temptation for Irish politicians to capitulate to American money, both when the United States government seeks to build nuclear submarine bases along the Irish coast (144) and, later, when Homer Mundy, the wealthy Texan, convinces the Irish government to turn the Connemara and surrounding areas in the West into a vast cemetery for Irish expatriates and their descendants (145–46). Thus, after several different types of family dramas, Friel closed the 1960s with a political play, and this interest in politics and the impact of Irish politics on individual lives was to become increasingly important to his plays of the 1970s.

CHAPTER FIVE

Plays of the Early 1970s

The Gentle Island (1971)

Helen Lojek's 'Brian Friel's Gentle Island of Lamentation' (1999) provides one of the most acute examples of how the broad historical context enhances our understanding of a play. Lojek introduces her reading of *Gentle Island* with a summary of the internment-related violence in Dublin as well as the growing tensions in Northern Ireland that would soon erupt on Bloody Sunday (48).[1] Writing at the same time as Lojek, F.C. McGrath additionally situates the play in a period characterized by Friel's 'anger toward Irish society', claiming that his recent move across the border into the Irish Republic in no way represented an embrace of the Irish culture or politics of the late 1960s (77).

This social ferment coupled with the playwright's growing experience and artistic maturation may explain why *The Gentle Island* has been seen as a watershed for Friel's career. D.E.S. Maxwell's 1973 book described the play as marking 'a new direction' for the playwright (100), while, writing fifteen years later, Ulf Dantanus more strenuously argues that the play marks a turning point for Friel: first, rather than being a mere 'presenter of a situation', with *Gentle Island* Friel 'has begun to take on the function of interpreter as well'. Second, perhaps because of his growing mastery of dramaturgy, Friel's work displays 'a less pronounced urge towards "supra-realism"…non-realistic techniques imposed on the framework of the play' (132). Similarly, in his 2011 book, Anthony Roche traces the origin of Friel's trademark use of stage space to this play: 'the interior and exterior are presented side by side, with neither absolutely prevailing, though the external occupies two-thirds of the space' (108), which is a division of space generally used in *Aristocrats* (1979), *Dancing at Lughnasa* (1990), and *The Home Place* (2005).

Maxwell initiates one of the most durable interpretive frameworks for *Gentle Island* in his reading of the play's dismantling of the pastoral tropes associated with the Irish West (95–96). This approach is refined by Dantanus as the cultural 'contrast between the West of Ireland and Dublin' (128), as staged in the opposition of the Sweeneys of Inishkeen, the bare island off the Ballybeg coast, and Peter and Shane, the gay couple on holiday from Dublin. The play's depiction of homosexuality was also radical for early 1970s Ireland. As I point out in my 2007 book, homosexuality was illegal in the Republic until 1993, so the play's portrayal of the homosexual couple Shane and Peter is especially important in the history of Irish theatre (114).[2]

While a recognition of the play's violence dates back to Maxwell's discussion (97–98), José Lanters is the first to systematically examine it. Her 1996 article 'Violence and Sacrifice' explores how the play ritualizes violence through the use of scapegoats, primarily seen in Philly's beating of Shane and Sarah's later demand that Shane be punished for having sex with her husband Philly (167–69). Helen Lojek's 'Brian Friel's Gentle Island of Lamentation' consolidates and extends these interpretive threads of the play's anti-pastoralism and violence by focusing on the play's 'basic pattern—intruder disrupts closed community' (50). Not only does she demonstrate how often Friel used it in his earlier stories and later plays, she also convincingly argues that Friel knowingly incorporates references to both the American and the Irish West (50–53).

Andrews is the first of the play's readers to explore how *Gentle Island* is also a play about storytelling; in fact, he sees this as the first of Friel's many important uses of 'contrapuntal narratives', in which plays are about a character's ability to deceive and prevent the audience from recognizing a single correct or authoritative version (126). Andrews cites the unresolved disagreement between Manus and Sarah over how he lost his arm as indicative of the play's repeated juxtaposition of 'romantic fictions of the past' and their 'ironic reworking' (125). Also, he is the first to single out Shane, the clever outsider who charms and disrupts the islanders, as a transgressive character 'deliberately mixing idioms, breaking the rules, refusing the magical function of story' (127).

In 'Telling Tales: Narratives of Politics and Sexuality in *The Gentle Island*' (1996), Michael Parker offers the most thorough analysis of the play's word choice and narrative structure. Not only does he offer a painstakingly careful and revealing analysis of the play's depiction of narratives, from '"readings" of the island' (146) and narration of events to the iteration of folklore and personal history, he also provides an acute exploration of the play's reliance on such words as 'truth' (145), the terms used to describe the island (151–52), and the way language conveys patriarchal structures (155–59). This view of *Gentle Island* as primarily concerned with telling stories, particularly anti-pastoral ones, dominates the subsequent, brief treatments of the play from Corbett's interest in its 'linguistic repression' (45–46) through Higgins assertion that its 'characters understand themselves in terms of the stories they tell' (24).

The Freedom of the City (1973)

Bloody Sunday

The Freedom of the City, dramatizing the story of three Civil Rights marchers killed by British soldiers in Derry, is one of the first plays to depict the Troubles,[3] the low-grade civil war that engulfed Northern Ireland from late 1968 until the paramilitary ceasefires of 1994.[4] In an 1982 interview with Fintan O'Toole, Friel admitted that the play was written in reaction to the murder of thirteen civilians on Bloody Sunday on 30 January 1972: 'To be there on that occasion and...to have to throw yourself on the ground because people are firing at you is a very terrifying experience'. Indeed, he admits that the play emerged 'out of some kind of heat and some kind of immediate passion that I would want to have quieted a bit before I did it'.[5] Depicting a riot, the callous response of British soldiers, and the miscarriages of the legal system, the play was uniformly criticized by the English and Northern Irish press as 'unconvincing', 'overzealous', and 'mawkish propaganda'; likewise, it met only muted support in the Dublin press (Dantanus, 140).[6] Nevertheless, the play has also proved surprisingly popular, and in the first twenty years after its premiere, it was professionally staged twenty times in ten countries.

In his book's treatment of *Freedom*, written less than a year after its premiere and in the early days of The Troubles, Maxwell follows Friel's statement that the subject of the play is poverty (104). In this, he cites Skinner's assertion that Lily marches because 'it's about us—the poor'; he also uses this theme to explain the prominence given to the character Professor Dodds, an American sociologist and expert on the culture of poverty (103–04). In the next monograph on Friel, Dantanus wishes to de-emphasize this sociological view of the play, saying 'it is not about poverty'; rather, he flatly states that it is 'about the minority population in Ireland', and thus about different strata of the Catholic population (134). While he strives to avoid a clearly anti-British reading of the play, Dantanus discusses the relationship of the action to the actual events on Bloody Sunday and the play's commentary on the infamous Widgery Report that exonerated the British soldiers (134–37). Writing more than a decade after Dantanus, Bernice Schrank's article, 'Politics, Language, Metatheatre' (2000) expands this general association between the march and the play to demonstrate how comprehensively *Freedom* incorporates not just the diverse events that defined Bloody Sunday but also the march's cultural context (123–28).

While Dantanus offers the most sustained attempt to compare the play's depiction of the murder of three protesters in Friel's fictitious 1970 march to the actual events on Bloody Sunday in 1972, Richard Pine was the first critic to strenuously attempt to shift the focus from the events of Bloody Sunday to the findings of the *Report* of the Widgery Tribunal, the official investigation ordered by Parliament and published in April 1972, barely three months after the event. Pine's claim that the play was not written in response to Bloody Sunday but 'in response to the Report of the Widgery Tribunal' (1999, p. 134) was argued with greater particularity by McGrath, who pointed out that, with the exception of the American sociologist and the Irish street singer, all the characters who comment on the play's action 'have counterparts in the list of witnesses who testified before the Widgery tribunal' (106). Similarly, in his book's explication of the play's origin in Friel's 1970 draft provisionally titled 'The Mayor's Parlour', Anthony Roche adds that Friel was revising this manuscript during the weeks that the tribunal was conducting its interviews and finished the play within a month after the report was published (2011, p. 115).

The Judge and Professor Dodds

This shift in focus from Bloody Sunday to the Widgery Report coincides with a critical interest in the diverse choric characters who comment upon or attempt to interpret the action. In this respect, the Judge has attracted considerable interest because of his statements' close relationship to those of Judge John Passmore Widgery (McGrath, 106–08). Tony Corbett has offered the most thorough reading of Friel's Judge, pointing out that the Judge 'speaks first and last' and appears in eight scenes throughout the play, with four soliloquies (2002, p. 147). Corbett carefully considers the class prejudices and English biases that pervade the Judge's interrogations of policemen, army personnel, and the proceeding's coroner (147–49). However, well before McGrath and Corbett detailed the Judge's faults, Andrews declared, '*Freedom* is … an exposure of the bogus language of the corrupt state authority *and* of the equally bogus language of traditional Nationalist mythology' (130). His reading of such characters as the Priest, the Balladeer, and the RTE commentator focuses on how their attempts to co-opt the trio's tragedy into a nationalist agenda 'shamefully' presents an ideological opportunism rivalling that of the Judge (135). In his *Theatre and the State in Twentieth-Century Ireland*, Lionel Pilkington further argues that

■ The fact-finding objectivity of the Judge (or Widgery) cannot be singled out for condemnation or satire because, Friel's play insists, it is just one version of the distorting process of representation in general. (199)[7] □

Finally, the play's American professor Dr Philip Alexander Dodds has also attracted considerable interest beginning with Dantanus's attempt to explain him as Friel's attempt to 'counterbalance' the Judge (136). He sees Dodds as a generally trustworthy spokesman on the culture of poverty, and some subsequent treatments of the character, for instance William Jent's 1994 article 'Supranational Civics', largely agree with him. While a desire to problematize Dodds's role in the play does not start with F.C. McGrath, his lengthy discussion of the character's relationship to the actual anthropologist Oscar Lewis and his detailed analysis of Dodds's main lectures raises many questions about his trustworthiness (1999, p. 111–18). Indeed, after considering the dissonance between the play's violence and the professor's academic detachment, McGrath concludes, 'we must ask ourselves whether Dodds's detachment is any less insidious than the more obvious injustice of the Judge' (118). This more sceptical view of Dodds is followed by Pilkington (2001, p. 201), Fulton (70–72), and Corbett (2002, p. 150–51) in their further developments of this basic analysis. However, while carefully comparing Lewis's writing to Dodds's statements, Maria Szasz argues that Friel uses this academic as a powerful tool to 'break the audience's emotional connection to the play' and force the audience's focus onto poverty (116).

Lily, Skinner, and Michael

The earliest critical interest also focused on Lily, Skinner, and Michael, the three marchers who took shelter in the Guild Hall, found their way to the mayor's resplendent office, and were later summarily executed by British forces as they surrendered. While the critical responses have long recognized the astute dramatic conditions created by Friel's decision to establish in the opening tableau that they are dead, Richard Rankin Russell, in his *Modernity, Community, and Place* (2014), employs Jacques Derrida's theory of 'hauntology' to effectively describe how the play stages a 'companionship between his ghostly characters and his audience, creating a 'politics of memory' that binds us together, the living and the dead' (98). And his subsequent discussion emphasizes that, by being ghosts, the demands made by Lily, Michael, and Skinner are both more pressing and more authentic for the audience (99–102). In 1980, in the first article published on the play, Elizabeth Winkler maps out the significant traits defining these characters; she is especially interested in juxtaposing the two young men and the manner in which their conflict 'echoes the clash of opinions within the early civil rights movement concerning the use of provocation and violence' (21).[8] The tensions that develop between Michael and Skinner, which are 'partly political, partly personal', and the way Friel uses Lily to prevent an irreconcilable breach between them, are carefully chronicled by Michael Parker in his 1999 article 'Forms of Redress' (285–91).

While Lily appears to be a straightforward embodiment of the uneducated, domesticated poor, Friel criticism has developed surprisingly complex discussions of her character. For example, though Parker considers Lily important to defining the generalized, unambitious working class (284–85), Elmer Andrews considers her the play's 'most dramatically appealing character', and he finds the combination of her deep emotions and her 'instinctual, uneducated' speech indicative of Friel's emerging 'dissatisfaction with language', which will become especially notable in *Translations* and *Dancing at Lughnasa* (132–33).[9] Helen Fulton also explores Lily's language, but she does so to reveal how church and state have socialized her to internalize 'the patriarchal hegemonic view of women as innately less intelligent and less able than men' (77). Conversely, in his 1999 study of the playwright, Richard Pine claims that Lily 'is one of Friel's most successful creations, and certainly one of those to whom we feel the greatest sympathy' (139). This sympathy, for Pine, arises out of not just her humour, but also her dogged devotion to her eleven children, which for years has motivated her desire to march (138–39). Tony Corbett roots such audience sympathy for Lily in her similarity to Sean O'Casey's Juno, from *Juno and the Paycock* (1924), one of the most important plays of the Irish Renaissance. Like various earlier counterparts, she strives to provide for her family despite poverty and her shiftless husband, and she does so with surprising humour and common sense (2002, p. 144–45).

The interpretive problems posed by Skinner have also concerned the scholarship more than the other male marcher Michael. While Winkler describes him as the only character with deft political insight, she nonetheless claims that he 'is certainly no revolutionary' (20). Fulton agrees with Winkler's assessment but asserts that Skinner represents the educated middle class, though he is acting as a 'class traitor' (78).[10] Michael Etherton even more closely highlights the contradictions inherent in Skinner's character: though he was turned out of grammar school, he quotes Kipling and Shakespeare.[11] Yet Etherton claims that in his oft-cited speech about 'the poor' to Lily, Skinner makes 'the central statement of the commitment of the playwright' (169). In addition, by connecting him with the sociology of B.F. Skinner, Corbett seeks to explain Skinner's contradictory character by describing him as 'one who has been negatively conditioned by his environment' (146–47). Although the consensus view is that Skinner is no true 'hooligan', even though Michael so accuses him, in my 2007 book on Friel, I argue that Skinner closely fits the model of a 'Sixty-niner', the young man who joined the Provisional IRA following the Battle of the Bogside (110). Indeed, in his ability to function amid a teargas attack, to articulate Marxist theory, and to anticipate the army's response to their actions, Friel suggests that he is an example of a significant group present at Bloody Sunday (108–10).

Finally, more than any play up to this point in Friel's career, *Freedom* experiments with overlapping narratives, mixing reportage with 'epic' structure, while assertively following a Brechtian strategy to alienate the audience.[12] Less than ten years after the play's premiere, Klaus Birker offers the first reading of the politics of the play's staging and scenography; however, Bernice Schrank details the political impact of Friel's use of horizontal as well as vertical space (128–38). In an attempt to more fully explore the play's ideological spatial definitions, Anthony Roche uses Michel de Certeau's *L'invention du quotidien* [*The Practice of Everyday Life*] (1980) to explore how the play's delineation of space link storytelling and space in a polyvalent manner that both isolates and interconnects micro-scenes upon the stage (116–21).

Volunteers (1975)

Volunteers is Friel's play about suspected IRA activists imprisoned by the Irish Republic under its controversial internment policy, initiated in January 1974, which allowed it to incarcerate those suspected of violence (Boltwood 2007, 98–99). After its premiere in April 1975 at the Abbey Theatre, this play was infrequently staged abroad, usually in American regional theatres, and not staged again in Ireland until the Cork Theatre Company revived it in 1987. While the play has attracted only limited critical attention, it marks a milestone in the relationship between Friel and the then-emerging poet Seamus Heaney.

In response to the very poor reviews that the Abbey production received, Heaney wrote 'Digging Deeper' (1975), a robust defence of the play first published in the *Times Literary Supplement*. Friel had sent Heaney a copy of *Volunteers* in manuscript in late 1974 and, as described by Christopher Murray in *The Theatre of Brian Friel* (2014), 'after he had read the play he put together all "the bog poems and Viking Dublin poems that were to hand"... and found he had a book ready for Faber, that is, *North*' (67). As a result of Friel and Heaney coming together over *Volunteers*, their professional acquaintance grew into a close, lifelong friendship.[13]

In his review, Heaney establishes one of the most enduring strategies for reading the play: the association of its main character Keeney with Shakespeare's Hamlet:

> ■ The action—or, more precisely, the interaction—centres on Keeney, a man who has put an antic disposition on, for Viking Ireland, like Denmark, is a prison. He is a Hamlet who is gay, not with tragic Yeatsian joy but as a means of deploying and maintaining his anger. (*Selected Plays*, 215) □

The play's reader will recognize that Heaney's observation merely follows clues provided in the play. In her 1986 article 'Digging into History', Ruth Niel develops this idea, arguing that both Keeney and Hamlet seek deeper knowledge about the nature of reality in their pursuits of truth (42), and this argument's general outline is followed by subsequent critics such as

Andrews (145), McGrath (1999, p. 126), and Murray (2014, p. 65). However, Keeney is considered noteworthy beyond his Shakespearean connotations; in his chapter on Friel in *Celtic Revivals* (1985), Seamus Deane recognizes that Keeney embodies a Frielian type that came to the fore in the 1970s. Like Shane in *The Gentle Island* (1971), Skinner in *Freedom* (1973), and Eamon in *Aristocrats* (1979), Keeney is an outsider who puts 'an antic disposition on' (169). Andrews captures the common thread of these characters when he describes them as 'fiction-specialists, impresarios, symbol-conscious commentators, obsessive role-players, Protean spirits, anguished doubters, dreamers with an almost compulsive resourcefulness' (145). More than the other critics, Andrews is especially detailed in his analysis of Keeney's complex character, which varies from the jocular through the disinterested to the disgusted (145–47).

Writing in the wake of such 'language plays' as *Translations* (1980) and *The Communication Cord* (1982), Dantanus proposes that the seeds of Friel's interest in language and society can be found in *Volunteers* (154). Similarly, in his 1991 article, Rudiger Imhof argues that one of the play's main purposes is to show how characters explore 'reality…by dint of linguistic categories' (87). Moreover, Imhof demonstrates how the play's characters employ words to define and limit themselves and their place in society. In his 1999 book, McGrath presents the most comprehensive survey of the functioning of the play's various forms of language: arguing that the play explores 'the relation of language and narrative to history' (126), he focuses on Keeney's limericks (127), 'banter' (129), and the various stories that he concocts about other prisoners and even the Viking corpse that is part of their archaeological dig (131–32).

The earliest criticism notes the importance of the play's two main props, the Viking corpse and jug, which are used to comment on Irish history and identity. Many subsequent commentators have, in essence, agreed with Niel's argument in 'Digging into History' that Lief is 'the most important symbol of the play' because of the way it comments upon the condition and implied fate of the five prisoners who have volunteered for the archaeological dig, which itself is accepted as a metaphor for Irish history (42). For Dantanus, the prisoners and the Viking corpse 'are all victims of internecine strife and ferocious tribal feuding', an appreciation of which is essential to the play's commentary on Irish history (156).[14] Indeed, taking their cues from Keeney's mock tour for imagined schoolchildren of the dig's historical layers, the interplay between the past and present has been seen as a central element of the play by such critics as Niel (37), Dantanus (156), and especially Pelletier, who sees this play as initiating the focus on History that is later developed in *Translations* (158–60).

While there has been only modest critical interest in the play after 2000, Corbett's book presents the most comprehensive survey of its themes, which is most useful for its attentive exploration of each of the IRA prisoners (165–66) and their speculations concerning Lief (169–71). In addition, Roche's 2014 book provides a detailed comparison of the play to David Storey's *The Contractor* (1969), a play about workers' attitudes towards labour (93–98), and Chu He's 'Brian Friel's Explorations of Trauma' (2014) explores how this theme manifests itself in the play's portrayal of history and the characters' actions (125–29). While these last two plays were the most political of his career, Friel's next plays, starting with *Living Quarters* (1977), would assertively return to the family and especially the powerful psychological demands placed upon children by domineering fathers.

CHAPTER SIX

Living Quarters (1977) and *Aristocrats* (1979)

Living Quarters (1977)

In *Brian Friel, Ireland, and the North*, I note that Friel makes a major dramaturgical shift starting with *Living Quarters*: Friel's plays from 1969 to 1975 rely upon overwhelmingly male casts, with forty-three male and seven female characters (115); however, with its focus on Anna, Helen, Miriam, and Tina, *Living Quarters* abruptly shifts to sororal narratives—plays about groups of sisters—that will be followed by such works as *Aristocrats* (1979), *Three Sisters* (1981), and *Dancing at Lughnasa* (1990). Moreover, Friel's sororal plays almost always include a single son and an emotionally fragile brother; this is even seen in nascent form in *Philadelphia, Here I Come!* (1964) when Gar's Aunt Lizzy laments, 'He's my sister's boy—the only child of five girls of us'.

Friel subtitles *Living Quarters* 'after *Hippolytus*', thus directly associating his play with the Greek tragedy by Euripides. Michael Etherton is the first commentator to summarize the play and consider the nature of Friel's debt to the ancient tragedian; after commenting on the manner in which 'the [Euripidean] ending is inverted' by the death of the Theseus figure Frank, he reflects on Friel's foregrounding of destiny as the play's theme (175–76). In his article 'Translating the Past' (1993), Alan Peacock seeks to assess how Friel recasts Euripides' original with a 'middle-class, Chekhovian format' that allows him to make 'radical changes in idiom, theological and psychological premises, and plot' (116). For Peacock, Friel's changes are less important than his ability to employ Chekhov to introduce

■ a comedic lightness of treatment which avoids parody but allows the stark, arbitrariness of myth to be tempered by a more socially and psychologically defined view of human motivation and destiny. (119–20) □

Michael Lloyd, in 'Brian Friel's Greek Tragedy' (2000), offers an interpretation of the play that more attentively compares the major characters and themes of *Hippolytus* and *Living Quarters*. While he makes sensible comparisons of Theseus to Frank Butler and Phaedra to Anna, his work is especially skilful in finding similarities in the unlikely pairing of Hippolytus and Ben (245–46). Similarly, his discussion of Sir's ledger as a secular version of Hellenistic fate addresses a major concern for anyone reading the play (249–50). Appearing in the same year as Lloyd's article, Redmond O'Hanlon's 'Brian Friel's Dialogue with Euripides' provides an examination much more concerned with exploring how Friel's play adapts to his play such ancient Greek concepts as *anagnorisis* [recognition] (108–10), fate (110–11), and the working of the human psyche (116–19).

In 'Brian Friel's Rituals of Memory' (2007), Robert Tracy explores the impact of the 'Cambridge Ritualists' of the early twentieth century on such figures as W.B. Yeats, T.S. Eliot, and Tyrone Guthrie, and through them on Friel as well. Tracy combines this tradition of tragedy as commemorative re-enactment of heroism or guilt with the importance of enacting ritual that Friel himself learned during his three years in a seminary. All of this illuminates death and the role of ritualized commemoration in such plays as *Living Quarters*, *Faith Healer*, and *Wonderful Tennessee* (399). In the case of the former, the audience quickly understands that the play depicts not Frank's last day, but 'one of a series of re-enactments of that day', stressing both the hero's tragic death as well as the multitude of minor family rituals that define the Butler clan (401–02).

In his 2014 study of Friel's career, Christopher Murray declares that *Living Quarters* takes its inspiration from Luigi Pirandello's *Six Characters in Search of an Author* (1921), and, in doing so, 'Friel turns his back on Brecht' (71). This Pirandellian turn is most apparent in the creation of the character Sir, who exists only in the overlapping psychological space created by the Butler family as they endlessly relive the events that led up to Frank's suicide. Ulf Dantanus is the first to assert that 'Friel's play is dominated by the character of Sir', and he sees him as the director, an agent of 'a higher authority', and even 'a metaphor of the writer at work' because he is in sole possession of the 'ledger' that infallibly details everything that leads to Frank's death (142–43). This view of Sir as surrogate for either fate or the author has dominated the subsequent criticism, as can be seen in the discussions of Etherton (176–77) and McGrath (1999, 139–44), while Andrews is the only commentator who attempts to argue that Sir's version is both limited and only a version with no more authority than those posited by other characters (140–41).

In his 1990 monograph, George O'Brien is the first to shift critical attention to Anna, Frank Butler's young second wife whose affair with his son leads to Frank's suicide. Indeed, he makes the bold claim that only Anna, and not Sir, 'is in possession of the whole picture' and 'she alone has the mettle to articulate' the Butler family's emotional immaturity (91). In his 2014 study of

Friel, Christopher Murray labels Anna the play's *femme fatale*, 'an enigma', who uncovers the inadequacies of both Frank and Sir (74).[1] Conversely, my reading of the play in my 2007 monograph is the only one to focus on Frank apart from his associations with Theseus. Rather, I argue that, in both his hubris and disastrous fall, 'Frank embodies the challenge facing Friel's entire generation … to "define our Irishness"': 'he must find opportunities for military heroism in the aftermath of Ireland's centuries of contradictory service both as agents of the British empire and rebels against English hegemony' (120).

Finally, both Anthony Roche and Christopher Murray offer insightful readings of the play's setting or production. Roche considers the ramifications of Friel's division of the stage into a free-flowing interior and exterior, which combines the theatre practices of both Pirandello and Ibsen (2011, p. 122–23). In discussing his claim that Frank is a 'false hero', Murray recalls his reaction to the play's premiere production, which he saw in a preview performance. This reading of *Living Quarters*, and Frank in particular, relies on Ray McAnally (1926–89), who played the Irish soldier in the original production and who, in Murray's view, created a Shakespearean connection: 'he played Macbeth. But […] he had no Macduff strong enough to make a fight of it' (77).

Aristocrats (1979)

In his summary of Friel's career shortly after his death, the eminent theatre critic Fintan O'Toole, in an appreciation entitled 'The Truth According to Brian Friel' (2015), noted that *Aristocrats*, *Faith Healer*, and *Translations* were all 'premiered within an extraordinary period of 18 months in 1979 and 1980'. In other words, *Aristocrats* is generally seen as the first of the playwright's trio of great plays that established him as one of the world's foremost living playwrights. Indeed, in *The Irish Times'* online tribute to the playwright, Peter Crawley includes it as one of the 'Seven Key Plays' for anyone seeking to understand Friel's career. Similarly, the Irish director and scholar Patrick Burke, who has seen 'all of Brian Friel's original plays, translations and adaptations from *The Enemy Within* in 1962 to *The Home Place* in 2005, twenty-two of them in their premiere productions', ranks *Aristocrats* fifth in the list of the playwright's seven 'Masterworks' (2006, p. 120). However, if the play is less well known outside of Ireland, this is because it is seen as a more narrowly 'Irish' play in its themes, and it has never emerged from the shadows of the other two plays of 1979–80.

While *Aristocrats* initiates Friel's greatest artistic period, the play is seen as a culmination of diverse trends. For example, in his 1995 book, Andrews argues that it concludes a series of plays beginning with *The Gentle Island* that portray an Ireland in which 'an old order is disintegrating' (149). Although this 'oppressive, patriarchal authority' collapses, the younger generation is portrayed as unpre-pared to assume control over their country's future. For many commentators, the flawed representatives of this struggling younger generation are character-ized by what Andrews refers to as a line of 'Protean Playboys' (123) and what in *Celtic Revivals* Seamus Deane more prosaically calls men with 'liberated and liberating intelligence' (169): Shane in *The Gentle Island*, Skinner in *The Freedom of the City*, Keeney in *Volunteers*, and Eamon (or Casimir) in *Aristocrats*.[2]

In a more limited way, such writers as O'Brien, Pine, Roche, and Higgins emphasize the profound similarities between *Aristocrats* and the play that directly precedes it, *Living Quarters*. Roche's 2006 article 'Family Affairs' offers a point-by-point comparison of the families, each of which is defined by a widowed father who dies, three sisters, and one brother, whose relationship with his father is 'fraught with Oedipal overtones' (46). Higgins provides the best sum-mary of how such themes as 'the tortured dynamics of a family, the "burden of the incommunicable", historical determinism, the multiplicity of realities, memory, and enabling/disabling fictions' are developed in both plays (42–43).

Sources and Influences

The scholarly consensus is also that *Aristocrats* is Friel's most overtly Chekho-vian play. As early as 1973, James Coakley had posited Friel's debt to Anton Chekhov (1860–1904), the Russian playwright who authored such psycholog-ically nuanced drama as *Uncle Vanya* (1897) and *Three Sisters* (1901), plays that Friel himself translated for 1981 and 1998 productions. However, the extent of his debt to Chekhov has only slowly emerged. Whereas, writing in 2010, Geraldine Higgins can confidently refer to Friel as the 'Irish Chekhov' (3), references to Friel's affinity to the Russian master's pacing, setting, and family dynamics were absent from studies before the mid-1980s. As will be discussed later, Friel criticism throughout the 1980s focused on the centrality of lan-guage in his plays, and the importance of Chekhov's influence was seriously explored only beginning in the 1990s, in chapters and articles by such scholars as Christopher Murray, Richard Pine, and Alan Peacock.[3] Perhaps the most perspicacious explication of *Aristocrats* as Friel's 'most "Chekhovian" play' is provided by Richard Pine in 'Friel's Irish Russia' (2006), where he explores the mood of this play about family and silence: 'a state of mind for those who experience "the great silence" of the house-as-affect' (110).

Along with the play's Chekhovian character, much of the criticism reliably makes reference to the connection between *Aristocrats* and his story 'Foundry House', which was first published in the 18 November 1961 issue of *The New Yorker* and subsequently in his story collections *The Saucer of Larks* (1962) and *Selected Stories* (1983). Both Dantanus and O'Brien draw their readers' attention to the play's origin in this story only in passing. Conversely, McGrath asserts that a comparison of the story to the play demonstrates how greatly Friel's 'epistemological and linguistic sophistication' had increased in the seventeen years between the two related narratives (1999, 155). The fullest comparison of the two is offered by Jacques Tranier in '"Foundry House" et *Aristocrats* de Brian Friel' (1992), an article that attentively identifies and compares all the major themes common to the story and play such as the confrontation of old and new social orders, the decline of the Big House, Friel's use of consoling fictions, physical decay and self-deception. While a similarly nuanced and detailed comparison is lacking in English, John Cronin's 'Donging the Tower' explores how the play broadens and complicates the story's one-dimensional explication of the gentry's social decline, as well as how the Battle of the Bogside (12–14 August 1969) changes the manner in which the play develops the story's latent political context (9–12). Finally, Anthony Roche provides a perceptive, albeit brief, discussion of how elements of the story's narrator, Joe Brennan, are split into two of the play's characters: Willie Diver and Eamon (2011, p. 77–78).[4]

The most frequent comparison of 'Foundry House' to *Aristocrats* focuses on the common scenes of patriarchal collapse: in the story, while listening to a tape-recorded message from his daughter who is involved in African missionary work, old Mr Hogan hoarsely cries out her name and collapses; in the play, a grotesque and dishevelled Father is drawn into the study by the sound of his missionary daughter's taped message, dying on stage after emitting 'an almost-animal roar'. O'Brien argues that the dramatic working of this scene produces 'a more complex [and] more decisive' turning point for the family and its members' own perceptions of their future (25–26). Although Roche considers the differences in the two portrayals of patriarchal figures and their collapses (75–76), Corbett focuses on how the two recordings emphasize the discrepancies between the aristocracy's view of its own condition and the more realistic views embodied in patriarchal collapse (2002, 85).

Judith

Although the criticism has focused on three male characters (Casimir, Eamon, and Tom), in the working notes for the play Friel's attention is concentrated on the three O'Donnell sisters (Claire, Alice, and Judith): 'A persistent sense that the play is about three aging sisters', later distilling this to 'Judith-Alice-Claire; and Father'.[5] Although Friel further comments that 'the one constant is Judith', Andrews is the first critic to consider her importance:

> ■ Judith speaks for the reality of decline, poverty and sickness. She is the one who has taken responsibility for Father and for looking after Ballybeg Hall....In remaining 'indifferent' to the violence in the North and in regarding politics as 'vulgar', the Catholic 'aristocracy has, in her view, rendered itself socially irrelevant.

For the first time Friel includes a serious countermovement which opposes itself to defeat and inevitability. (155) ☐

Murray as well points out in his 2014 study that 'Judith is the strongest of the family and the one on whom the whole play depends' (129). In an analysis that differentiates this Frielian heroine from her Chekhovian and Shavian predecessors, Murray explores Judith's strange mix of self-effacing family sacrifice with life-defining acts of rebellion (129–30). In my book, I expand these treatments of the character into a more comprehensive analysis of the play's portrayal of the plight of women in 1970s Ireland, which depicts them as 'doubly subordinated' by the family at home while they are similarly deprived of political autonomy in public (135–37).

Casimir

Despite Judith's reserved centrality to the play, the criticism has persistently found her emotionally fragile brother Casimir, who has emigrated to Germany, the play's most compelling character. He has been memorably described as 'Friel's worst mythomaniac' (Dantanus, 165), an 'impresario of fictions' (Andrews, 153) and 'the greatest of Friel's fantasists', whose temperamental roots extend back to Will Logue in Friel's earliest play, *A Doubtful Paradise* (Roche 2011, 22). For Dantanus, Casimir's 'self-knowledge' allows him to find a place for himself in this world of collapsed aristocracy; however, subsequent discussions have taken less laudatory views of him. For Andrews, he is a character 'pathetically lacking in self-confidence', who attempts to compensate for his insecurity by resisting reality:

> ■ Though more of an *ingenu* than Shane or Skinner, he is still kin to those other Protean playful spirits. He survives because of his playfulness and his constant readiness to adjust to change: but also because of his recognition of his own limitations. (154) ☐

McGrath extends Casimir's powerful ability to mythologize beyond himself to the broader Ballybeg Hall, arguing that for the world of the play it is not important whether the O'Donnells' illustrious past is historically true; rather, Casimir is seduced by family lore, and in this reading everything he does can be seen to buttress the family myths that sustain him and frequently enthral others (1999, p. 150–52). However, Corbett points out that though Casimir may be 'the spirit of the house', his actual memory is very limited; in the play's first scene, he fails to recognize Willie as his close childhood friend or even to recall the day they were swept out to sea together (2002, p. 77–78).

While equally viewing Casimir's 'inaccurate and hazy memories' as problematic from a historical point of view, Maria Germanou, in 'An American in Ireland' (2004), persuasively argues that these fantasies 'define the conception that the aristocracy had about its own identity' (266). In contrast to Tom's scientific view of History dominated by verifiable evidence, Casimir fashions a fictional history that expresses emotional truths despite some factual errors (265–68). In his 1993 study of Irish literature, *Changing States*, Robert Welch also delves into Casimir's mania for history, seeing it as a type of a neurotic obsession with establishing continuity and control over the intersection of 'the past, his narration and the present' (232). Thus, once Casimir's inaccuracies have been exposed by Tom near the play's end, Welch explains the unexpected 'air of jubilant relaxation' as resulting from the return of the play's world to one 'where what is actual is real' (234). Similarly, in his recent reading of the play, Roche employs Slavoj Žižek's Lacanian theory of fantasy to posit that Casimir's fantasy of the O'Donnell past, which is never anything more than a 'tentative aspiration', is all the more powerful because it possesses 'a kind of truth' (2011, p. 80). Moreover, the extravagance of Casimir's stories allows the audience to witness the extent to which the world of the Irish aristocracy associated with the Big House has passed.

Eamon

Eamon, the child of the village who married into the family, has similarly been seen as a thematically revealing character. In his 1988 book Dantanus refers to him as the play's 'catalyst' (169), while in his *Brian Friel* O'Brien similarly identifies him as a 'pivotal character' (93). In the early criticism's fullest assessment of his role in the play, O'Brien argues that Eamon's actions are central to redefining this Big House family to accommodate future Irish society:

■ He is the one who breaks defining, image-laden barriers. He marries into the O'Donnell family. He breaks diplomatic ranks. He ... is entirely committed to his work as a Probation Officer, and insists on Uncle George coming to London to live. He reveals to Tom Hoffnung the identity of Father's wife. (94) □

However, despite Eamon's awareness of the O'Donnells' historic failures and falsehoods, O'Brien recognizes that he has fallen under the spell of the Big House nonetheless. Andrews similarly recognizes him as a contradictory character, at once rebellious as well as subservient. However, for Andrews, Eamon has less critical awareness of how much he is in thrall to the O'Donnells' 'aristocratic dream'; indeed, he significantly recognizes that, when Father collapses, it is Eamon, not any of the O'Donnell children, who rushes to catch him (151).
    Tony Corbett offers the most thorough analysis of Eamon to be found in the later criticism. While he too recognizes that Eamon often expresses surprisingly

sentimental devotion to the house, Corbett's treatment brings out more of the character's antipathy towards it. For example, he aptly highlights how Eamon fails to fit in with established O'Donnell decorum (2002, p. 80) and is able to articulate how the family has failed in its traditional role as patron of Ballybeg (81). However, Corbett perhaps rightly roots the source of Eamon's ambivalent feeling in the fact that 'his family were forced to emigrate' from the village, leaving him to be raised by his grandmother, a servant in the O'Donnell Hall (82). Even in Murray's recent book on Friel, there is the impression that the criticism has not successfully explicated this character and is still searching for the framework to better understand him. In him Murray sees 'a complex figure, a new type in the second half of the twentieth century': the working-class rebel reminiscent of Jimmy Porter in John Osborne's *Look Back in Anger* (1956), but one—to quote Eamon—who has been 'educated out of our emotions' (131).

Tom

Finally, Tom Hoffnung, the American academic who is conducting research on the family and the history of the Catholic Big House in Ireland, has also attracted considerable critical attention, starting with McGrath's work in 1999. In his analysis, Tom's greatest purpose in the play is to expose the multiple factual inaccuracies of Casimir's stories, which pose as the compendium of family history (154). However, this does not allow Tom to assume a position of authority in the play because, in a much-quoted comment, Eamon assures the O'Donnells that 'There are certain things, certain truths...that are beyond Tom's kind of scrutiny' (155). Writing just a few years after McGrath, Corbett points out that Tom resembles Sir from *Living Quarters* in that his questions elicit revelations about the family (2002, 76). However, Corbett resists the assumption that Tom is endowed with Sir's authority or insight; indeed, he points out that there is something essentially dead about his form of history: 'his study...connects the family with the past and with the countryside, not with the present' (75).

Germanou's 'An American in Ireland' presents the most theoretically refined attempt to assess Tom's role as historian within the play. His emphasis on establishing the 'facts, dates, and names' of the family's past events reveals that he represents History as a social science (265). But in her reading of the dynamic between Tom and Casimir and Eamon, who are both guardians of O'Donnell folklore, Germanou argues that Tom fails in his attempt to capture history 'as "it really was"', because 'Tom is constructed as a split self' in a disciplinary sense: he craves understanding of the family's social significance, but such knowledge evades the dry material found in estate papers and family records (267). Indeed, she too considers Tom's work as ultimately flawed because he renders it 'an object of study distant from the present' (268).

Maria Szasz's extensive survey of Tom's role in the play forms a useful complement to Germanou's more conceptual discussion of the play's various historians. Szasz initiates her consideration of Tom by exploring the evolution from Friel's first academic, Dr Dodds in *Freedom of the City*, to this more personable and compassionate historian (120), and in her main analysis she meticulously documents every significant exchange between Tom and the play's major characters. Although she assesses the implications of Tom's questioning of Casimir in an especially nuanced manner (120–23), her work is more valuable in the way she opens up the discussion to consider his relationships with Eamon (124–27), Alice (127), and Judith (127–28). Indeed, she brings out the complex relationship that evolves between Eamon and Tom from one defined by Eamon's distrust to, oddly, the point when he 'becomes Eamon's confessor' (126).

Father

In reflecting on the plays of the 1970s, Pine observed in his 1999 book, *The Diviner*, that 'Friel is almost too concerned with pursuing the relationship of father and son' (155). While this theme has been recognized in the criticism of such plays as *Philadelphia, Here I Come!* and *Living Quarters*, it is especially relevant for this play where the patriarch is known only as 'Father', appearing in the play largely as a disembodied voice that interrupts the play's action and strikes fear in Casimir. An early article on the topic, Marilyn Throne's 'The Disintegration of Authority', surveys the theme in five plays from *Philadelphia* to *Translations*, including *Aristocrats*. Elmer Andrews' treatment of Father stresses the character's contradictory nature: he 'continues to exert a strange power' over his family despite his 'state of incontinent and utterly dependent senility' (149). Andrews also considers the importance of Father's appearance in the play's most dramatic moment, when he is drawn to the stage to die by the taped greeting from the family's missionary daughter who has been in Africa for several years (150). In his 1999 discussion of Father, McGrath argues that Casimir's 'neurotic conflict' arises from the psychological link between his debilitating dread of his father and his love for the family's grand heritage (150–52). Corbett even more forcibly asserts that 'the house, as symbol of authority, is inextricably linked' with Father, and his book provides the most detailed analysis of Father's outbursts in Act 1 and the staging of his on-stage death in Act 2 (83–85).

Music

Finally, while there are few nuanced discussions of Friel's use of music in *Aristocrats*, the topic broadly is important to Friel studies, especially in light of the centrality of music to such later plays as *Dancing at Lughnasa* (1990), *Wonderful Tennessee* (1993), and *Performances* (2003). Harry White's 1990 article on Friel's use of music in *Modern Drama* broadly juxtaposes the aims of *Aristocrats* to those of *Philadelphia* as 'at once more pervasive and somewhat less abundantly suggestive' (556). However, White narrowly focuses on Chopin, both as a celebrity who appears in O'Donnell lore as well as a body of music that gives meaning to Claire's 'ruined' past potential as a concert pianist and her 'pathetic' present as she prepares for her 'ludicrous marriage' to a local grocer (557). In his 1995 book, Andrews recognizes that the figure of Chopin also establishes strong resonances with Casimir, whose name is Polish and whose memories are frequently associated with the Chopin melodies Claire plays (155). Considering the arc of Friel's career from his critical vantage point in 2011, Roche sees the return of music to a place of dramatic importance as vital to the evolution of his career, and he opines that Casimir's sister's playing of Chopin allows Friel to allude to 'an incestuous attraction between the two' (82). More significantly, Andrews recognizes a significant shift in music that occurs after the death of Father: Claire 'vows never to play Chopin again' and 'the music of high culture is replaced by the popular song, 'Sweet Alice'. Andrews argues that the siblings' singing of this folk-song so loved by their mother signals their freedom from Father and the family's rejection of their past elitist culture (156–57).

The two plays discussed in this chapter allowed Friel to find balance in his longstanding interests in politics and family, but in his next play, *Faith Healer* (1979), he creates an unremitting study of three private lives bound by tragedy.

CHAPTER SEVEN

Faith Healer (1979)

Despite the enduring popularity of stage productions of *Dancing at Lughnasa,* such eminent Irish commentators as Roy Foster recognize *Faith Healer* as 'argu-ably Friel's greatest play', while Declan Kiberd even claims that it 'may well be the finest play to come out of Ireland since J.M. Synge's *Playboy of the Western World*' in 1907. Likewise, the Irish director and theatre critic Patrick Burke places it first in his list of the author's seven 'Masterworks' (121). Indeed, the list of professional productions summarized in the descriptive catalogue for the Brian Friel Papers housed in the National Library of Ireland similarly sug-gests the play's importance: in spite of its notoriously failed premiere at New York's Longacre Theatre in 1979, in its first twenty years the play has enjoyed forty professional productions in ten countries and seven languages, including important productions in 1992 at The Royal Court and in 2006 with the Gate Theatre's touring production with Ralph Fiennes as Frank Hardy.

Anthony Roche's 2011 *Brian Friel* provides an invaluable summary of the play's complex development, starting in early 1975, through several drafts with such titles as 'Bannermen' and 'The Game'. Commenting on the mul-tiple manuscripts for *Faith Healer* in the Friel archive, Roche points out that 'nowhere … is there a greater transformation or a greater degree of structural modification and development between the first drafts and the final script' (155). Roche adds that, for a playwright notoriously unwilling to share his work in progress, Friel solicited a great variety of opinions on the play's form and content as it developed. At the suggestion of the actor Niall Tóibín in 1976, Friel added the monologue spoken by Teddy, and he similarly fol-lowed the producer Oscar Lewenstein's later advice to end the play with a second monologue delivered by Frank Hardy, the play's faith healer (156). However, Roche asserts, basing his claim on the copious notes for the play in the national archive, that this advice did not change the play's story: 'his notes further reveal that the plot and characterization were fundamentally in place from the start' (157). In his book's chapter on *Faith Healer*, Richard Rankin Russell becomes the only other commentator to explore the drafts to better understand the play. He argues that when Friel developed 'Bannermen' into Frank's final monologue of the finished play, he creates a more ritualized narration by adding phrases to emphasize Frank's intentional self-sacrifice and repetition to slow the scene's pace (2014, 138–39).

Another indication of the play's importance is the number of essays and chapters on the play, as well as the rapidity with which they appear. Whereas the first treatments of such plays as *Philadelphia* and *Volunteers* were published more than a decade after their premieres, the first article on *Faith Healer*, 'Language Play: Brian Friel and Ireland's Verbal Theatre' by Richard Kearney, was published barely four years after the premiere at the Longacre Theatre, New York, in April 1979. Indeed, in the three years from 1983 to 1985, the play was discussed in articles and chapters by the rising stars of Irish criticism—Kearney (1983), D.E.S. Maxwell (1984), Seamus Deane (1985), and Declan Kiberd (1985)—and their arguments established the discussion topics for decades to come.

Kearney's essay would make the robust argument that *Faith Healer*, *Translations* (1980), and *The Communication Cord* (1982) 'constitute not just a theatre *of* language but a theatre *about* language' (24). In a chapter on Friel in *A Critical History of Modern Irish Drama* (1984), considering the plays Friel published since his 1973 study of the author, Maxwell explores how *Faith Healer* continues Friel's exploration of memory by boldly leaving the incompatible recollections of the play's characters unreconciled (201–03). The following year (1985), in an article entirely devoted to the play, Kiberd reads it as an extended allegory for the artist struggling with his gift.

Sources and Influences

Although viewed as a play unique in its ground-breaking reliance on monologues, speculation concerning the play's origins emerged even in the earliest criticism. Not only in his 1985 article, but also in his 1999 and 2005 discussions of the play, Kiberd asserts that *Faith Healer* 'creatively misinterpret[s]' the Deirdre legend of the medieval Ulster tale 'The Exile of the Sons of Uisneach' (1999, 632), which was also the subject of Synge's *Deirdre of the Sorrows* (1910). In the same way that Joyce's *Ulysses* establishes a 'reverberation' of Homer's *Odyssey*, Kiberd argues, Friel reimagines the tragic heroine Deirdre as Grace, one who becomes heroic 'for the pain which she must endure with her partner' as they wander. In his brief return to the topic in *The Irish Writer and the World* (2005), he further develops this analogy by associating Frank with Naoise, the 'attractive but weak young man' for whom Deirdre abandons her people, and by placing Frank's manager Teddy in 'the same role as Naoise's brothers in Synge's play' (167). Writing about the play in his book, Richard Rankin Russell cites another possible Old Irish influence for the play by identifying Frank not with Naoise, but with Cuchulain, the legendary warrior of the Ulster epic *The Tain*. By so doing, Russell aims to portray Frank, like Cuchulain, as 'the embodiment of a province increasingly torn by sectarian strife' (127).

In her article 'Unveiling the Vice' (2006), Giovanna Tallone sees diverse thematic similarities between *Faith Healer* and such medieval morality plays as *Everyman*, *Magnyfycence*, and *The Castle of Perseverance*. Most broadly, she identifies *Faith Healer* as a 'revenant drama', as in *Everyman* and the pervasive Dance of Death setting, in which 'dead characters tell stories of different deaths' that have religious overtones (128). However, Tallone more thoroughly details an interpretation of Frank Hardy as a medieval Vice character, 'a master of words' who uses language to seduce other characters and establish an intimate relationship with the audience (129–30). Thus, she subsequently connects Frank with Merry-Report in John Heywood's *The Play of the Weather* or Vice in *Hickscorner*, a 'reciter of alliterative lists of place names' used to charm and disarm other characters (133–35).

An equally persuasive view of the play is first briefly sketched out by the playwright Frank McGuinness in '*Faith Healer*: All the Dead Voices' (1999) where he declares that in this play Friel, 'not Yeats, is truly the last Romantic' (62). He claims that, with its focus on love's destructive and transcendent powers, the 'dramatic vision' of this play is 'quintessentially Romantic' (61). Moreover, he proposes that Friel 'draws on one of the great images of the movement to create Frank's death': the disrupted wedding of Coleridge's 'Rime of the Ancient Mariner' (1798). But in Friel's 'ironic reworking' of the setting, the wedding guests kill both the mariner and the albatross (62). McGuinness's observation is rigorously explored in Bruce Wyse's 'Traumatizing Romanticism in Brian Friel's *Faith Healer*' (2004). While he more specifically associates Coleridge's wedding guests with Friel's McGarvey, the play's crippled wedding guest whom Frank fatally encounters in Ballybeg (453), Wyse is more interested in exploring Frank as the solipsistic 'asocial "genius"' of Romanticism (448), 'the "lawless genius" who displays an "artless spontaneity"' (449). In a persuasive and detailed argument, Wyse connects Coleridge's assertion that the poet creates a peaceful 'oneness' in the human mind to Frank's ability to use his power to create a meditative contentedness in those he heals:

■ Recalling the amazing cure of ten in the Methodist hall in Glamorganshire, Teddy keenly observes that there oddly 'was no shouting or cheering…he had given them some great content in themselves as well' (359). In his last night alive, amidst the conviviality in the lounge bar in Ballybeg, Frank bestows this same 'content' on his loyal manager. (451) □

Finally, Wyse describes Frank's peacefulness and enlightenment as he approaches the men who will murder and dismember him as akin to Coleridge's assertion that epiphany is the very aim of art (454). Indeed, as Frank approaches them, Wyse sees him realize the Romantic sublime, which combines heightened understanding, unity with all beings, a tranquil observation of the forces around him, and intimations of the divine (456–59).

Of course, several scholars have argued that Friel's own plays are part of the background to *Faith Healer* as well. In one of the earliest analyses of the play, Michael Etherton asserts that not only were *Aristocrats* and *Faith Healer* premiered in the same year, but 'they could be thought of as the same play', though told in markedly different ways (183). At the core of this comparison is a senile judge approaching death, his bitter rejection of his 'radical daughter' (Judith in *Aristocrats*, Grace in *Faith Healer*), and the inability of the Big House to adapt to the challenges posed by modernizing Ireland and the rising middle class (184–86).[1]

However, the more common comparison of *Faith Healer* to Friel's earlier play *Crystal and Fox* was first posited by Robert Hogan in his 1983 collection of essays, *Since O'Casey* (183). Similarly, while noting points of contact to such plays as *Freedom of the City* and *Living Quarters*, George O'Brien devotes several sentences to his claim that *Faith Healer* is 'a condensed and more intense version of *Crystal and Fox*' (1990, 100). In her 1997 book, Martine Pelletier claims that all the dramatic elements that Friel was not able to realize in *Crystal and Fox* are brought to full development in *Faith Healer*: 'Tous les elements que le dramaturge n'était pas parvenu a maîtriser de façon satisfaisante en 1969 dans *Crystal and Fox* sont repris avec talent, conviction et maturité' (64). As with Etherton's analysis, Pelletier focuses her comparison on Grace, but in this case the comparison is made to Crystal; both women embodying a tragic grandeur by virtue of their capacity to sustain their love for the bitter men they share their lives with (65).

The most sustained comparison of the two plays is offered by Giovanna Tallone in her essay 'Restless Wanderers and Great Pretenders' (2006). More fully than in any previous discussion, Tallone identifies the broad similarities that link the two plays:

■ Both plays are based on marginal characters inside a travelling show.... In both, the central character is tormented by different forms of restlessness. Both are based on sacrifice and annihilation. In different ways both reconstruct the past.... In both an undercurrent of violence is evident and takes various forms. (38) □

After detailing such broad thematic similarities, Tallone devotes the remainder of the article to a comparison of Fox Melarkey to Frank Hardy, exploring their shared brooding temperaments (42–42), a similar use of language (45–46), their comparable methods of showmanship (51–54), and their equally tortured relationships with their wives (55–57).

Frank Hardy as Artist and Christ figure

From the earliest to the most recent readings of the play, the most frequent assumption is that Frank Hardy represents the artist. Such an interpretation does not only rely upon Friel's own 1982 comment to Fintan O'Toole that Frank's healing gift is 'some kind of metaphor for the art, the craft of writing'.[2] In the play itself, Grace describes the people who sought Frank's help as 'his fictions', and near the end of her monologue she decries her own status as 'one of his fictions' (*Selected Plays*, 345, 353). Thus, Kearney concludes his 1983 consideration of *Faith Healer* with the declaration that Frank operates 'as a metaphor for the self-destructive impulses of the creative artist overobsessed with his own art', one whose tragedy results from his unhealthy, myopic devotion to writing (32).

Friel criticism until the late 1990s sought primarily to refine this association.[3] In his introduction to the *Selected Plays* (1984), Seamus Deane points out that Frank is a particular type of artist: 'the artist who is possessed by a gift over which he has no control' (20). And in the following year, briefly writing about the play in *Celtic Revivals*, Deane further adds that there is a 'strange' relationship between Frank's gift and his self-exile, that his gift to heal others functions only outside of his home country (173). While in his introduction Deane also mentioned that, for Friel, 'there is an inescapable link between art and politics … between eloquence and violence', Dantanus is the first critic to actually assert 'that it is the Irish artist in particular that is intended.'[4] In doing so, he ascribes a 'Celtic temperament' to Frank as opposed to 'the Englishness of Grace and Teddy' (174).

For the early criticism, Kiberd's 'Brian Friel's *Faith Healer*' (1985) offers the most nuanced examination of Frank as artist. For example, he notes that Friel uses Teddy, Frank's manager, to assess Frank as artist. In comparing him to the various animal acts that he had managed before Frank, Teddy presents Frank as a flawed 'performer' because he's inhibited by 'too anxious a self-scrutiny' (213), that he is 'far too self-analytical for his own good as an artist' (215). Moreover, Kiberd argues that under Teddy's influence Frank's powers decline as he slowly degrades 'his healing artistry to the level of mere performance'; having abandoned the purity of his calling, he becomes merely an entertainer who 'prostitutes his art' (218). This view of Frank as a flawed, troubled character is also developed by O'Brien, who argues that the play does not heroise Frank. Indeed, he claims that even Frank's successes do not compensate for 'his destructiveness', nor do they 'justify or explain his treatment of Grace' (1990, 101).

These discussions frequently make reference to the inherent spiritual context of Frank's gift; thus, it should not be surprising that the first article to fully explore the play as religious parable came early in the critical history with Paul Robinson's 1987 'Brian Friel's *Faith Healer*'. This very brief essay sketches out the arguments for considering Frank a Christ figure, because in part 'The prime analogue of the faith healer in Western culture is Christ' (225). Robinson fails to anticipate the complications of this interpretation, relying on the broad points that both Jesus and Frank worked miracles and sought their vocations among the downtrodden and each died 'at the hands of his own people' (225–26).

Returning to this comparison in his 2014 book, Richard Rankin Russell summarizes the possible arguments for considering Frank a Christ figure only to ultimately dismiss them as 'superficial similarities', even arguing that Frank 'experiences no grace' as he approaches his death (130). Without directly addressing this Christian context, Robert Tracy's 2007 article on the Cambridge Ritualists, discussed in Chapter 6, considers Frank at best as one of 'corn kings and vegetation gods', of J.G. Frazer's *The Golden Bough* (1922), who foresees his death, or at worst as one who must die because he 'impersonates' a god (404). Despite the duality he suggests, Tracy seems to opt for a less defined middle ground of Frank as 'a man for a time endowed with the powers of a god' who accepts the 'murder/sacrifice he about to undergo' (405).

Margaret Strain's article 'Renouncing Change' (2004) surveys the broad theological background for the play. To locate an Irish context, she reviews the relevance of such medieval Christian concepts as place-name lore (*dindshenchas*), the traditional role of the *filid*, or Irish poet, and even how Frank's miracles would have been seen by the early Christian church (64–68). The second half of her essay focuses on Frank's death: both his spiritual state as he prepares to meet his killers and his description of the courtyard. Using Michael Buckley's six stages of transcendence to interpret Frank's acceptance of his own death, Strain argues that Frank has achieved 'the awareness of God as ultimate Truth' (77–78), and his '"renouncing change" becomes an affirmation of the sacred and salvific' (79). Chu He expands Strain's focus on medieval Irish culture in her article 'Non-Modern Culture', where she considers Frank as a type of avatar of ancient shamanism in an inhospitable modern world. However, because of his limited access to his numinous powers, He views him as 'only a dysfunctional shaman … a pale reflection of the old shamanic tradition' in the modern world (99). This reading sees both Grace and McGarvey as aspects of the rational modern world antagonistic to ancient faith (101), but Frank's ritualized death is suffused with pre-Christian Irish imagery and marks his 'victory over the empirical reality he has battled throughout his life' (102).

Strain's description of Frank's willing entrance into the sacred space leading to his death (77–78) is one of the many attempts to understand the character's death as a type of ritual or transcendent event. Kearney's early assessment was that in death Frank becomes 'a hapless *Salvator Mundi* [Saviour of the World]' and 'the victim of his own…cautionary tale' (32); similarly, in 1988, Dantanus observed that Frank's death is 'a defiant act of self-destruction' after a failed attempt to find rejuvenation in Ireland (177). However, in his 1993 article 'Brian Friel: The Name of the Game', Deane proposes a radically different view: that 'Hardy heals himself' in death in 'a moment of the sublime, when everything that had been random and accidental is finally configured as destiny' (111). Andrews too continues this re-evaluation, albeit in a more equivocal manner, when he declares that Frank's death was his 'supreme fiction' (160). While he recognizes that, in these last days, Frank is 'exhausted and impotent', he nevertheless views Frank's death as his successful attempt to recast himself 'in biblical and apocalyptic terms' (160).

The most recent discussions of Frank's death continue this shift in the critical balance to a view that he achieves a type of dramatic and personal redemption in his encounter with the crippled McGarvey. In a skilful discussion of the incorporation of 'acted drama' in Frank's own description of his death, Nicholas Grene's 2009 article 'Brian Friel and the Sovereignty of Language' argues that the subtle addition of props and movement to Frank's monologue endows his final moments with 'authority and conviction' intended to 'leave an audience in the theatre unable to resist Frank's mood of awe and elation or the eloquence with which his secular martyrdom is so powerfully expressed' (44). In an examination, published the following year, of the *unheimliche*, or uncanny, in the play, Yu-chen Lin also pays particular attention to the props and stage directions incorporated into its final moments to explain how Frank 'has become his own fiction of the apocalyptic sublime' (82). Although she posits 'the interpretation that he heals himself', she nonetheless concludes that in his temperamental inability to admit to himself and mourn the deaths of those around him (mother, father, and child), he never frees himself from the compulsion to relive his trauma (83). Thus, for Lin, his redemption is partial at best.

The latest, longest, and most nuanced examination of Frank's death was offered by Russell in his 2014 book on Friel (113–44). Employing Victor Turner's theories of *communitas* relationships, Russell explores the circumstances of Frank's sacrificial murder, which is all the more paradoxical because, first, 'Frank wants to be killed' (115) and, second, the play depicts a society that considers itself 'beyond ritual' (114). Such a theoretical framework is especially useful for the reader because, by interpreting Frank as a liminal figure, moving from the physical into the spiritual world, Russell is able to explain why his failures to heal Teddy, Grace, and McGarvey on his final night in Ballybeg do not necessarily signal his failure as a sacrificial scapegoat for society at large (120–23). In this reading of the play, Frank's brutal dismemberment by his own people establishes powerful links with tales of communal strife in Northern Irish folklore that are hinted at in 'the common spiritual unity' that the play depicts between Frank and his killers (132). Indeed, because of this bond between the scapegoat and his community, Frank's death 'offers a different kind of closure than that of tragedy', one that promises a path to a Northern Ireland rejuvenated after the Troubles (141–42).

Grace

Faith Healer is dominated by Frank Hardy: his monologues open and close the play, and his death is the event upon which all narratives converge. With that in mind, it is not surprising that his spectre dominates the interpretations of his partner Grace as well. In her oft-quoted survey of Friel's female characters, 'The Engendered Space: Performing Friel's Women from Cass McGuire to Molly Sweeney' (1997), Claudia Harris has very little to say about Grace other than she 'is Friel's most compelling, fragile woman' (59). Similarly, Kearney's article only briefly outlines the broad contours of her relationship to Frank (29–30). Even though Kiberd's first and lengthiest analysis of the play seeks to establish its reliance on the Deirdre legend, the argument has little to say about Grace, the supposed Deirdre figure, herself (220–21). Indeed, when he next discusses the play fifteen years later in *Inventing Ireland* (1999), he subtly pivots away from the female-oriented version of the tale, Synge's *Deirdre*, to the male-oriented one, the medieval 'The Fate of the Sons of Uisneach' (631). However, unlike his earlier article, this later analysis generally establishes the outlines upon which this comparison rests, pointing out, for example, that both women commit suicide within a year of their lovers' murders (632).[5]

O'Brien views Grace and Frank as 'perhaps [Friel's] most sophisticated use of the familiar divided character', asserting that, unlike Teddy, Grace and Frank are both passionate, social outsiders who are equally 'divided against each other and ... divided in him—or herself' (1990, 101–02). In her article 'Gender and Identity' (1992), José Lanters similarly views Grace and Frank as defining intertwined, oppositional themes. Lanters argues that the *agon* between Grace and Frank relies upon the basic tension in which Grace embodies 'the neglected body' and Frank 'the dominant mind' (283). Thus, arising out of this dichotomy are 'sterility and fertility, death and renewal, destruction and creativity' (284), though in a complex way Grace's 'physical sickness and childlessness' is used to suggest her 'impaired' creativity in juxtaposition to Frank's sterility (285). When Strain briefly considers this pairing in her 2004 article, she does so to weave Grace into a theological interpretation of Frank's spiritual journey. First, she takes Frank's comment that Grace is his 'mistress' in a Dantean sense to suggest that 'she is the power who shapes and directs his actions' (70).

To this end, for Strain, Grace literally embodies Frank's need for Christian grace, God's 'self-communication to us' that potentially abides within us whether we reject it or not; Strain argues that we witness this virtue function through Grace especially when she abandons and returns to her truant mate (70).

McGrath's chapter on *Faith Healer* in his 1999 study is the first to attempt to disentangle an understanding of Grace's character from her relationship with Frank. Indeed, McGrath highlights the differences between Frank's view of her and her own self-descriptions; for example, while Frank describes Grace as 'a loyal, devoted appendage', Grace's own 'self-portrait resisted Frank's attempts to subject her needs to his own' (159–60). Similarly, whenever considering the play's most significant events—such as those in Kinlochbervie and Ballybeg—McGrath reliably identifies the differences between Grace's and Frank's accounts (and those of Teddy as well).

Significantly, throughout more than thirty years of criticism, Grace's version of events has uniformly been accepted. While such critics as Dantanus comfortably refer to Frank as a 'liar' (175), others silently adopt Grace's facts, as when O'Brien accepts Grace's claim to be Frank's wife rather than Frank's that she was only ever his 'mistress' (98). Even critics such as Nicholas Grene, who describes Grace as 'pathetic and evidently hopeless', believe her, and this is due in large part to the testimony of Teddy (42). While Teddy does contradict Grace on some details, he agrees with her on the play's crucial issue: the events at Kinlochbervie, which Grace remembers as the place where she delivered a baby that quickly died but Frank mentions only as the place where he received the news of his own mother's death.[6] In Teddy's version, he delivers Grace's baby himself because Frank walked away during the delivery; in Grace's version, Frank delivers the baby. Ultimately, though, Christopher Murray expresses the critical field's willingness to gloss over such a significant discrepancy: 'Outvoted two to one by the other witnesses, Frank must be lying' (86). Thus, even when generally aligning itself with Grace's versions, the play does not superficially employ Teddy to bolster Grace.

Memory and Language

Faith Healer is Friel's fourth play to focus on the events that led to the deaths of central characters who appear posthumously—the first being 'Winners' (1967), then *The Freedom of the City* (1973), and *Living Quarters* (1977)—so rather than action, the play recounts the characters' extended memories focused on events at Llanblethian (where Frank healed ten people), Kinlochbervie (where Grace may have delivered her baby), and Ballybeg (where Frank died). George O'Brien is the first to note an important dramaturgic shift in *Faith Healer*: the posthumous characters cannot be relied upon for the truth (1990, 98), or as Andrews puts it, 'There is no Sir and no ledger' to establish an authoritative version of events (158). Unlike in these earlier plays, discrepancies between the memories recounted by Frank, Grace, and Teddy destabilize nearly every aspect of the play. Whether remembering how 'The Way You Look Tonight' became the opening music for Frank's performances or whether Frank confronted the wedding guests with the claim that he could heal one of them, significant differences riddle the accounts reported by Grace, Teddy, and Frank.[7] Or, as David Barnett describes the state of the three characters' memories in his article 'Staging the Indeterminate' (2006), only the broadest outline of agreed-upon narrative exists:

> ■ While all three agree that Frank was a faith healer (whatever that might mean) and that Teddy was his manager, Frank denies that Grace was his wife....All three agree they went to Kinlochbervie, a village where something terrible took place, and that Frank was murdered in Friel's town of choice, Ballybeg. Almost everything else is a matter for conjecture. (376) ☐

While Grace, Frank, and Teddy differ on details of what happened in Kinlochbervie, their three versions agree on other details: there is no argument that Frank healed ten people in Wales and received a large sum of money as spontaneous recompense; likewise, there is no disagreement that, after a night of boisterous drinking, Frank leaves the bar to face the wedding guests and is murdered. However, the three accounts of events at Kinlochbervie interweave agreement and disagreement: even though Grace and Teddy remember Grace's stillborn baby, they disagree on other major details. Thus, throughout the 1980s, such critics as Maxwell and Dantanus are reluctant to probe the characters' memories after noting the general agreement between Grace and Teddy.

In her article on 'Gender and Identity', José Lanters notes that in associating Kinlochbervie with the death of his mother, Frank compounds 'the death of the past (the mother) and of the future (the child)' and that both deaths signify a failure in Frank's abilities as healer (285). After providing a detailed summary of the three versions of events at Kinlochbervie (164–66), McGrath also seeks to assess what we can learn about Frank from how he shifts his memory to a homecoming with his father over the death of his mother (1999, 167). Indeed, McGrath's analysis is especially acute as to how Frank's memories of his parents are woven throughout the text and, in his reading, all point to Frank's unresolved relationship to paternal authority, whether that be his own father, Grace's father, or his own prospects of becoming a father (167–68).

Conversely, Lin's article presents the most balanced attempt to understand the event's impact on both Grace and Frank. For example, assuming Teddy's version that Frank abandoned Grace during her labour is correct, Lin claims, 'Her invention of Frank's presence in this loss, however, suggests that her origin of trauma lies not so much in the infant's death as in Frank's deliberate refusal to share this loss' (79). Lin sees Frank's trauma as perhaps even greater than Grace's: first he cannot admit what transpired in Scotland and, second, in fabricating his complex memory of a visit home to his father, Frank expresses both patriarchal grief and more personal feelings of loss (79–80). In his recent book, Murray returns to Kiberd's observation that the audience witnesses Frank's 'deep guilt' when he stumblingly repeats 'Kinlochbervie' at the opening of his last monologue.[8] Murray takes Frank's difficulty as a powerful clue that the events at Kinlochbervie lead to those at Ballybeg: 'his own end must be seen as a form of expiation for what happened *there* [Kinlochbervie]' (87). In fact, Murray even claims that if Frank's remarks concerning Kinlochbervie in his two monologues are compared, the second will betray Frank's guilt over the birth and his callous part in it.

In his 1995 book Andrews presents the first attempt to analyse the effect of Friel's refusal to affirm a single Truth that can be combined to construct a reliable narrative. While asserting that there is 'enough coherence' to identify character and plot, he proposes that Friel uses *Faith Healer* to 'explore ambiguity and uncertainty, where he can refuse authoritarianism and demonstrate simultaneously his scepticism *and* his creativity, the limits of his art *and* its possibilities' (162–63). Following Andrews' attempt to explain the play's narrative strategy, McGrath proposes that Friel's intention is to demonstrate 'the role desire plays in shaping memories' (172). In this reading, each character develops memories that support a certain 'image of the self', so what we see is the impact that psychology and desire have upon memory.[9] Writing only a few years after McGrath, Corbett endorses his reading of the play but builds into it the Lacanian element that such an image of the self is a projection imposed from the outside, or to put it simply it is an 'other' (121). For Corbett, this attempt to construct a self can never be coherent because it reflects the struggle between the individual, Grace for example, and the others—Frank and Teddy—who endeavour to impose their versions of Grace upon her (121–22). Finally, writing in 2014, Roche employs Paul Ricoeur's idea that the self is developed out of an individual's response to the 'fragility of identity' and that solipsistic memory is crucial to resisting such an erosion of self:

■ In place of the 'inflexible rigidity of a character', which a more conventional dramaturgy would have enforced, the fluidity of the form allowed [the play's] people 'the slippage, the drift … the flexibility, proper to self-constancy'. (161)[10] □

Thus, in a manner compatible with these previous readings, Roche argues that Friel's heteroglossic text allows the reader to understand each character with a clarity that conventional drama cannot offer.

Employing the continental theories of postdramatic theatre associated with Hans-Thies Lehmann, David Barnett has suggested an alternative strategy for responding to *Faith Healer*. According to Lehmann, the sign of postdramatic theatre is that it is 'about the experience of a condition', not actions (382). Such an orientation to the play would encourage us not to expect that incompatibilities be resolved by the final curtain; rather, we would 'experience' the characters' 'common struggle with a painful past' whether each character is able to admit her or his sorrow or secretly represses it (383). Finally, in a way that opens potential readings of the text, Barnett argues that postdramatic theatre, like the stage of *Faith Healer*, does not represent the naturalistic world, but 'a 'space of remembering" (385). Thus, in Barnett's reading of the play, rather than choosing to believe one character or another or judging the characters' truthfulness based upon subjective criteria, we can accept 'four texts that are not marked by interpretive reduction, but by presentational plenitude, all true and false simultaneously' (386).

In making his argument, Barnett is very attentive to 'language as protagonist', moments in *Faith Healer* when 'it is not a person who speaks the language but the language that "speaks" the person'.[11] Indeed, Barnett's reading of the play requires us to see Frank, Teddy, and Grace not as characters, but as 'text bearers' (382). In this way, his essay reminds us of the very earliest discussions of the play when it was considered primarily a language play. The first discussions of *Faith Healer* were written when the critical community was coming to terms with the immense impact of Friel's next play, *Translations* (1980). This play and its companion *The Communication Cord* (1982) unequivocally stage the importance of language to history, culture, and individual identity. *Faith Healer*, with such rhetorical flourishes as the chanting of place names at the beginning of Frank and Grace's monologues, naturally suggested itself to an interpretative strategy based upon language theory. Thus, though in his 1983 article 'Language Play', Kearney claims that *Faith Healer* is part of a trilogy of plays exploring 'our ontological attitude towards language' (30), his brief discussion of the play covers less language-focused topics such as Frank as artist, ritual, and Frank's murder. Corbett is the first to attempt a language-theory analysis of the play when he considers the extent to which semiotics helps reveal the characters' struggles on a structural level (114–15). Corbett follows Andrews' earlier assertion that the chanting of place names is the play's most important enactment of Friel's interest in language (116). However, Andrews' earlier discussion is more revealing: he equates it to Gar's recitation of Burke's description of Marie Antoinette as an 'escape' and a 'longing for transcendence, for a break with historical reality' (161).

Finally, any summary of the *Faith Healer* criticism needs to mention Maria Szasz's detailed discussion of music in the play in her book *Brian Friel and America*. After identifying the three songs referred to in the play, she focuses on 'The Way You Look Tonight', which was not just the revival's theme song but, apparently, Teddy's favourite song as well (74–79). In 1995, Andrews passingly noted that Teddy was introduced singing this song rather than, like Frank and Grace, chanting place names; however, he considered this merely an indication of the Englishman's 'jaunty cockney manner' (161). Conversely, Szasz presents Teddy not as secondary to the relationship between Frank and Grace but as 'the most admirable character in *Faith Healer*' (79). By looking at the specific words that he sings and speculating on the reasons that he returns to the song throughout his monologue, she builds a persuasive argument for reading Teddy as a selfless character moved to anger and reverence by his great love for both Grace and Teddy.

Soon after its premiere *Faith Healer* was recognized as a major work by a playwright at the height of his talent, yet it was the next play, *Translations* (1980), that transformed how both critics and audience members viewed the playwright and his art for more than a decade.

CHAPTER EIGHT

Translations (1980)

There are several clues to the importance of *Translations* to twentieth-century Irish literature as a whole, and not just in Friel's career. In *Modern Irish Theatre*, Mary Trotter's guide to the field from 1891 to 2007, her section on contemporary theatre begins with *Translations*, treating it as a turning point for the island as a whole (157–58). Lionel Pilkington's brief discussion of the play's opening night in his *Theatre and the State* makes the even grander claim that the event 'marked an important shift in Northern Ireland's … political order' (210). Similarly, in his ambitious *History of Irish Theatre, 1601–2000* (2002), Christopher Morash treats the premiere of *Translations* on 23 September 1980 as one of the island's seven iconic events in his four-hundred-year survey (233–41).[1] Finally, in *Inventing Ireland*, his survey of Irish literature from the Irish Renaissance to the end of the twentieth century, Declan Kiberd devotes a chapter to the play (614–23), thus placing it on a par with such works as W.B. Yeats's *The Winding Stair* (1933).

In his overview of the play's reception in *The Politics of Irish Drama*, Nicholas Grene succinctly states that, despite the political confrontations of the 1970s, 'everyone loved *Translations*, critics and audiences alike', and the play was widely staged and admired in England, Ireland and Northern Ireland (35). Indeed, far from its being seen as an anti-English drama, the poignancy and attractiveness of the English character George Yolland attracted early English productions at the Hampstead Theatre (1981), the Theatre Wales (1982), the Birmingham Repertory Theatre (1991), and the Old Vic (1995). While the play was premiered by the Field Day Theatre Company, which was formed by Friel and the veteran actor Stephen Rea for the purpose of staging it, the Abbey also repeatedly produced it in 1983, 1987, 1996, 2000, and 2001.

In his 1999 study of Friel's career, Richard Pine claims that '*Translations* is more international than national' (183) and, in fact, it has also proven itself amazingly popular as a drama of the world stage. The Friel archive housed in the National Library of Ireland contains evidence of over sixty major productions in seventeen countries in the twenty years following the play's premiere. By comparison, while *Faith Healer* quickly overcame its failed premiere on Broadway, in the same period it was staged forty times in ten countries. *Translations* was soon produced by such prestigious theatres as the Avon Theatre of the Stratford Shakespeare Festival (1982), the Oregon Shakespearean Festival (1984), and the State Theatre of South Australia (1984). Moreover, it was particularly popular in places where minority languages competed against hegemonic ones, for example in Quebec (1983), Estonia (1985), Norway (1986), Ukraine (1996), Poland (1999), and Catalunya (2001).

Finally, whereas during the 1960s and 1970s there was generally a decade between a play's premiere and the first critical article to explore it, scholars turned to *Translations* with a startling rapidity.[2] Eitel Timm's article 'Modern Mind, Myth, and History: Brian Friel's *Translations*' (1982) appeared less than two years after the play's premiere and was quickly followed by Richard Kearney's 'Language Play' (1983) and Ronald Rollins' 'Friel's *Translations*: The Ritual of Naming' (1985). By the decade's close, *Translations* would be the subject of articles by Anthony Bradley (1985), Csilla Bertha (1987), Catherine Wiley (1987), and F.C. McGrath (1989), and it would be discussed at length in books by Robert Hogan (1983), Seamus Deane (1985), David Cairns and Shaun Richards (1988), Ulf Dantanus (1988), Michael Etherton (1989), and George O'Brien (1990). Indeed, as early as Christopher Murray's 1993 essay 'Friel's "Emblems of Adversity"' and Andrews' 1995 chapter on the play (166–67), critics found it necessary to discuss the play's body of criticism when formulating their own arguments. This is a critical fascination that has never flagged; despite the greater popularity of *Dancing at Lughnasa* and the continued popularity of *Philadelphia, Here I Come!* and *Faith Healer*, *Translations* remains the play that has generated the most sustained scholarly debates.

Language

In 'Language Play', published a mere three years after the play's premiere, Richard Kearney argues that Friel's portrayal of two language communities side by side has powerful ideological and philosophical underpinnings; indeed, Kearney's essay was to powerfully define the reading of this play and much of Friel's career for years to come. He claims that 'Friel's plays of the eighties' form 'not just a theatre *of* language but a theatre *about* language' and, for him, this is most true of *Translations* (24). Indeed, Kearney suggests as much by devoting more than twice the space to his analysis of this play than to all the other plays combined. While this article generally ignores the play's political context, it establishes many topics that will be central to the next four decades' discussions of language in the play. It should also be noted that Helen Lojek's

1994 article 'Brian Friel's Plays and George Steiner's Linguistics' marks the first comprehensive attempt to reinterpret the playwright's entire career from *Philadelphia, Here I Come!* (1964) to *Dancing at Lughnasa* (1990) as dominated by the meta-topic of language, unified by 'the idea of translation' (83). Often considering silence or arguments over memory as subsidiary elements of linguistic or cultural translation, Lojek proposes this as a unifying theme for a dozen plays as diverse as *Freedom of the City* (1973) and *Making History* (1988).

For Kearney, the play's central concern is to stage 'the mis-taken [sic] substitution of Irish by English' (42), a message fully explored in the final scene when Hugh opposes his son Owen's attempt to repudiate his work as translator for the English survey team:

■ in sober acknowledgement that what is done cannot be undone, Hugh determines to make a virtue of necessity by creatively refashioning the English language so as to make sense of the new landscape of historical fact. (42) □

In making this argument, Kearney surveys the many levels on which language and culture intertwine in the play's portrayal of Ballybeg, or Baile Beag as the Irish speakers refer to it: from the way Jimmy Jack's fluency in Greek and Latin reveals a 'harmony between word and world' (34) to the way Owen's playful imitation of his father allows him to employ 'that communal dialect which identifies its members' (36). Similarly, Kearney proposes the idea that the second act's two scenes present two attempts to establish cultural rapprochement through different and nuanced forms of translation (39–40).

Finally, Kearney asserts the importance of George Steiner's book *After Babel: Aspects of Language and Translation* (1975) to the play's meaning, and in his article's appendix he quotes seventeen passages from Steiner's book that 'Friel brilliantly contrives to refashion … in his native cultural and historical context' (39). Dantanus also accepts the centrality of Steiner to the play's meaning; in his reading, Steiner's insights allow Friel to deepen his fascination with culture and history, which we had seen in such recent plays as *The Gentle Island* (1971) and *Volunteers* (1975):

■ In particular, it was in [Steiner's] apparent belief in the relationship between language and mind that Friel was able to magnify and transcend a simplified and dogmatic interpretation of the historical confrontation between English and Irish. (189) □

The following year, in his book *Since O'Casey* (1983), Robert Hogan devoted a short section to Friel, who in his estimation had 'done more work of the highest quality' than any other Irish playwright who emerged in the 1960s and 1970s (128). But his reading of *Translations* treated 'the split-language device' as merely one of Friel's many dramatic 'devices', reminiscent of the 'split-personality' device of *Philadelphia* (131). In Hogan's estimation, this technical trick has no greater significance beyond its effect on the audience and had 'blinded some critics to a number of telling flaws in the play', especially the underdeveloped male characters and the inconclusive ending (131). However, Hogan's brief criticism of the play was one of the very few to so estimate it. Conversely, Dantanus's 1988 book, *Brian Friel*, offers a truly detailed reading of *Translations* as a play about language; he discusses the opening scene with Manus and Sarah (191–92), the courtship between Yolland and Maire (188), and Owen's casual attitude towards translation (190–91). Ultimately, for Dantanus, Friel seeks to establish that the English and Irish languages reveal their basic differences 'in the way they perceive reality' (193).

The 1990s saw F.C. McGrath, Robert Smith, Seamus Deane, and Richard Pine develop the most detailed and complementary support for Kearney's exploration of the impact of Steiner upon Friel. Smith's 1991 essay 'The Hermeneutic Motion in Brian Friel's *Translations*' provides a detailed, multi-level examination of Friel's use of Steiner.[3] Whereas Kearney had provided seventeen quotations from Steiner that he considered important to the play, Smith supplies seven such sections from Steiner side-by-side with passages from the play, allowing the reader to view how Friel condensed, rearranged, and dramatized ideas of language philosophy. Moreover, Smith's article displays an equally nuanced understanding of the way Steiner's themes express themselves in the play. For example, he notes that 'Steiner carries on an extended argument about the concept of "private language"', which he applies to the general dynamic that develops between Yolland and Maire (395–96).

Similarly, Smith considers how Steiner's ideas of 'presence' (396–97), 'copula and copulation' (398–99), and language as concealment (401–03) all unexpectedly inform the dialogue or staged action. Smith also explores Steiner's notion of the 'hermeneutic motion' that defines the relational stages that develop between translator and foreign language community (404–07). While this interpretive framework has obvious points of contact to Owen's role in the play, Smith also uses it to redefine Yolland as aspiring translator. Indeed, in this reading Yolland comes much closer to experiencing the '"rapture" of the translator' (406), and his tragedy both disrupts Steiner's paradigm and is useful for explaining Owen's personal and ideological evolution in the last act (407–08).

Using Saul Kripke's book *Naming and Necessity* (1980) as a means to interrogate the relationship of *Translations* to Steiner's theory of translation, in his 1993 essay 'Brian Friel: The Name of the Game' Deane wishes to examine the relationship of equivalence that emerges when a word is translated, when the 'mutilated version' of the original is born (107). On the one hand, Deane uses Hugh, whose linguistic abilities can be reduced to 'pedantry and pomposity', to embody one philosophy of naming. As the play's polyglot, Hugh does not equate words with things; his is 'a refusal of mimesis' in which words from one system (Irish) can be substituted into another (English) (108). Conversely, Yolland and Maire in their privileged moment alone in Act 2 scene 2 embody Deane's other possibility; theirs is 'the only [intersection] in the play' when names are pure, free from meaning or the need to translate: 'The names of the lovers, the place names and the naming of the time they desire for each other is all the language they need' (109). However, Deane asserts that such a moment is fragile, and we as the audience witness its dissolution in the cultural transition from Irish to English.

While McGrath's 1989 article 'Irish Babel' provided a detailed survey of Friel's debt to Steiner, his 1999 book *Brian Friel's (Post) Colonial Drama* seeks to develop a more nuanced view of the, by now generally accepted, relationship of philosopher to playwright by incorporating Homi Bhabha's postcolonial theories. Bhabha's *The Location of Culture* (1994) is especially useful for McGrath, allowing him to move from Steiner's abstract discussions of language communities to the disproportional power dynamic of the Irish situation:

■ Bhabha, however, goes well beyond Steiner's observation by theorizing a reinscribed, non-mimetic narrative of identity that emerges performatively from the boundaries of conflicting cultures.

　 Bhabha's theoretical stance can also account for Ireland's complex and unique situation as both past and present colony located within the boundaries of the first world. (5) □

In discussing *Translations*, McGrath notes that the act of translating is central to both Steiner and Bhabha, but he argues that Bhabha 'theorizes the inevitability of mistranslation … and the inevitable existence of untranslatable residue' (183). McGrath locates examples of the untranslatable throughout the play, from Yolland's concern that 'the language of the tribe will always elude me' (186) to the renaming of Bun na hAbhann to Burnfoot (189) and, especially, to Sarah's silence at the end of the play (192).

Likewise, McGrath employs Bhabha to emphasize that 'mistranslation is endemic to colonial situations', where reference is always to the language of the Other (188). The scene in Act One where Manus and Owen offer drastically different translations of Lancey's official statements provides McGrath with the richest opportunity to explore how language works in the play and to propose that both Manus and Owen create partial translations that reflect their respective ideological orientation; in short, 'the translations of both Owen and Manus are acts of subversion' (185). Finally, it should be noted that in her 1995 *Acting Between the Lines*, Marilynn Richtarik provides a targeted discussion of Friel's adaption of Steiner's philosophy to nineteenth-century Ireland (33–35).

When Roche first considers the play, in his 1994 book *Contemporary Irish Drama*, he places the language issue within the context of staging traditions, specifically how such Shakespearean plays as *Henry IV* and *Henry V* stage multiple languages to an audience. He looks at *Henry IV Part One*, where English and Welsh speakers are presented side by side (245–46), and the love scene in *Henry V*, where Shakespeare has Henry speak basic French to court his French bride (247). This preparatory analysis allows Roche not only to consider how such theatrical norms condition the audience of *Translations* to make stereotyped assumptions about the initial cultural dynamics of the opening scene (246) but also to highlight Friel's decision not to present spoken Irish as a quaint form of English. As his discussion of the play moves into the two scenes in Act 2, Roche shifts his attention to the manner in which Friel silently expands the linguistic strategy of *Translations* to include words that are actually spoken in Irish (249–50, 252–53). However, these two scenes—one focusing on Yolland and Owen, the other on Yolland and Maire—offer a tentative reconciliation of English and Irish that collapses in the last act once Yolland mysteriously disappears (254–55).

Roche's reading of *Translations* marks not so much a departure from a reading based upon Steiner as a maturing, or broadening, to expand the discussion of language from the theoretical to analyses of the drama's dynamics. Just as Roche seeks to explore the interplay of languages in the play, W.B. Worthen also endeavours to better assess the actual staging of language in his essay 'Homeless Words' (1995). Worthen's overall goal is to better describe the type of English spoken in the play, which he asserts is a form of Irish English 'that keeps its language "other" to audiences whose English isn't Irish' (32). Focusing on such phrases as 'everyone'll end up as cute as the Buncrana people' (where 'cute' means clever or educated), Worthen claims that the play's reliance on a vocabulary and syntax that differs from standard English allows Friel to write dialogue that, outside of Ireland, would be heard as 'an oddly estranged tongue' (33). This also allows him to establish a difference between the regional English used by the people of Baile Beag and the more formal version spoken by Lancey.

Worthen's article is also noteworthy for expanding the discussion of language beyond the opposition between English and Irish to consider the play's 'three language-realms—classical (Greek and Latin), colonized (Irish), and imperial (English)' (31). Not only is he interested in exposing the juxtaposition between spoken Greek and Irish English on stage, as in the play's opening moments, which suggest a 'parallel between the two "heroic", lost cultures of Athens and Ireland' (31), he is also interested in the implied hierarchy between the two. Especially in the latter half of the play, Worthen argues that we witness the greater resilience of this earlier language which, Friel implies, will survive the death of Irish (32).

Clearly, as Roche and Worthen demonstrate, once discussions move from the abstractions of language theory to the specifics of Irish and English in

Irish history, cultural imperialism enters into the interpretation of the play. Josephine Lee's 1995 essay 'Linguistic Imperialism' demonstrates that such interpretations must contend with a play that does not readily support black-and-white readings. Lee repeatedly claims that *Translations* opens with a depiction of Baile Beag as 'a linguistic Eden', 'a linguistic paradise', in a 'linguistic Golden Age' (172–73), and that the two scenes of Act 2, in their diverse ways, clearly establish that translation, even for such bilingual speakers as Owen and Hugh, is difficult and fraught with opportunities for failure. However, if her reading argues that translation and shared understanding fail, the final moments of the play, in which Hugh declares his intention to learn the region's English names and teach Maire the English language, establish that 'English becomes a language of Irish unity' (179).

Toponyms

Language is nowhere more evident in the play's action than in Act 2 scene 1, when Yolland and Owen attempt to replace the Irish names for towns and topography with English alternatives. The scene opens on their attempt to find a translation for Bun na hAbhann and includes Owen's exposition on the meaning of Tobair Vree, and why it might be untranslatable. In his 1983 article, Kearney argues that Owen's suggestion to use 'Burnfoot' as the English replacement for Bun na hAbhann demonstrates that translation 'closes off rather than discloses' meaning (38). In a similar vein, McGrath states that 'Burnfoot' is Friel's example of how arbitrary the Ordnance renaming process could be (189). However, Roche notes that in Scots Gaelic 'burn' means 'river', so the renaming is not as arbitrary as some assume (303).

In Timm's 1982 article, 'the loss of language is also the loss of mythical imagination' (453); thus, when Yolland and Owen decide to leave the name *Tobair Vree* as it is, he reads this scene as a vital turning point at which Owen comes to recognize the near 'sacred' quality of names (451). Lee considers it equally significant for Yolland because here he first asserts his belief in a Romantic integrity to names (176). In his treatment of the play, Andrews momentarily reflects on Tobair Vree to observe that, while names are not arbitrary, many place names lack a 'natural' reference and are 'rooted in extra-linguistic reality' (170). Considering this issue in his book, McGrath adds that Friel includes this digression to demonstrate that forces other than culture also contribute to the erosion of language (190). As the discussions of *Translations* become increasingly refined, these scenes are subjected to greater analytical nuance. For example, Pilkington asserts that *Tobair Vree* is ironically already an Anglicized name because 'the letter 'v' is not used in the Irish alphabet' (214).[4]

History

In my *Brian Friel, Ireland, and the North*, I argue that earlier critics had failed to grasp just how extensively the 1980s marked a decade when Friel became fascinated with Irish history, especially the 'small voice' of remote and shifting local histories as opposed to the history of government and party politics (161–63). To that extent, *Translations* initiated a marked shift in Friel's career: for the first time since 1962, he would set a play not in contemporary Ireland but in the past. While *Translations* is set in 1833, his next plays *Making History* (1988) and *Dancing at Lughnasa* (1990) would be set in 1591 and 1936 respectively. Furthermore, though he wrote fewer original plays in the 1980s, his artistic departures were more numerous and varied than at any other point in his career. In 1981, the Field Day Theatre Company staged his first translation, his version of Chekhov's *Three Sisters*; he edited and wrote the introduction for Charles McGlinchey's *The Last of the Name* (1986), a memoir by a local weaver and tailor who lived from 1851 to 1954; in 1990 he published *The London Vertigo*, his adaption of *The True-Born Irishman* (1761) by the seventeenth-century playwright Charles Macklin, who was born close to Friel's home in County Donegal.

However, despite Friel's own interest in history and the theatrical success of *Translations*, the play was not popular with historians, especially J.H. Andrews, the author of *A Paper Landscape: The Ordnance Survey in Nineteenth-Century Ireland* (1975), the book that provided Friel with the setting for his play and the inspiration for such characters as Owen, who was based on the historical John O'Donovan, and Yolland, based on the historical Lieutenant Thomas Larcom. A little more than two years after the play was premiered, Andrews participated in a roundtable discussion with Friel at St. Patrick's College, Maynooth, which was published in the 1983 issue of *Crane Bag*, where Andrews criticized the play for its historical inaccuracies.[5] In response to Andrews' criticism, Friel took the very uncharacteristic step of publicly defending of his play, noting that the goals of writing a history play are different from those of writing history: 'Drama is first fiction, with the authority of fiction. You don't go to *Macbeth* for history' (119).[6]

Coincidentally, the very first article published on *Translations*, Eitel Timm's 'Modern Mind, Myth, and History' (1982), explores the tension between history and fiction, or in Timm's words 'history and myth' (448), the first being a way to know one's place and culture that is 'learned, literate and conscious', the second 'lived, illiterate and unconscious' (449–50). In Timm's reading, the play stages the conflict between myth and history nowhere more clearly than in the debate over toponyms. The debate over how to find an English equivalent for Tobair Vree and the ultimate decision to keep the Gaelic, whose meaning is obscure even to Irish speakers, marks for Timm the play's defence of 'mythic imagination' (450–52). In her 'Poetry and Politics in Northern Ireland' (1986), Edna Longley is also interested in the dynamic between history and myth in the play; however, in this reading, the play is neither innovative nor in control of its manipulation of history: 'the play does not so much *examine* myths of dispossession and oppression as repeat them' (190). Moreover, Longley asserts that *Translations* fails to even capture the past, merely translating 'contemporary Northern catholic feeling into historical terms' (191). In this, Longley sees the basic cultural strategy not only of the play but of Seamus Heaney's *Wintering Out* (1972), Tom Paulin's *Liberty Tree* (1983), and Field Day as a whole (191–92).

In his 1990 study of Friel, O'Brien makes the first attempt to place the play within a more concrete historical context and to avoid the more abstract discussions of the roles of fiction and history. Indeed, in exploring the nature of early nineteenth-century hedge schools, he points out that by using this more realistic setting Friel undermines 'the stereotype of the Irish peasant— drunken, fighting, cohabiting with pigs, craven, superstitious' (103). While the two historical events that undergird the play—the Ordnance Survey and the 1831 Education Act that established national schools—are routinely mentioned, Tony Corbett's 2002 analysis of the play consider both as equal elements of the history of Irish subjugation most evident in the Statutes of Kilkenny of 1366 and the series of Penal Laws beginning in 1625 (21). He adds some historical detail both on the nineteenth-century hedge schools and on post-Independence attempts to revive the Irish language (21–23).[7] In his *Art of Brian Friel*, Andrews also turns our attention to concrete historical details, to recognize that one historical detail may have distinct different meanings for the Irish and the English. To demonstrate this, Andrews points to the year 1789, which Yolland wistfully remembers as 'Year One', the day the Bastille fell and a new world was born, while Hugh remembers it as the year of the failed Irish uprising, when the old order reasserted itself (170–71).

While clearly addressing the specificities of Irish history, Richard Rankin Russell's *Modernity, Community, and Place* considers the play against the backdrop of Western Europe's eighteenth-century transition into Modernity. While rooting his argument in readings of Friel's earlier stories and plays, Russell frames Friel's historical drama as expressing an environmental philosophy that valorizes Ireland's vanishing parochial, agrarian communities. Thus, Russell calls our attention not merely to the temporal and physical settings of the play (during harvest and in a barn full of farming implements) but also to the many conversations that highlight the play's rundale society (163–68).

Sources and Influences

Throughout the 1980s, the critical community was myopically concerned with two texts in the background of *Translations*, Steiner's *After Babel* and J.H. Andrews' *A Paper Landscape*; thus, the play's other possible sources and analogues were left almost entirely unexplored until the 1990s. R.K.R. Thornton started the process of exploring other Irish plays that form the context for Friel's drama with his 1991 article 'Friel and Shaw'. In the interviews and working notes for *Translations*, Friel does not mention George Bernard Shaw's *John Bull's Other Island* (1904) as an inspiration; nonetheless, Thornton instructively notes the issues shared by the two plays. For example, both plays portray the British imperial incursion into Ireland initiated by such Englishmen as Shaw's Thomas Broadbent and Friel's Captain Lancey (226–27). Likewise, Thornton argues that, while seemingly relying upon caricatures of Irish identity, both playwrights attempt to broaden the 'definition of what it means to be Irish' (228).

At the end of the 1990s, Nicholas Grene returns to the potential of reading *Translations* in the ideological wake of Shaw's earlier comedy. In the first chapter of *The Politics of Irish Drama*, he identifies three plays that embody the most representative attempts to 'deliver the true Ireland' both to the Irish themselves and the English: Dion Boucicault's *The Shaughraun* (1874), Shaw's *John Bull*, and Friel's *Translations* (6). Boucicault's successful Victorian comedy of cultural reconciliation between the English and Irish is clearly another Irish play that can be instructively compared to Friel's drama. For example, in these three plays about English adventurers who find themselves unexpectedly love-struck with an Irish woman, the role of the Irish 'go-between'—Boucicault's Conn, Shaw's Doyle, and Friel's Owen—drastically shifts in its tone and function to reflect the Irish political attitude towards the English (41–42). Similarly, the resolution of these three stagings of 'the colonial…dream of intermarriage' says much for Grene about the political orthodoxy of the era when the plays were written (43).

In her chapter, 'Decent Chaps', Elizabeth Butler Cullingford also focuses on the relationship of Friel's play to *John Bull* and *The Shaughraun*, along with such other works as Boucicault's *Arrah-na-Pogue* (1864) and Brendan Behan's *The Hostage* (1958), in a wide-ranging exploration of Irish portrayals of 'stage Englishmen who fail to operate as villains even when the piece is anti-colonial' (37).[8] Her argument adds psychological detail to our understanding of the Yolland-Marie relationship (55), and it valuably draws our attention to the structural similarities between *Translations* and *Ryan's Daughter* (1970), an iconic David Lean film about 'an identical erotic triangle': a British officer, an Irish schoolmaster, and the 'colleen' (53). In his 2011 book, Roche also notes the importance for recognizing the romance between Claire and Molineux in *The Shaughraun* as the model for Maire and Yolland. Although his treatment is brief, he valuably summarizes how the melodrama's attention to politics, language, and place re-emerge in Friel's drama as well (135).

Owen

In the play's original production that toured fourteen Irish towns and cities from Derry and Belfast in the North to Cork and Dublin in the South, Owen was played by the young actor Stephen Rea who, together with Brian Friel, formed the Field Day Theatre Company and would appear as lead actor in its productions throughout the 1980s.[9] After being appointed to the board of directors of the company in 1981, Seamus Deane was the first to discuss Owen as the play's central character. In his introduction to Friel's *Selected Plays* (1984), he describes Owen as 'the recognizable Frielian outsider who has the intimacy of an insider' (21). In his chapter on Friel the following year in *Celtic Revivals*, Deane places Owen in a long line of Friel's heroes, from Columba and Gar O'Donnell to Frank Hardy, who are torn between the love of home and the call from abroad. In Owen's case, it is 'our love to the failed world (Ireland) [and] our respect for the conquering world (England)' (171). Indeed, like Skinner in *Freedom*, Owen fails in his attempt to overcome his impoverished background to achieve the heroism of which he is capable.

Dantanus is another early commentator who sees Owen as 'the key figure' for the Irish audience because his dual life in Anglicized Dublin and Gaelicized Baile Beag places him on the cusp of 'the clash between two languages and two cultures' (197). Writing a decade later, Declan Kiberd also sees Owen as 'by far the most complex character on stage'; however, he argues that he is a much less torn figure (619). In Kiberd's analysis, our clearest understanding of Owen comes when we recognize that he is modelled upon Larry Doyle in Shaw's *John Bull's Other Island*, 'a pragmatic fact-facing Irishman who…has enough of the rebel in him to sense that, if the Irish are to fight successfully, they had better master the language of their colonizers'.[10]

Other commentators since the 1980s consider Owen a more complex and suspicious character. While Kearney calls him 'a master of what Kavanagh called "the wink and elbow language of delight"', he nonetheless views him as fundamentally a 'duplicitous' figure (36–37); in a qualified judgement Wiley considers him 'not entirely a traitor' (60).[11] When O'Brien patiently analyses his character in his 1990 study, he notes his importance to the development of the play's action, but he explores his role to point out his frequent short-comings and lack of insight into the political role he plays (104–06). Indeed, in perhaps the most dismissive interpretation of the character, he says of Owen's initial act of translating Lancey's words,

■ Owen's rough translation of this and the rest of what Lancey says is made with a casualness that suggests that he is indifferent to the survey's ultimate meaning or that he simply has a general sense of Lancey's words and cannot fully comprehend their applicability to a world…apparently, proof against change. (106) □

While Cullingford is not as critical of Owen, she recognizes in his 'efficiency, cynicism, preference for English employers and lack of heterosexual enthusiasm' the type of Irish lackey common to such earlier plays as Shaw's *John Bull* (54). Similarly, in his *Theatre of Brian Friel*, Murray struggles to grasp Owen's character in his paragraph on him: on the one hand citing his 'mercuriality' and duplicity, while also describing him as a dreamer with 'beguiling innocence' (114).

By far the darkest interpretation of Owen is offered by Anthony Roche in his 2011 *Brian Friel*. Noting Friel's earlier portrayals of strong male friendships in *The Enemy Within* (1962) and secret homosexual desire and violence in *The Gentle Island* (1971), Roche considers 'the strong structural and thematic affinities' between the plays, ultimately focusing on Owen's friendship with Yolland. As had Cullingford, Roche notes that 'absolutely nothing is said about his emotional and sexual life', and he uses this observation to inform his reading that Act 2 scene 1 'balances and parallels the love scene between George and Maire … with the long intimate interlude' between Owen and Yolland (146). Indeed, Roche even proposes that, in his statements concerning Yolland's disappearance in Act 3, Owen may be concealing the reasons for his strange absence from the Chatach family *ceili* the night before (147).

Hugh

In his 2014 book, Christopher Murray mentions that, in Friel's earliest ideas for the play, 'Hugh was intended as the main character', but, while writing the play, Friel developed Owen at his father's expense (113). Thus, for many commentators, Hugh's nature and role is difficult to assess. He is memorably described by Richard Kearney as the play's 'minister of names', 'the transmitter, guarantor and guardian of the community's cultural identity' (34), but, despite this seeming praise, he describes Hugh as a figure locked in the past and limited by it. Another early commentator, Catherine Wiley, considers Hugh 'emblematic of his nation' (57). She sees him as strenuously attempting to manage Baile Beag as it is 'being dragged into the modern colonial world', but, in her view, he is too encumbered by 'nostalgic blarney' to decisively aid his town. For different reasons, Dantanus also struggles to reconcile Hugh's seeming dramatic importance with his character's temperamental weaknesses. Although he criticizes him for his 'pomposity' (187, 189), he recognizes that Hugh often quotes Steiner's book verbatim in Friel's effort to crystallize the play's issues (193).[12]

Conversely, O'Brien does not view Hugh as a figure of painful or poignant ambivalence; rather, he compares him to Manus Sweeney in Friel's earlier *Gentle Island* (1972), a 'king of nothing' (107). O'Brien summarizes the ways that Hugh's ambitions and plans 'fail' over the course of the play, leading him to the conclusion that 'Hugh himself [is] "imprisoned in a linguistic contour"' (108). Nicholas Grene takes an equally negative view of Hugh in his 1999 book; however, it is Hugh's pedantry and 'high-flown English' that, for Grene, signal his character flaws (44). In fact, based on his reading of Hugh's preference for using a Latinate vocabulary, he claims that Hugh's 'language … is really English from the beginning', which for him is a sure clue of Hugh's weaknesses as a character.[13]

Writing in 1995, Andrews offers the earliest full examination of Hugh; however, admitting that 'Hugh is a large and complex creation', he finds the character difficult to assess (177). On the one hand, he claims that Hugh is fundamentally conservative and narrow minded. For example, while he plans to run the national school 'exactly as he had run his hedge school' for decades, Andrews finds his attitude to education and his students typified by laziness and chauvinism. To that end, Andrews specifically criticises Hugh for dismissing the English language as 'plebeian', yet quizzing his students on the etymology of English words when convenient (175). Andrews sees Hugh as equally vacillating in his perspective on the Irish, at times taking 'a surprisingly critical view of the Irish' when talking with Yolland; at other times disparaging English culture compared to the Irish (175).

Nonetheless, Andrews repeatedly speculates that Hugh speaks for Friel: 'he would seem to voice Friel's acceptance of the English language' (177), and some of his views 'seem to have Friel's endorsement' (178). Hugh refrains from joining in Manus's passionate complaints against the arrival of the English in Act 1, and Andrews especially praises his openness to the new emerging order in Act 3 (177–78). Indeed, he views Hugh's recitation of Virgil's *Aeneid* in the play's final moments as indicative of his ability to 'use the past to enlighten present dilemmas and obtain a perspective on them' (178).[14] Yet, after finding much to praise in the character and his putative embrace of the 'fusion of Gaelic and English traditions', his section on Hugh closes with a retreat from any such endorsement:

■ We are forced to consider the possibility that Hugh's civilised, classical balance, his serene, speculative, even-handed rejection of anything in particular, may, in fact, be a recipe for political inertia and, thus, for passive submission to the oppressor. (179) ☐

Appearing in the same year as Andrews' book, Lee's article 'Linguistic Imperialism' only briefly discusses Hugh, yet she presents one of the most laudatory assessments of his character. For her, even his entrance in Act 1, returning slightly drunk from celebrating the christening of Nellie Ruadh's baby, affirms 'the security and order of this world' before the advent of English (173), and his faults throughout the first two acts are forgiven because of his 'tragic self-consciousness' (174).

Finally, with an interpretation that complements Andrews', she too considers his closing lines as bearing special importance, as emphasizing to the audience that the glory of a great civilization like Carthage, even if it is all but erased, does not die with its language. Rather, in the Irish case, its new English tongue will be the vehicle for the story of Gaelic Ireland (178–79).

In his 1999 book, McGrath follows Andrews and Lee to express a less equivocal respect for Hugh; indeed, he too claims that 'Hugh is much closer to Friel' than any other character, because like the playwright he neither clings to old Gaelic tradition nor styles himself a convert to English. Rather, he chooses to 'reappropriate the English language for Irish culture', which is what McGrath sees as the Field Day project overall (193). For McGrath, Hugh's faltering recitation of the first lines of Virgil's *Aeneid*, as the play ends, expresses Friel's own fatalism (194). However, it is a fatalism laden with some irony because, McGrath points out, Virgil wrote his epic to celebrate the victors (imperial Rome), while Hugh's recitation is taken as a melancholy lament for the defeated (Gaelic Ireland).[15]

In his detailed treatment of Hugh in 2001, Pilkington is the first critic to argue that Hugh's character does not so much evolve in the course of the play as that Friel slowly reveals Hugh's nature to the audience. In this reading, Friel uses Act 2 to betray Hugh's intentional irony regarding Irish culture; to quote the play he is 'deliberately parodying himself' (213). Pilkington asserts that had Yolland not been drunk, he would have recognized Hugh's warning to distance himself from Irish culture (214). However, in the third act, Hugh's statements to Jimmy Jack, Marie, and Owen and his final monologue emphasize the material and cultural advantages of accepting the coming of English (215–17). Indeed, Friel suspends Hugh's recitation of *The Aeneid* 'quite literally, in mid sentence' to change the question away from whether Irish culture will survive after the English conquest to one of redefining Irish nationalism 'not in terms of anti-imperialism but, like Hugh's unfinished syllogisms, as a modernizing, and apparently open-ended project of cultural recovery' (217).

Maire

In the earliest criticism of the play, Maire was recognized as the play's tragic figure. For Kearney she is representative of an 'emerging generation of aspiring peasants tired of treading the timeless mudtracks of oppressed Gaeldom' (35), but her appearance in the play's final scene in desperation and distraction is symbolic of her state as a person ostracized from both communities (41). Kearney carefully reads the details of her final scene, both her recitation of the imaginary English map taught to her by Yolland and her very placement on the site where the ordnance map had earlier been spread, as indicative 'of the tragic historical fact that in the colonial conflict between England and Ireland the time was out of joint' (41). Etherton recognizes that her desire to learn English has little to do with the politician Daniel O'Connell's argument that learning English will empower the Irish and much to do with her desire to acquire the basic skills to leave Ireland (203). Andrews develops these interpretive strands, declaring that 'Maire is the principal spokesperson of the forces of modernisation' (174). He sees her as a character who consistently 'questions traditional "Irish" habits of mind' and demonstrates an intellectual forcefulness rarely seen in Friel's characters (173–74).

While Maire has been recognized by various critics as an important character, she was not made the focus of a sustained analysis until Lauren Onkey's 'The Woman as Nation' (1997). An exchange between Manus and Jimmy Jack early in the play, during which they compare the medieval Irish heroine Grania to Athena, becomes vital to Onkey's interpretation of Maire. In both medieval legend and the dramatic version co-authored by W.B. Yeats and George Moore in 1901, Grania was known as a romantically assertive woman who repudiated her arranged marriage to the aged king Finn to run off with his warrior Diarmuid, which ultimately leads to his death, her despair and suicide, and 'disorder in the community' (165). Early in *Translations*, Maire is portrayed as temperamentally similar to the legendary heroine in her surprising independence: she is the only native of Baile Beag eager to learn English and emigrate; she has the temerity to argue with Hugh; and she romantically rejects Manus in favour of Yolland (163–64). Thus, Onkey sees Maire's resolve to choose her own lover and leave Baile Beag as operating with the same thematic force as the medieval tale, with the same tragic result. Indeed, near the end of the play when Jimmy Jack discusses his own intention 'to marry outside the tribe', Onkey argues that he is making a plea to Maire 'to accept that she has tried to do what cannot be done' (166).

Yolland

Dantanus states that Yolland 'can be seen as the key figure for an English audience', and his naïve attempt to navigate the English and Irish extremes that threaten to engulf the action make him the play's most sympathetic character (195). In this assessment of Yolland, Dantanus echoes Kearney's 1983 treatment of the character, where Kearney first identifies the audience's sympathy for Yolland's 'naïve and positivistic belief that there might exist an ideal system of translation … a prelapsarian naming process, similar to that of Adam' (39).

Roche treats Yolland as the play's central figure in his 2011 book in a chapter that carries the subtitle 'An Inquiry into the Disappearance of Lieutenant George Yolland' (135–50). Even in Yolland's most celebratory moments—when in a sign of genuine friendship Owen reveals the Irish version of his name to him—Kearney sees 'a hint of the disillusioning reality to follow'. Like many other commentators, Roche views Yolland's naïveté as a trait that associates him with 'the second generation English romantic poets', thus making him susceptible to the charms of Baile Beag's 'landscape, language and spirit' (*Contemporary* 251). In this sense, Roche sees a major opposition between Lancey's 'Lockean empiricism, fired by industrial and colonial expansionism' and Yolland's temperamental kinship with Wordsworth. In his recent book, Russell considers Yolland's Romanticism as indicative of his basic anti-modernity: by adopting the Baile Beag's 'organic rhythms' and pre-industrial lifestyle, Yolland aspires to become a 'hybrid character' who exists in both English and Irish languages and cultures (190–91). Ultimately, while Russell assumes Friel's sympathy for Yolland, he is 'sacrificed' because, like Frank Hardy in *Faith Healer*, he represents a doomed resistance to a 'worldview' that emphasizes 'quantitative rather than qualitative aspects of our experience' (191).

Roche has observed that throughout the play 'different men step into the dramatic limelight and hold centre stage for a time'; in other words, *Translations* resists any simple attempt to construct 'a hero' (2014, 136). Not surprisingly, as with the summaries of Hugh and Owen, critical opinions of Yolland vary. Thus, as early as Lee's 1995 article, Yolland is seen as a naïve tool of English imperialism:

■ Yolland must be read as political; as an Englishman and a gentleman, he can exist in no other capacity other than as imperialist, either in Bombay or in Ireland. Although sympathetic, he is also culpable.... (178) □

In his chapter 'Friel Translating', which appeared in his 1999 study of Irish literature, Kiberd considers Yolland perhaps the most self-deluded character in the play; Kiberd points to Yolland's nostalgia for the world before 1789 and his feeling that his arrival in Ireland suggests to him that he has returned to the *ancien régime* (621). Moreover, Kiberd employs Edward Said's *Orientalism* (1978) to describe Yolland as a type of stock colonizer who, despite his good intentions, pursues 'the hopeless stupidity of the attempt to impose a foreign grid on Irish reality' (619). Even his love for Maire Chatach recalls nothing more clearly than the imperialist's '"ritual infatuation"...with some mysterious woman of the native tribe' (620). In short, in Yolland's character Kiberd reads an 'aristocratic fetishism' for a receding 'anti-modern, anti-democratic' world (621).[16]

While accepting the basic tenets of this interpretation of Yolland as a Romantic, my 2007 book discusses the importance of recognizing Yolland's true historical model. Just as Friel relied upon the Ordnance's historical Colonel Colby for his character Captain Lancey, he used Thomas Larcom as the basis for George Yolland. Throughout the course of his long career in Ireland, Larcom studied Irish while directing the renaming project and 'advocated greater Irish influence in the Survey' (160). I argue that Friel transformed this influential Hibernophile who served for almost twenty years into the short-lived Yolland because of his suspicion of 'benevolent Englishness' (166). Indeed, I contend that in such plays of the 1980s as *Translations* and *Making History*, English characters who support Irish causes and seek Irish spouses see their efforts thwarted and their lives tragically ended (166–69).

Yolland and Maire

The love scene between Yolland and Maire (Act 2 scene 2), despite the fact that they do not share a common language, has been viewed by many as the play's most important scene.[17] Dantanus claims that here 'the theme of communication receives its finest and most ironic expression' (188). For him, it is an ominous turning point for the play because this attainment of 'love between two individuals ironically ruptures any hope of communication in the larger context between the two nations and languages'. Writing in 1999, McGrath also considers this scene as staging 'the implicit but ill-fated ideal of the play' that two cultures can communicate across language barriers (186). In his *Modernity, Community, and Place*, Russell considers this the play's 'crucial moment' as well (182). Harking back to passing comments made by Grene (43) and Cullingford (169), Russell asserts that their exchange of place names allows Maire and Yolland to 'realize the intricate way in which they are now connected' (182). Nevertheless, he observes that 'the irony is strong' because she wishes to learn English while he is committed to an enterprise that plans to eradicate the very Irish words they recite.

Clearly, with the critical tradition of reading a heavy dose of irony into this scene, there is a tendency to articulate the characters' failure as well. Lee points out that any notion that Yolland and Maire create a 'shared world' is an impression of the audience alone; the characters recognize none of their shared words and coincidence of ideas (177). Similarly, in her 2004 article 'Carrying Across into Silence', Suzy Clarkson Holstein posits that 'perhaps they can fall in love...only because they do *not* speak the same language' (7). If they did, she argues, they would recognize that they disagree on their basic perceptions of the world and even whether to remain in Ireland.

However, Murray responds to this growing pessimistic reading of the scene in 'Palimpsest: Two Languages as One in *Translations*' (2006), which presents perhaps the most detailed and nuanced reading of the scene. In a play obsessed with the act of 'writing…written over an effaced writing' (100), Murray first argues that this scene triumphantly affects its audience because of its 'release of feeling, so that the audience is drawn in' (103). In achieving this, he asserts that primarily 'it is not the words but the sounds that matter', but for the scene to progress the characters must also share a single language—place names (103–04). Finally, he astutely notes that at this point, and until they touch, they no longer speak to each other: 'Friel says in his stage directions that each of them speaks almost to himself and herself' (105). Such a reading ultimately suggests that the audience should not use Yolland's subsequent tragedy to ironize this earlier part of the play.

Finally, Elmer Andrews' analysis of this scene expands our understanding of it within Friel's career. First, by comparing it to scenes between Lily and Skinner in *Freedom* or the sisters' ecstatic dance in *Lughnasa*, he suggests that, when Yolland and Maire leave the dance together, the scene 'opens up a lyrical space that presses back against history' (172). In fact, Andrews pushes back against the dominance of the language theory of the play by asserting that in this scene Friel is attempting to free himself of language, seeking 'forms of communication which are free of the social contaminations of ordinary language' (173).

Sarah

In the earliest defence of the play, Seamus Heaney's review in 1980, he posits that Sarah has a significance that far outweighs her minor role; indeed, he likens her to Cathleen ni Houlihan, a seemingly defenceless woman who calls men to revolution and martyrdom (1199). Despite her limited role, such critics as Michael Etherton argue that she 'completes the structure of relationships that encompasses the theme of language', and by focusing on the changes of her relationship to Manus throughout the play, he claims that 'the bleakness of her characterisation…reflects the emotional contour of the whole play' (205). Similarly, the idea that Sarah's importance far outweighs her role in the play is supported by Roche, who mentions in his 2011 book that, in the play's early drafts, her character was named Unity (140).

In an attempt to incorporate Heaney's view into a structure suggested by Steiner's observation on silence and oppression, McGrath posits in his early article on the play that Sarah alludes to the hidden Ireland that was only beginning to re-emerge at the end of the period defined by the Penal Laws. He equates Sarah's return to silence at the play's end with 'Kurtz's "the Horror, the Horror" [in Joseph Conrad's *Heart of Darkness* (1902)] and the Ouboum of the Malabar caves [in E.M. Forster's *A Passage to India* (1924)]' as marking a culture's recalcitrant refusal to translate itself into the Master's language (192).[18] Writing soon after McGrath in his article 'The Hermeneutic Motion in Brian Friel's *Translations*', Robert Smith also views Sarah as integral to a Steinerian reading of the play. For him, Sarah is Steiner's 'autistic child' locked in a 'speech-battle' with a threatening 'master' (399). Thus, Sarah resists speaking to Lancey at the play's end not because she finds him intimidating but because she intuitively recognizes that a name is part of the 'ritual formula of the tribe; possession of it confers power'.

All these readings, from Heaney to Smith, focus on what each critic considers Sarah's representative moment in the play and extrapolate a symptomatic interpretation of her character. Clearly, one element shared by all is the belief that Sarah, this most minor character, in some way represents her people—whether that be Heaney's view of her as Kathleen ni Houlihan, McGrath's Gaelic Ireland, or Smith's tribe. Conversely, in her 1997 discussion of women in the play, Lauren Onkey undertakes a much more probing reading of Sarah's significant moments in the play that declares its intention to resist *a priori* interpretations of 'her many silences and ambiguous gestures' (169). For Onkey, to read Sarah in the 'woman as nation' tradition effaces her identity within the play and especially the way that her love for Manus operates dramatically (168–69). Such a reading interpretively opens up her most important acts for Onkey: not just the 'hesitant love scene between the two' that initiates the play, but her crying for Manus when she witnesses Yolland and Maire's love scene. Ultimately, Onkey's reading is especially skilful in its treatment of Sarah's various actions in the final act, from her frequent glances towards the room where Manus packs to her sphinx-like smile at Owen at the end of her confrontation with Lancey. Indeed, attempting to overturn the conventional reading of the confrontation between Lancey and Sarah, Onkey posits that Sarah's smile suggests that Lancey has had little psychological impact on her and shows her 'refusal to be simplified'; that her lapse back into silence has more to do with Owen's complicity with the English and Manus's departure than Lancey's attempted intimidation (170). As a sort of coda to Onkey, Suzy Holstein opines that in Friel's dramaturgy 'not all silences are clear defeats' (8), and Sarah's silence 'may be the only remaining, rational response' (7).

Minor Characters

Manus is largely ignored in the early criticism, aside from Andrews' comment that Manus stands as a stubborn Nationalist who, at the play's end, becomes the 'pathetic victim of his own inflexibility' (180). Although Manus has never emerged from the shadow of his father and brother, in his 2002 book Corbett is the first critic to claim he is 'the touchstone of the play' (23). As a figure marked out as 'lame' in an agrarian society, Manus is Baile Beag's 'outsider' from the drama's very beginning. Moreover, when Manus defends the trick that Doalty has played on the soldiers, asserting that it indicates 'a presence', Corbett states that he foreshadows the outcome when all the town's people become outsiders: 'Manus feels, already, that they have lost their presence in Baile Beag' (23).[19]

Richard Harp's 'Manus and *Oedipus*' (2002) also endeavours to make Manus relevant to the play's interpretation, arguing that on many levels the figure is defined by his self-destructive loyalty to family and place. Harp argues that Manus's tragedy results in large part from his inability to free himself from the authority of the father who accidentally crippled him; this suffocates his ambitions and disrupts his plans to marry Maire (25–27). Moreover, by adopting the identification of Sarah with Cathleen ni Houlihan, Harp is able to explore the extent to which Manus resembles the character Michael Gillane who, in the famous nationalist play *Cathleen Ni Houlihan* (1902) by W.B. Yeats and Augusta Gregory, joins the 1798 uprising and loses his life because he has been bewitched by Cathleen (28–29).

Anthony Roche provides a rich and significant discussion of the Donnelly twins in his 2011 book. While several critics have commented in passing on how these absent characters suggest the violence that lurks beyond the town's borders, Roche comprehensively surveys the instances in the play in which the mention of their name reduces a scene to silence or raises the issue of insurgent violence; similarly, he argues that the shadow of their influence leads us to re-interpret the comical antics of their friend Doalty in a threatening light (141–43). Roche also looks forward to *The Home Place* at the end of Friel's career to consider its portrayal of Fenian secrecy and anti-English intimidation (142).[20]

Politics

Through the influence of Seamus Deane and Richard Kearney, who first presented the idea in the *Crane Bag* in 1977, Field Day advocated the notion that the company sought to define a political and cultural 'Fifth Province', an alternative to the historical division of Ireland into four provinces, that would navigate between Catholic and Protestant, Nationalist and Unionist.[21] Indeed, in 1982 interviews with Ray Comiskey for *The Irish Times* and Fintan O'Toole for *In Dublin*, Friel embraced the Fifth Province as Field Day's intention to bridge political divides by distancing itself from Ireland's traditional ideological antimonies:

■ Field Day is not about changing the North—I hate using grandiose terms like this—but in some way the very fact that it's located in the North and has its reservations about it, and that it works in the South and has its reservations about it, it's like, as somebody said, an artistic fifth province.[22] □

In short, especially because the Field Day Theatre Company was associated with a Catholic playwright and Catholics dominated the board of directors, it strenuously sought to avoid associations with Irish nationalism and especially Northern nationalism.

Interpretations of *Translations* were soon swept up into the politics of the Troubles, after the rise of the Provisional IRA and the Shankill Butchers in the 1970s, amid rising communal violence.[23] For example, in his 1985 article 'Friel's *Translations*', Rollins views the play's cultural politics in the starkest terms:

■ the British imperialists will perform a frontal lobotomy upon the village of Ballybeg and the rest of the country, instantly reducing the Irish to cultural illiterates, to tongue-tied children uncertain about their identities. (36) □

In 'Poetry and Politics', an article also originally published in 1986, Edna Longley uses equally strong language to criticize the play's 'fossilised' ideology. She claims that Hugh 'embodies the play's pervasive nostalgia for "what has been lost"...for Ballybeg as a kind of Eden' (191). While she sees Hugh as the dreamer as opposed to Owen 'the doer', she comes very close to claiming that Hugh represents the Field Day board overall: 'Field Day, like Hugh, "dreams of a perfect city" as well as a promised land'.

When he discusses the play in his 1999 study of the politics of Irish drama, Grene attempts to shift and broaden this view of Baile Beag as a Gaelic culture undiluted by outside influences. Not only does he agree that, despite the possible irony of Hugh's statements, Friel depicts a 'hedge-school culture' embodying a continuity with 'an unchanging pre-colonial Celtic past dating back to time immemorial' (39); he also speculates that Friel may even hint that Baile Beag preserves a 'pre-Christian as well as pre-colonial and pre-modern' culture (39–40). Thus, one of Grene's conclusions is that the play portrays the inexorable colonial process that will 'leave the Irish people spiritually and psychologically dispossessed' (42).

However, even as early as the 1980s, less nationalist views were strenuously argued as well. In her article 'Recreating Ballybeg' (1987), Catherine Wiley admits that the play captures a transitional moment in the colonization of Ireland: 'history must be not only translated, but from now on enacted in English' (59). Yet she recognizes that the results are mixed for both colonizer and colonized. For example, she posits that Jimmy Jack and Hugh attest to the fact that Ireland 'cripples or somehow incapacitates those who are born' there (58). Likewise, with Yolland especially in mind, she is the first to argue that the colonizers are humanized by their encounter with the Irish (59–60). A more nuanced view is taken by David Cairns and Shaun Richards the following year. In one of the earliest sustained attempts to apply Postcolonial theory to the Irish cultural experience, Cairns and Richards in their book *Writing Ireland* (1988) assert that the play resists a simplistically reductive idea that Gaelic Baile Beag 'was a kind of Eden' before the advent of English (147). While they admit that the events stage Ireland's 'transition, or translation, from one mode of time and experience to another' through 'the exercise of colonial power', they see the final positions of Hugh and Owen as offering unexpected commentaries on possible Irish responses to this English expansion. On the one hand, Owen, who has 'betrayed his origins' through his English employment, embraces Irish armed resistance to the English, while his father Hugh 'takes the more highly charged decision' to teach English and accept the new English names (147–48).

Andrews opens his book's review of *Translations* by invoking Kearney's notion that the play's portrayal of language stages antonymous philosophical and ideological differences: the Gaelic view that language expresses cultural rootedness and 'the hermetic core of being', versus the more utilitarian English approach, with 'no time for…hidden origins of meaning or community' (170–71). Yet, Andrews recognizes that even in the first scene the play undermines 'any straightforward Nationalist' interpretation of Baile Beag before the coming of English by having Maire argue that the politician Daniel O'Connell, who was known as 'The Liberator' for his efforts to empower the Irish, has urged the Irish to learn English (171). Indeed, Andrews argues that by making Yolland central to the action, the play 'asks us to consider the colonial mentality in a positive and sympathetic light' (171). While not invoking Andrews by name, Kiberd's chapter on *Translations* in his book *Inventing Ireland* also seeks to describe a nationalism that is anything but straightforward. Unlike earlier writers, Kiberd makes a sharp distinction between Friel as a Northern writer, a Northern nationalist, and the Republic's nationalism. Thus, in Kiberd's reading, the portrayal of language in *Translations* does not make this a 'language' play but a political play, because Friel, like the poets Seamus Heaney and John Montague, 'grew up in a state where the speaking of Irish was a political act, and where a person who gave a Gaelic version of a name to a policeman might expect a cuff on the ear or worse' (616). That Hugh agrees to adopt and teach English, the colonizer's language, shows that 'the pragmatists outnumber the dreamers when the chips are down' (619).

My own article coming at the end of the 1990s, 'Swapping Stories about Apollo and Cuchulainn' (1998), marks the beginning of a more assertive trend to read the play against the grain of Irish nationalism. Pointing to the Gaelic characters' general ignorance of Irish mythology (575), Hugh's preference for

Latin in the classroom and as the language for his own poetry (577), and the hedge school curriculum that closely resembles its English counterpart (578), I argue that the play seeks 'to dispel the nationalist myth of a past Gaelic purity, predicated upon the Romantic belief in an *echt* Irishness' (578). In his 2001 book *Theatre and the State*, Pilkington furthers this proposition, arguing that the play should be properly read as advocating an 'anti-republicanism' (220). In Pilkington's careful reading, Friel's drama builds towards a rejection of history as narrative, which in Act 3 is equally represented by Jimmy Jack's obsession with Athena and Owen's with a return to the Irish language (215–16). Rather, in the final act, Hugh champions the reality of 'history as fact', and by accepting the English language, and eventually English culture, Hugh rejects the social and economic decay of Gaelic culture's 'delusive quixoticism' (217).

Translations ended the most productive and acclaimed artistic period of Friel's career, and retrospectively the 1980s seem somewhat the antithesis of the 1970s: a decade of a few minor or unsuccessful plays. The next chapter will explore the playwright's struggle to sustain his vocation amid the increasing demands placed upon him as director of a new theatre company and, eventually, Irish senator.

CHAPTER NINE

Plays of the 1980s

'The American Welcome'

Six months before the premiere of *Translations*, in March 1980, the Actors The-atre of Louisville presented 'The American Welcome' as part of a series of short plays in a festival entitled The American Project. The monologue was commis-sioned to run between five and ten minutes and consumes barely two pages in its printed form (appearing in *One on One: The Best Men's Monologues for the Nineties*); not surprisingly, in such a long and complex playwriting career, this short piece has received scant attention.

Ulf Dantanus presents the only treatment of the play to appear in the twenti-eth century (180–81), and along with an extensive quotation he establishes the play's setting: an unnamed 'great British dramatist' travels to the United States to meet the director of his play, only to discover that the director has hired an American playwright to adapt the play's language into colloquial American Eng-lish and to rewrite the monologue into a play with four characters (180–81). In her 2013 study *Brian Friel and America*, Maria Szasz provides the most detailed and informative treatment of this short play. Indeed, her examination even includes details for the contract and commissioned payment (150–51). Her analy-sis also probes the brief play to reveal the manner in which it engages with the themes of *Translations*; for example, she notes that the American director uses eight different names for the playwright, while the silent playwright is given 'no voice' (152). Similarly, she explores how the director has overseen a process of 'translating' the play from British into American (153).

Three Sisters and Friel's Russian Plays

In 1981, Field Day premiered Friel's translation of Chekhov's *Three Sisters*; this marked the first time that the playwright authored a translation, and for many it confirmed his close dramatic and thematic debt to the Russian writer. During

98

the remainder of his career, he was to have two other translations of Chekhov staged: *Uncle Vanya* premiered at the Gate Theatre in 1998, and a version of 'The Bear' (first performed 1888) presented at the Gate in 2002. 'The Bear' was the second of a trio of one-act homages to Chekhov performed between 2001 and 2002, the first being 'The Yalta Game', a dramatic adaptation of Chekhov's story 'Lady with Lapdog', and 'Afterplay', Friel's fantasy meeting between Sonya from *Vanya* and Andrey from *Three Sisters* (see Chapter 12). Friel's interest in Russian literature also manifested itself in his translation of *A Month in the Country* (first published 1855), a play by Ivan Turgenev (1818–83) premiered by the Gate in 1992, as well as in his dramatic adaptation of Turgenev's novel *Fathers and Sons* (1862), which was first staged by National Theatre, London, in 1987.

Friel's published interviews affirm that he started reading Steiner's *After Babel* as he struggled with translating Chekhov, though he did not actually start his version of *Three Sisters* until *Translations* was all but finished. While he does not reveal why he undertook this challenge at this point in his career, the Friel Papers show that he suggested the project to Joe Dowling, a director with the Abbey Theatre, late in 1979. In my *Brian Friel, Ireland, and the North*, I point out that Friel's interest in *Three Sisters* dates at least to 1963, when he attended Tyrone Guthrie's rehearsals of it at the Guthrie Theatre (216).

Critical examinations of Friel's Russian translations and adaptations have been few. Dantanus provides a useful summary of Friel's intention to create an Irish translation free of the formal British phrasing that, in Friel's view, characterizes the versions that were available to the average Irish theatre company (183–85). After reviewing an example of how Friel attempts to 'localize' a speech by Natasha, Dantanus speculates that such changes may help the play appeal to 'audiences in places like Maghera, Galway or Tralee (where, among other places, the play toured)' (185). A more comprehensive analysis of Friel's work as translator emerges in Richard York's 1993 article 'Friel's Russia', where he compares Friel's translation of Chekhov's play to his adaptation of Turgenev's novel *Fathers and Sons*. York begins his essay by recognizing Friel's attempt to offer 'a riposte to the hegemony of British English' in his translations at the same time that they 'bear witness to a deep fidelity to the originals' (163, 167). Moreover, throughout the article, York also explores the different strategies that Friel employed in the distinctly different challenges of translating a play, on the one hand, and condensing and reorganizing a novel, on the other (167–76).

When Robert Tracy entered the field in 1999, in 'The Russian Connection', his discussion of *Three Sisters* is placed in the context of the greater textual liberties evident in Friel's version of *Uncle Vanya*. As with the earlier critics, he notes Friel's 'Irishisms' that he posits are used to 'attractively naturalise the speech of Chekhov's characters' (69). However, unlike previous readers of the play,

Tracy discusses *Three Sisters* more as part of a trilogy beginning with *Translations* and ending with *The Communication Cord* (68–71). For example, he notes that his construction of Vershinin and Tuzenbach is shaped by 'Friel's mistrust of that "language of aspiration" that Hugh defines in *Translations*' (71). The last section of Tracy's article explores the greater freedom that Friel employed in his *Uncle Vanya*, which premiered more than fifteen years after *Three Sisters*. While asserting that he 'does no real violence' to Chekhov's original, Tracy enumerates the scenes in which Friel greatly intensifies intentions and emotions that Chekhov left unexpressed (73–75).

Later that year, David Krause sought to overturn these admiring assessments of Friel's work in 'Friel's Ballybeggared Version of Chekhov'. Krause offers a corrective to the praise of Tracy and York based on a fundamental question:

■ While it was valid for Friel to protest against the use of affected Edwardian or Bloomsbury speech rhythms for Chekhov's play, why did he presume that all he had to do to solve the problem was to include a good dose of Irish speech patterns in his own 'translation'? (634) □

First, Krause questions whether Friel can legitimately describe his *Three Sisters* as a translation at all, because, by the playwright's own admission, he does not know the Russian language and relied on six existing translations (635). More importantly, however, Krause objected to Friel's 'anti-British' assertion that English words 'spoken in the theatre were dangerous to the Irish people'. Krause follows these broad concerns with others based on more particular readings of the play. For example, he points out that Irish idiom is used almost exclusively by 'the servile or socially inferior characters' and asks whether 'deliberately or inadvertently' Friel's play conformed to 'a demeaning' portrayal of the Irish (636). He also contends that Friel coarsened such characters as Masha (638–40) and Olga (643–45). In exasperation over what he perceives as Friel's departure from Chekhov's tone, he asks, 'Has Friel made indecent vulgarity an Irish thing?' (640).

Only one of the books or essay collections published after 2000 does more than mention these translations or adaptations in passing: *The Cambridge Companion* (2006) which contains Richard Pine's 'Friel's Irish Russia'. Pine writes from a perspective that encompasses of all of Friel's Russian translations, adaptations, and 'other notional "Russian" projects', including a few that he never completed; thus, he presents the reader with the fullest overview of Friel's relationship with this body of literature (105). In a manner informed by his personal friendship with the author, Pine is able to skilfully map out a broad range of personal affinities between Friel and Chekhov, ranging from similar biographical elements to the themes that define them both, such as 'the dispersal of households' to their common 'search [for] childhood' (106–07). After surveying the Chekhovian atmosphere of *Living Quarters* and *Aristocrats* (110–11), Pine considers *Three Sisters* and *Uncle Vanya* as examples of Friel's attempt both to translate the originals and to develop 'a more interpersonal and Irish relationship' between characters than was possible in the originals (112).

The Communication Cord (1982)

Both essays in the programme for the premiere of *The Communication Cord* establish the play's fundamental reliance on *Translations*. In the first, 'Commencement' by Tom Paulin, nearly the entire first page is taken up by the reproduction of Hugh's reminiscence of his role in the 1798 rebellion, which appears near the end of the play, and Paulin's subsequent discussion stresses the importance of *Translations* to the meaning of *The Communication Cord*. Indeed, he even points out that the newer play 'redresses or counterbalances some of the more *völkisch* pieties which *Translations* inspired'. Similarly, the next brief essay, Deane's 'In Search of a Story', defines *The Communication Cord* as 'an antidote to *Translations*' in its very second sentence. Their readings of the play clearly reflected the views that Friel himself asserted in interviews with Fintan O'Toole and Ray Comiskey at the time of the play's debut. Thus, the conventional interpretation for Friel's farce was set, and in the intervening decades few have departed very far from this assumption.

When Richard Kearney's carefully argued 'Language Play' appeared in *Studies* the following year (1983), he stated that

> ■ both plays conspire to present us with a fascinating genealogy of the process of human speech.... The fact that the former play is composed in *tragic* tones, while the latter is written as a *farce*, is itself an indicator of Friel's tragic-comic realization that there is no going back on history; that the best that can be achieved is a playful deconstruction and reconstruction of words in the hope that new modes of communication might be made possible. (46) □

In short, Kearney emphasizes the diverse correspondences that structure *Cord*. For example, Tim Gallagher, the struggling graduate student in Linguistics, combines aspects of Hugh and Manus, while Senator Donovan is 'a sort of modern antitype of Jimmy Jack' (49–50). Finally, for Kearney, the main character is Jack McNeilis, a modern Owen: a 'successful, suave, and self-assured barrister from Dublin' (47). He describes him as 'a dealer in identities' and 'master of modern pragmatism' who cynically exploits his family's cottage and its associations with cultural authenticity to advance his schemes (49).

Far more than in any earlier discussion of the play, Elmer Andrews is eager to point out how *Cord* shares traits with Friel's previous plays apart from *Translations*. Not only does Andrews generally associate this farce's political tone with *The Mundy Scheme* of 1969 (193), but he is especially interested in making the case that Jack is heir to Friel's 'earlier playboys', Gar, Shane, Skinner, Keeney, and Casimir, though he allows that Jack is less sincere than those earlier characters (194). In her 1997 book, Pelletier also seeks to broaden the play's relevant references, arguing that its comparison to *Mundy Scheme* reveals Friel's maturation in the development of comic rhythm and character (189). In a more limited view, Kathleen Ferris points out, in her article 'Brian Friel's Uses of Laughter' (1997), that Tim resembles earlier 'academic experts' whom Friel satirizes such as Dr Dodds from *Freedom* and Dr King from *Volunteers* (128).

State-of-the-Nation Play

While the play's subordinate relationship to *Translations* has been assumed from the time of its premiere, *The Communication Cord* has increasingly been read as a state-of-the-nation play. In his 1988 study *Brian Friel*, Dantanus focuses on the farce's portrayal of the various fault lines within Irish society of the 1980s, especially the modernized East and the agrarian West, as well as the nation's 'muddle of insincere and unthinking attitudes to the Irish past' (204). Indeed, rather than focusing on the play's depiction of language, Dantanus is more interested in describing Senator Donovan as the 'hypocritical and confused' cipher of official Ireland (204–05). Writing in 2000 Kathleen Hohenleiter also considers Donovan as the embodiment of the Irish state, but in her treatment it is an Irish state that has '[internalized] British representations of Ireland as a rustic vacation spot' (379). Indeed, when Donovan is later caught in the cottage's cow tether, she claims that Friel intends his audience to understand that the state is 'chained to a phony signifier of cultural heritage...forced on the community by colonization' (380).

In their *Writing Ireland*, Cairns and Richards broaden this view by considering *Cord* within the broader context of Field Day itself. They explore the relationship of the play to the intention of such Field Day figures as Declan Kiberd and Seamus Deane to use their essays in *The Crane Bag* 'to put an end to national artifice and illusion' that undermines society in the Republic (149). Cairns and Richards find Kiberd's discussion of Lionel Trilling's opposition between 'sincerity' and 'authenticity' especially illuminating for the play. The stage directions describe the cottage as 'too "authentic"' and this ersatz authenticity forms the backdrop to the play's excoriation of 'national platitudes' that imprison and humiliate the characters who attempt to manipulate them, such as Senator Donovan and Jack McNeilis (148–50).

Etherton's *Contemporary Irish Dramatists* offers a brief appraisal that combines Kearney's focus on language with Dantanus's critique of contemporary Ireland, seeing the play as concerned with both the 'sterile' romanticism of 'the present Irish *petit bourgeois* state' and the 'arid English language' that coarsens its people (208). In this overview of the play, the most important aspect is the relationship between Jack and Tim, which playfully recalls that between Owen and Manus (206). Tim Gauthier's essay on Friel's Field Day plays, 'Authenticity and Hybridity' (2002), also considers the issue of authenticity and language in *Communication Cord*, but in his reading the issue is most blatantly revealed in language. For example, Jack is especially skilful in his ability to speak with a 'sense of the authentic', while the linguist Tim character more awkwardly, if not transparently, seeks to mimic Jack's lies (356–57). Ultimately, Gauthier uses his analysis of the verbal strategies of Jack, Tim, and the senator to reinforce the by-now conventional interpretation that the play ironically stages the failure of the romanticized past to represent the Irish present (357).

The critical interest in *The Communication Cord* as a play about the Irish state may explain why several commentators have seen Senator Doctor Donovan as important to it. Compared to the play's young hero (Tim) and the hero's foil (Jack), Donovan is admittedly a secondary stock figure. Nonetheless, O'Brien sees him as Jack's double: not only have they shared the same girlfriend in their careers of philandering, but they also 'form a culturally manipulative twosome' in their common willingness to cynically exploit Irish cultural traditions (110). Kathleen Hohenleitner argues that Donovan is the farcical version of Owen of *Translations*, asserting that his name is an intentional allusion to John O'Donovan, the historical translator who accompanied the Ordnance Survey of Ireland and who serves as the background figure for Owen (377).

Noting that Donovan carries two potent indicators of social prestige—he is a 'doctor' and a 'senator'—Tony Corbett in his 2002 book presents a detailed exploration of the multiple examples of the character's insincerity and hypocrisy. However, he argues that Donovan, in his glorification of the Irish past, is the political heir of Eamon de Valera (1882–1975), and he finds considerable resonance between Donovan's attitudes and the ideals expressed in de Valera's famous St Patrick's Day speech of 1943 (91–92). In his *Brian Friel*, Roche also notes that Donovan represents a consummate politician and skilful manipulator of his public image. Roche associates him not with de Valera but with Charles J. Haughey (1925–2006), Ireland's most controversial and successful politician of the middle century (181–82). Moreover, Roche presents Donovan as the play's icon, a 'monstrous figure' proving that all Irish culture as well as its heritage are cynically exploited and easily sold to foreigners (182–83). In my book, I also draw attention to Donovan's power and his two titles, describing him as the 'hyper-competent Northerner who has overcome poverty to excel in two professions and rise to the pinnacle of Irish influence' (148). Many minor details in the play suggest that Donovan is the play's model of professional success that Jack subconsciously emulates.

The collapse of the cottage at the play's end has also been seen by various critics as Friel's statement about contemporary Ireland. Andrews' book considers the falling in of the roof as Friel's attempt to exorcise the 'false myth' associated with the Irish 'attachment to the past' (195). In 'Brian Friel's Uses of Laughter', Kathleen Ferris takes a decidedly darker view of the ending, seeing this depiction of contemporary Ballybeg as 'that marginal world where comedy borders on tragedy'; she asserts that the cottage's falling in 'suggests a crumbling, disintegrating society' (128–29).

If possible, my treatment of this play in *Brian Friel, Ireland, and the North* is even darker than Ferris's. Rather than accepting the play as about contemporary Ireland, I argue that it is Friel's examination of relations between the South and the North, with Jack and Claire representing Northern identity, Susan and Tim Dubliners of the South, and Donovan as a Northerner who has made his life in the South. Such a reading brings out the naïveté that characterizes these Southerners, making them easy prey for the romantic designs of the Northerners (147). Indeed, I argue that Claire shares Jack's calculating and exploitative traits: at no point does she express love for Tim but rather declares her intention to spoil his romantic designs on Susan, claiming that 'I going to enjoy' disrupting his plan (149). Thus, when Friel claims that 'the Northern thing [will] complete' Irish identity, my reading of the play argues that he views the typical Southerner as easy prey of the North's clever and more calculating people (150).

Language

Despite the references to the play in Kearney's essay on Friel's 'Language' plays, the first actual discussion of the topic came in 1991, when Richard Pine identified Erving Goffman's *Forms of Talk* (1981), with its discussion of 'the dance in talk', as vital to the play's explication (251). Martine Pelletier expands Pine's observation in her 1997 study of Friel, where she argues that Goffman's analysis is the model for Tim's unfinished thesis. Moreover, for her, the play stages a Goffmanian conflict between the two functions of language: the first as information vector and the second as vehicle for the expression of identity (189).[1]

In his 1995 study of Friel's plays, Andrews attempts to identify concrete correspondences between the two plays in a manner reminiscent of Kearney's 'Language Play'. For example, Andrews is attentive to the way that *Cord* uses 'nicknaming' as a degenerated form of 'the mystical *caerimonia nominationis*', or naming ceremony, found in *Translations* (192). Likewise, 'the frenetic babble of French and German...and various forms of Irish-English' and the similarly vacuous dialogue when characters repeat or echo earlier lines all constitute for Andrews the farce's intended lampooning of the gravity of *Translations* and its treatment of language (192–95).

However, Andrews recognizes that *Cord* moves beyond *Translations* in one important aspect: the ending offers the idea that 'words...may not matter all that much' in human communication. Indeed, the kiss shared by Tim and Claire in the play's final moment demonstrates something more basic and powerful than this farce's portrayal of semantic corruption (196–97). Gauthier also stresses the importance of comparing the final dialogue between Tim and Claire to that between Yolland and Maire. Seeing it as a rebuttal to those who romanticize language, he contends that this portrayal of language's inadequacy undermines the very fear that English, the colonizer's language, has the power to alter Irish identity (358).

Making History (1988)

Evaluated from the perspective of subsequent staging history, *Making History* is one of Friel's least successful plays, with very few productions outside Ireland. Indeed, it has not been uncommon for critics such as F.C. McGrath and Kathleen Hohenleitner to remark on the play's reputation as 'a bad play, a boring play, an overly intellectual play'.[2] In his essay 'O'Neill's Last Tape' (2002), Ulf Dantanus describes the mid-1980s as a period of considerable artistic frustration for the playwright (119). The six-year gap between *The Communication Cord* (1982) and *Making History* (1988) is the longest artistic dry spell of Friel's career; the demands placed upon him as a theatre company's founding dramatist and spokesman made substantial demands on his time, and increasingly he found himself at odds with the other directors.[3] Thus, the mid-1980s is a period marked by his editing of Charles McGlinchey's memoir *The Last of the Name* (1986) and by his adaptation of Turgenev's *Fathers and Sons* (1987) but no original work. Although the interim late in his career between *Give Me Your Answer Do!* (1997) and *Performances* (2003) is of a similar length, in the latter case he filled the years with such short works as 'The Yalta Game' (2001) and 'Afterplay' (2002).

History

In the first treatment of *Making History*, barely two years after its Field Day premiere, O'Brien notes that the play is a significant departure for Friel. He has concluded his 'sequence of language plays' and turned his attention to history; while noting that *The Enemy Within* (1962) was his only earlier work in the genre, O'Brien asserts that *Making History* provides a more complex view of history:

■ Not since *The Enemy Within*, where the author explicitly eschewed history, has Friel directed his attention to an important figure in Irish history, and in none of his plays has he addressed the subjects of historical action self-consciously undertaken and historiography deliberately commissioned. (119–20) □

Considering the controversy over Friel's disregard for historical accuracy in *Translations*, it should not be surprising that the first sustained examination of *Making History* was by the historian Sean Connolly, in an article entitled 'Translating History' (1993). Connolly quotes at length Friel's statement in the programme that he 'kept faith' with 'the imperative of fiction' rather than 'historical "fact"' (159), and his article begins by outlining the discrepancies between the chronology of O'Neill's historical life and the dramatic portrayal (159–60).[4] Furthermore, he claims that Friel's depiction of O'Neill's as a pragmatic strategist relies upon Sean O'Faolain's portrayal of him in *The Great O'Neill* of 1942. Ultimately, while he freely notes the historical problems, Connolly considers *Making History* a 'more restrained and even-handed' treatment of history than he found in *Translations* (161).

Although midway through his chapter on the play, McGrath dismisses *Making History* as failed theatre (220), he nonetheless presents the most thorough exploration of the play's relationship to O'Faolain's study to be found in Friel criticism. As the first commentator to bring a reading of O'Faolain's book to a reading of the play, McGrath recognizes that O'Faolain's portrayal of O'Neill's intention to create a European Ireland is analogous to Field Day's 'desire to Europeanize Irish culture' (216–17). And while he considers Friel's O'Neill less psychologically nuanced than O'Faolain's, McGrath establishes the various ways in which the playwright is indebted to the historian (211–15). He also skilfully charts the manner in which Friel's play diverges from O'Faolain's history. As noted in the following sections, McGrath points out that Friel presents very different views of Lombard as historian and of O'Neill's love for Mabel; moreover, he even argues that Friel presents O'Neill as a representative of 'a hybrid Anglicized Irish culture', while for O'Faolain he embodied 'a Europeanized Gaelic culture' (230).[5]

Discussions of history in the play have also considered Friel's historiographical method, and in *The Diviner* (1999) Richard Pine was the first to suggest that in this play Friel shifts his attention from Steiner's fixation on the word to Paul Ricoeur's idea of myth (207). While Corbett obliquely alludes to this in his discussion of Lombard as myth-maker (12–13), Roche attempts the first sustained engagement with the topic, using Ricoeur's *Memory, History, Forgetting* (2004) to unpack Friel's complex explorations of the relationship between memory and history in the play (163–66). In this reading, O'Neill's memories of his years with the Sidney family in Shropshire and his formative relationship to his English wife Mabel are juxtaposed to Lombard's determination to 'impose "a pattern"' on Hugh's career that omits such ties to the English (164).

Language

Despite the dominance of the criticism exploring this play's relationship to history, both as an academic discipline and a narrative strategy, Helen Lojek's article 'Brian Friel's Plays and George Steiner's Linguistics' makes the first, and perhaps the most convincing, argument that the play continues Friel's fascination with Steiner's *After Babel*. In her reading of Steiner 'all history is translation', and Lombard echoes none other than the hedge school master Hugh when he speaks of 'imposing a pattern on events' through language (93). Indeed, when Steiner claims that 'the historian 'makes history''', Lojek wonders whether she has found the impetus for the play's title (94).

Robert Welch mounts a persuasive argument that the play's use of language merits careful analysis in his 1993 chapter on Friel. Welch brings to our attention the manner in which O'Neill fluctuates between courtly English and his native Tyrone accent; indeed, he variously notes O'Neill's skilful deployment of Renaissance tropes, whether that be translating his friends through the language of flowers or reciting his highly stylized statement of submission (237–39). Appearing in the year following Welch and Lojek, Andrews' book describes the play's debate about the writing of history as ultimately a debate about language. Whether it be both the English and Irish calling each others' leader a 'Butcher' or broader debates about individuals' portrayal in Lombard's history, Andrews demonstrates the importance of specific words and their perceived meaning in the play's discussion of history (203–05).

Hugh O'Neill

Andrews' 1995 study of Friel presents the first and fullest exploration of the character of Hugh O'Neill. In a reference to Friel's 1962 play about Columba, Andrews refers to O'Neill as 'plagued by "the enemy within"', but in this reading O'Neill repulses any expectation that a unified self will be created (206). Indeed, O'Neill is able to navigate the shoals of English and Irish political intrigue precisely because he knowingly manages the English and Irish sides of his character (204–05). However, O'Neill's actions cause dissonance between the English and the Irish views of him; thus, Andrews notes that 'Ironic juxtaposition is a major compositional principle in this play about multiple identity, dual citizenship, conflicting allegiances' (206).

McGrath's detailed comparison of the play to O'Faolain's history includes a comparison of the two views of O'Neill as well. Although McGrath recognizes that Friel retains many examples of O'Faolain's 'calculating, intellectualized' Renaissance man, who capably assesses his political situation, he faults the playwright for making him too much of a Romantic figure moved by his passions (219). Yvonne Lysandrou also seeks to recover O'Neill as Renaissance thinker in her article 'Hugh O'Neill as "Hamlet-Plus"' (2006). Quickly outlining the superficial similarities between Hamlet and O'Neill (95), Lysandrou's core argument explores the importance of 'stasis', or the inability to act, to both figures, as well as their shared tension with their surrogate fathers—Claudius on the one hand, and Sir Henry Sidney on the other (97, 100–01).

Tim Gauthier pursues O'Neill's dual heritage in his 'Authenticity and Hybridity', where he argues that this icon of Irish independence and culture must be seen as a hybrid of Irish and English. More than merely presenting O'Neill as a product of his Irish heritage and English fostering as an adolescent, Gauthier provides diverse examples where O'Neill argues that he knowingly identifies and exploits English stereotypes of Irish behaviour to undermine the ability of the English to manipulate him. In one example, when Mabel's sister is lambasting him for being a treacherous ally, O'Neill recounts the earlier military alliance that found him fighting in support of the English (360–61). Since this play portrays O'Neill as culturally hybridized more than two hundred years before *Translations*, Gauthier posits that there may not be 'authentic' Irishness in Friel's history of Ireland: 'if O'Neill, in 1590, is a hybrid, how far back would one need to go to find someone authentically Irish?' (364).

Peter Lombard

The discussion of history in the play easily leads to a focus on Peter Lombard, the play's archbishop and historian. The historian Sean Connolly considers him 'Friel's attack on the pretensions of the historian', specifically the type of historian who criticized *Translations*. Indeed, Connolly alleges that Lombard, rather than serving as champion of historical facts, is the historian who 'distort[s] the past in order to serve the needs of the present' (163). The literary critic Elmer Andrews is no less dismissive of Lombard; he claims that, even if we sympathize with Lombard's desire to unify the Irish with his chronicle, 'There is something of Shakespeare's distaste for the "politician"' in Friel's portrayal (207).

Conversely, McGrath argues that Friel diverges most from O'Faolain in the play's positive view of Lombard; he argues that the author's idea of history, as stated in the programme, 'contains some of the same language he gives to Lombard's historiographical utterances in the play' (229). McGrath claims that in the play's final scene, which juxtaposes the demoralized O'Neill to the archbishop, 'Lombard, not O'Neill, becomes the representative of the sophisticated European intellect' (230). McGrath goes so far as to identify a poststructuralist historiography in *Making History* and argues that Lombard is a spokesman for historical relativism, for the position that there is no authoritative history for any set of facts. Writing in 2002, a few years after McGrath, Corbett views Lombard as neither villain nor hero but as myth-making historian. He looks to the historical archbishop's *De Regno Hiberniae* (1632) to better understand Friel's dramatic portrayal of him as an ideologue who sought to blend Irish nationalism and religion (12–13).

Mabel Bagenal

Writing in 1990, O'Brien is the first to recognize the importance of Mabel to the play. Seeing her as much more than an example of the play's discussion of race, he points to Act 1 scene 2, where she carefully and presciently argues against O'Neill's rebellion, as her 'finest hour' (118–19). However, it is this very portrayal of Mabel that McGrath objects to in his comparison of the play to O'Faolain's history. McGrath claims that Friel unconvincingly departs from O'Faolain's view of O'Neill as Ireland's first intellectual man of the Renaissance by forcing a love story into the play (220). Because he believes that 'Mabel is not convincing' as a character (222), McGrath finds her hallmark role as O'Neill's political advisor and her new-found understanding of Gaelic culture too improbable (221).

Conversely, writing nearly fifteen years after McGrath, Roche argues that O'Faolain's history reveals an anti-English bias that misrepresents the role of the historical woman. He takes issue with O'Faolain's repetitive portrayal of her as a 'girl', or 'poor child', out of her depth (166–67). Indeed, Roche points out inconsistencies in O'Faolain's history that suggest that the historical Mabel had just the type of influential role with O'Neill that Friel provides her in the play. In his 2014 book, Murray even more strenuously argues for Mabel's importance to the play, even though she appears in only three scenes (98–102). Indeed, he claims that she dominates *Making History*, 'making that play woman-centred' (102). In his analysis of the scene where Mabel argues against Lombard's call for open war against England, Murray describes her as 'a woman Shaw might have created': insightful, reasoned, and intellectually superior to the men around her (101).

In his essay 'Homesick for Abroad' (1995), Jochen Achilles further argues that Mabel stands as Friel's paradigm for someone able to overcome a narrow identity as either English or Irish (442). In other words, she is both, and she embodies multiculturalism 'as an achievement rather than as a disgrace' (438). Conversely, as I argue in my book, the two English characters of the 1980s, Yolland in *Translations* and Mabel, seem to propose the 'challenge to Irish society posed by benevolent Englishness' (166). In the former case, Friel changes Andrew Larcom, who had a career of almost thirty years as 'the first 'Mountjoy superintendent to identify himself with Irish interests', into the short-lived and ineffectual Yolland. In this reading, Mabel is like Yolland in that she is a character whose ability to benefit Ireland is cut short by her own untimely death (166–67).

The London Vertigo (1990)

The London Vertigo is Friel's one-act adaptation of Charles Macklin's *The True-Born Irishman* (1760), which the Gate Theatre premiered at Andrew's Lane Theatre in 1992. Although it was first staged two years after *Dancing at Lughnasa*, it was finished considerably beforehand. Indeed, a letter in the Friel Papers, from Friel to 'Arthur', mentions that the Field Day Company gave the play a reading in 1987, almost two years before *Lughnasa* was written.

John McVeagh's '"A Kind of *Comhar*": Charles Macklin and Brian Friel' (1993) provides the most detailed summary of Macklin's life as an Irish actor and playwright who enjoyed a long and successful career on the London stage from the 1720s into the 1780s (216–25). However, Andrews' treatment of Friel's *London Vertigo* in his 1995 study remains the fullest examination of the play and its relationship to the themes that define Friel's career. Andrews' account is especially useful in analysing how Friel compressed Macklin's play from five acts to one and reduced the number of themes and characters to give the work greater focus. Similarly, he compares Macklin's dialogue to Friel's reductions to demonstrate the effects the latter achieves (237–39). While he briefly alludes to how this depiction of mid-Georgian Dublin's obsession for London slang and fashion resonates with the themes found in *Translations* (236), his discussion is more concerned with the portrayal of Murrough O'Doherty and his wife Nancy, whose marriage is struggling with her desire to adopt fashionable English traits which he adamantly opposes (236–37). Although Andrews notes that Friel introduces Murrough's direct address to the audience to change the play's tone, he claims that the play's most decisive modernization is the 'kind of "feminist" rewriting' that refuses to fully condemn Nancy's 'unruly female energies' (241).

The remaining criticism of the play is both scant and brief. For example, in his book *The Diviner*, Pine mentions how the play casts English culture as the Other to the Irish, and Anglophilia becomes a 'madness', or vertigo, that people must be cured of (253). Likewise, in *Le théâtre de Brian Friel* (1997), Pelletier points out that London becomes the source of linguistic and cultural deviance and Dublin the redoubt of mainstream values (265–66). In a broader discussion of *Translations* and *Making History*, I point out how Friel has excised Macklin's critique of 'Irish "patriots"' and other issues of nationalist politics to create a domestic comedy without the original's political awareness (164–65).

Whether one considers *Making History* or *London Vertigo* as Friel's last play of the 1980s, the decade closed quite differently from the 1970s, which had ended with the most important plays of Friel's career so far. Although Friel had not written even a moderately successful play during the 1980s, by May of 1989 he was working on a play that would, once again, be celebrated throughout the English-speaking world—*Dancing at Lughnasa*.

CHAPTER TEN

Dancing at Lughnasa (1990)

As 1990 dawned, Friel seemed a playwright in decline: the three masterpieces that marked 1979 and 1980 were long behind him, and, aside from *Translations*, the 1980s had been a decade of a very few indifferently received plays, several translations and adaptations, and distracting managerial work for the Field Day Theatre Company. However, when *Dancing at Lughnasa* premiered at the Abbey Theatre on 24 April 1990, it re-established him as one of the greatest playwrights of his generation.[1]

The play transferred to London's Royal National Theatre in October 1990 and won the 1991 Olivier Award for Best Play; similarly, it won three 1992 Tony Awards (Best Play, Director, and Actress) for the Plymouth Theatre production that ran from October 1991 through October 1992. Perhaps more impressively, *Lughnasa* received sixty-nine separate professional productions in thirty nations between 1990 and 2000; not only was it staged in twenty-one European countries, but it was even produced as far afield as in Japan, Kenya, South Africa, Argentina, Uruguay, and Israel. By comparison, after its first twenty years, *Translations* had been staged sixty times in seventeen countries. Even after twenty-five years, *Lughnasa*'s status as Friel's most popular play has endured, as is affirmed by the eminent theatre critic Michael Billington, who included it in his *The 101 Greatest Plays from Antiquity to the Present* (2015).

While the initial reviews for the premiere production show 'that *Lughnasa* was certainly liked' (50), Patrick Lonergan has attempted to explain how this 1990 production quickly became recognized as Friel's 'golden production' (47). He persuasively details how the setting and music combined with social and economic trends that will define the 1990s to create a theatre experience that mirrored Irish society (43–47). With productions in Dublin and tours of the country by the Abbey throughout the 1990s (1990, 1991, 1992, 1999, 2000), *Lughnasa* became the play of the decade; in fact, Lonergan argues that the 1999 Abbey production 'was not so much a revival as a reprise—a celebration of Friel … and a transforming Ireland' (53).[2]

Autobiography

Friel waited to give his earliest interviews about *Lughnasa* for more than a year after the play's triumphal premiere; his first was with Mel Gussow for *The New York Times* in late September 1991, followed the next month by Julie Kavanagh for *Vanity Fair* and John Lahr for *Vogue*. While Friel mentions the relationship of the play's five Mundy sisters to his own aunts, to whom the play was dedicated, only Gussow's interview uses the term 'autobiography' in reference to the material.[3] The subsequent criticism has generally adopted the idea that the play's autobiographical content is defined by these portrayals of Friel's aunts. However, only Roche in his 2011 book investigates the general contours of this autobiographical content, and he mines the Friel archives for details concerning Friel's uncle, Fr. Bernard Joseph MacLoone and his aunts Kathleen, Margaret, Rose and Agnes (170).

My 2007 book marks the only attempt to explore the more direct autobiographic kernel that would identify Friel with the illegitimate Michael and Friel's father Patrick, a teacher and city councillor from County Tyrone, with the Welsh wastrel Gerry Evans (174–75). While I initially look to Friel's *Irish Press* and *New Yorker* stories to identify the author's 'conflicting emotions' towards his father, we can better apprehend the extent to which Michael overcomes patriarchal authority (175) by comparing him to Friel's previous portrayals of embattled sons such as Gar in *Philadelphia* or Casimir in *Aristocrats*.

Sources and Influences

In 'Marking Time' (1993), Fintan O'Toole discusses *Lughnasa* as marking Friel's attempt to turn away from history and politics, his dramaturgic staples of the 1970s and 1980s, and he compares Friel to Arthur Miller and Tennessee Williams, two playwrights who faced a similar mid-career disillusionment with politics (207). While he suggests that *Lughnasa* and Miller's *Death of a Salesman* (1949) employ a 'continuous present' for similar purposes, he finds Friel's play most intricately indebted to Tennessee Williams's *The Glass Menagerie* (1944), and for him the connections are 'reasonably obvious':

■ The use of the narrator as a device for the suspension and conflation of time, the elegiac tone of the narration, the use of a mentally disturbed young woman (Laura, Rose) whose sexuality takes on a critical edge, the guilty departure of the narrator, the sense of a family trapped as an anachronism in an increasingly hostile world, the persistence of old ceremonies, and, above all perhaps, the use of music. (209) □

In his 1995 book, Elmer Andrews echoes O'Toole in his brief comparison of Friel's narrator Michael to Williams's Tom Wingfield; indeed, he suggests that both characters romanticize the past for similar reasons (219).

In his 1997 article '"Recording Tremors": Friel's *Dancing at Lughnasa* and the Uses of Tradition', Murray situates the play within a different dramatic tradition: the Abbey Theatre's realist tradition of the 1930s through the 1950s. Of course, he notes that the repeated intrusions of the narrator, Michael as an adult, undercut the play's realism, but he also points out that *Lughnasa* overturns the traditional expectation for 'marriages and happy endings' established by decades of the Abbey's peasant plays (29). Two years later, in his 'Friel and Synge' (1999), Roche observes the way that the descriptive landscape of greater Ballybeg beyond the Mundy's house suggests Friel's debt to Synge's portrait of the Aran Islands (155–58). In his book *Modernity, Community and Place*, Richard Rankin Russell builds upon Roche's observation to argue that Friel's portrayal of the Mundy sisters also draws upon Synge's play *Riders to the Sea*, first performed in 1904 (210).

McGrath initiates his chapter on Friel by identifying the play's reliance on two of the playwright's stories from the early 1960s: 'A Man's World' (1961) and 'Aunt Maggie, the Strong One' (1962). Although McGrath surprisingly fails to explore the play's debt to the stories, he mentions the appearance of Rose in the former and, of course, Maggie in the latter (235). Similarly, he suggests that the play's narrator Michael has his origins in Bernard, a character in 'Aunt Maggie' most notable for his determination to preserve his memories for future uses. While Richard Pine notes that the play's framing device reminds him of the short story's structure, he considers the play most thematically akin to Friel's *Philadelphia, Here I Come!* (*The Diviner*, 271). In Pine's view, both plays split the young male protagonist (Gareth and Michael) into two to meditate on memory and the act of committing events to memory (274). Moreover, he sees Gar's absent mother repeated in Michael's remembrance of his mother and sisters.

In my 2007 book, I discuss *Lughnasa* as a third and final exposition of the paradigmatic problem of Irish identity posed by *Translations* and *Making History*. Just as Maire Chatach and Hugh O'Neill were tempted to abandon their Irish identity for the perceived benefits of Englishness, as represented by the English characters Yolland and Mabel, Chris is similarly tempted by Gerry, a Welshman with a distinctly English accent, who promises her relief from Ballybeg's repressive society and her child legitimacy. Although, according to Michael, his mother's future life was grim and impoverished, by comparison to the fates endured by Maire and Hugh, Friel's portrayal of Chris Mundy presents the only successful union of Irish and English lovers in the playwright's career (171–72).

Memory and History

The relationship of Friel's history plays to accepted historical chronologies and historiographical practices was central to the reception and much of the criticism of such plays as *Translations* and *Making History*. Thus, with yet another play set in the past—this time 1936—we should expect this line of critical interrogation to continue. However, in the first article to pursue it, O'Toole's 'Marking Time' (1993), we witness a deliberate challenge to the idea that any of these plays are history plays at all. Rather, this article boldly claims that we have 'misread Friel's plays as history plays' (204). For O'Toole, *Lughnasa* is a play that replaces history with the operation of memory and the associated threat of forgetfulness. Moreover, O'Toole points out that, by dismissing historical events to the remote horizon of the play's action, Friel uses the autobiographical memory play to stage 'an image of ahistorical time' that collapses past, present, and future into a now that is always also the remembered past (210–11).

Anthony Roche returns to this argument in his 2011 study, where he asserts that *Lughnasa* is Friel's 'most powerful fusion of memory and history' (171). While he notes the play's engagement with the social politics of the 1930s (175), he nonetheless considers Michael to be one of Friel's most 'limited and compromised' narrators, primarily because the boy Michael in 1936 could not fully understand the adult events that he witnesses (172). Roche highlights Friel's working note wondering whether Michael's memory functions in 'its own reality', and to that end Roche explores the possibility that as narrator Michael acts as a type of bridge between his childhood and adult selves, between individual and collective memories (173).

Pine asserts that, throughout his career, Friel explored two types of memory: private recollections, as in 'The Child', Friel's first story of 1952, and the public memory, which is most fully manifested in *Making History* (*The Diviner*, 270). While *Lughnasa* retains elements of the public memory's different kinds of truth, Pine considers the play's focus to be on Michael's memories of 1936 as his 'homecoming' (272). Indeed, for Pine, Michael's narration creates a hierarchy of the play's different types of memory, allowing him to present the overarching authority of his memories compared to his aunts' less reliable memories of more past dances and his uncle's even more elusive memories of colonial Ryanga (272–73).

Andrews firmly situates his reading of the play not in memory but in the social malaise of 1930s Ireland (220–21). Indeed, he usefully suggests how the era's politics, revealed in de Valera's new Constitution for the Irish state and the Public Dancehalls' Act, inform an understanding of the play's increasingly repressive social milieu. Anna McMullan's 1999 article 'In touch with some otherness' is also conscious of O'Toole's criticism of Friel's static view of history, focusing on his claim that in both *Making History* and *Lughnasa* Friel rejects accepted views of history (95). In McMullan's perspective, these plays, and

Lughnasa in particular, reveal the bias inherent to the 'dominant narratives' of the state, and she explores Friel's focus on the individual and the local.

In her 1999 article '*Lughnasa* after *Easter*', Catriona Clutterbuck reorients our view of the play's historicity by situating the action in the 1960s (113–14). Noting that Michael is described in the *dramatis personae* as a 'young man' and his 1929 birth, she argues that he must look back from the vantage point not of 1990, but the very late 1950s or early 1960s, and she views the play as an assessment of the repressive society that Ireland was emerging from in 'the run-up to the fiftieth anniversary celebrations of the Easter Rising' (114). In her analysis, Michael looks back on the recent 1940s and 1950s, to an Irish society—or, in her words, a 'domestic zone'—that was threatened by 'the Catholic Church, large-scale industrialisation, and right-wing…politics' (111).

Postcolonialism

In his exploration of the play's Dionysian mood, McGrath identifies the Dionysian with premodern culture, and especially 'the Celtic temperament' as described by the Victorian essayist Matthew Arnold and by William Butler Yeats. McGrath uses this background to assert that the Irish government of the 1930s 'mimicked the values esteemed by the colonizer…in the stereotype it constructed for the Irish' (245). In other words, McGrath gestures towards postcolonial theory to explain the similarity between the stereotypes of Irish irrationalism propagated by English imperialism and adopted by the newly independent Irish state (245). Writing in 2002, Margaret Llewellyn-Jones in *Contemporary Irish Drama* similarly identifies a postcolonial context for the play. In her brief reading, she establishes Uncle Jack as having 'most significance for postcolonial readings' (36). She argues that he has been sent home not only as a punishment for adopting the Ryangan religion but also for having rebelled against British colonial authority. To that extent, she views the regimental 'tricorn hat with plumage' that he exchanges with Gerry as a particularly problematic signifier of the way that English influence both lingers and is rejected in the play (36–37).

However, in her 2006 article '*Dancing at Lughnasa* and the Unfinished Revolution', Helen Lojek observes that the play's idealization of Ryangan society, replete with a Great Goddess and fully incorporated 'love-children', suggests that the play is best considered an expression of 'neo-colonialism' rather than postcolonialism (87). While not expressly responding to Lojek, Geraldine Higgins rejects the contention that the play imposes a 'crude postcolonial parallel between Ryanga and Ballybeg' (86). Rather, she claims that *Lughnasa* reveals the tenacious 'pagan energies' that survive in Ireland despite Christianity's 'deadening homogeny.'

Paganism

Friel's early interviews stress 'paganism' as the play's dominant theme. In his 1991 conversation with John Lahr the playwright declares, 'I think there's a need for the pagan', later adding, 'whether we want to call it religion or the acknowledgement of mystery or a salute to the otherness, it can be enriching'.[4] Moreover, not only does the play's title make reference to the pagan Irish festival of Lughnasa, but the Abbey Theatre's programme accompanying the premiere included an excerpt from Máire MacNeill's anthropological study of the survival of this pre-Christian celebration, *The Festival of Lughnasa* (1962). Indeed, even before the publication of Friel's interviews, the first article on *Lughnasa*, 'In touch with some otherness' (1992) by Alan Peacock and Kathleen Devine, explores the significance of the 'older beliefs, superstitions and observances' that permeate the play.

Peacock and Devine see paganism's passionate expression of spiritual longing throughout *Lughnasa*, but perhaps nowhere more forcibly than in the wireless radio, which they claim is 'explicitly associated with Lugh' (115), the ancient Irish god Lug Lamfada or Lug Samildanach, who plays a prominent role in many of the most archaic tales of Ireland's mythic prehistory in *Lebor Gabála Érenn* (*The Book of the Taking of Ireland*). Peacock and Devine's careful reading of the play allows them to trace the many pre-Christian elements that permeate it: not just the fundamental importance of dance (117–20), fertility (118–19), and Father Jack's role (122–23), but also the play's more incidental use of iconography and even the word 'pagan' as a playful jibe between the sisters (118).

However, in 'Recording Tremors', Murray notes that paganism is placed in conflict with Christianity, and this is sharply defined by the play's two priests: the parish priest, who never appears on stage, and Father Jack. Murray observes that this opposition suggests the rather straightforward opposition of 'good shepherd' to 'corrupt priest' common to P.V. Carroll's plays of the 1940s, but he quickly establishes Friel's departure from this model.[5] While the parish priest fires Kate from her job as school teacher because of her brother's perceived apostasy, Father Jack presents 'a rich and complex set of associations' (34). As someone who recommends polygamy to his sisters and fondly remembers Ryangan pagan festivals, Jack has 'lost his identity, and in this respect he is modern Ireland personified'. In Murray's reading of the play, Jack promises a model by which the other characters can restore their direct access to spirituality through a paradigm suggested by the director Richard Schechner, the author of such works as *Between Theater and Anthropology* (1985); however, he argues that Jack's influence fails to prevent the social disintegration and economic collapse that devastates the family at the play's end (37–38).

McGrath's chapter 'Dionysus in Ballybeg' offers the most comprehensive survey of the diverse ways that 'the pagan' is incorporated into the play. While McGrath echoes earlier criticism by summarizing the Celtic god Lugh and his thematic relationship to the wireless (235–38), his focus is on the play's expression of the 'Dionysian impulse for chaos and the irrational' as described by Friedrich Nietzsche in *The Birth of Tragedy* (1872).[6] For McGrath, the Dionysian is strongly associated in the play with sexual desire, and he charts how each of the Mundy sisters struggles with libidinous desire (239–41). However, he reserves his most detailed analysis for Gerry, who, for McGrath, is 'the most Dionysian character in the play' because of his association with music and dance (241). In the examination that follows, he focuses on how Gerry's arrival disrupts the Mundy household and, most strongly, on detailing his relationship to Chris and Agnes (241–43).

Ritual

In discussing the elaborate process by which Father Jack exchanges hats with Gerry, Peacock and Devine suggest that Gerry becomes 'the unconscious inheritor of a priestly or even god-like role' (123). This observation allows them to make the broader argument that *Lughnasa* has a vital place among Friel's many plays that explore self-sacrifice as the path to self-realization. While they recognize elements of this in such early plays as *Crystal and Fox* (1968) and *The Freedom of the City* (1973), they see a more substantive link between *Lughnasa* and *Volunteers* (1975) and *Faith Healer* (1979). Such a reading of the play aligns Gerry's inexplicable desire to risk death in the Spanish Civil War loosely with Pyne's imagined stories of Lief, but much more specifically with Frank's description of his own ritualized death (125–26).

Richard Pine looks specifically to Victor Turner's *From Ritual to Theatre* (1982) to create the anthropological context for surveying the play's view of Ryangan religious practice, the vestigial survival of the Celtic Lughnasa festival, and the condition of Irish society (268). Borrowing from Turner's model, Pine sees *Lughnasa* as 'a sacred drama in the Yeatsian spirit' which transports the audience into a 'liminal situation', or rite of passage, that creates the circumstances through which the audience can achieve a reformed understanding of ritual in modern society (268–69). Ultimately, Pine considers dance the primary vehicle through which ritual functions; indeed, he asserts that dance, being more 'primitive' than words, is more closely associated with Victor Turner's 'thudding of ritual drums' (269). Indeed, for Pine, dance denatures such linear discourses as history and language, because dance is 'the hidden unknown thing' that expresses an ineffable emotion without a historical analogue or verbal description (275).

Dance

Peacock and Devine (117) remark that dancing is a central aspect of Maire MacNeill's description of the survival of Lughnasa celebrations in early twentieth-century Ireland. Noting this importance, they trace the diverse ways that the play deploys dance both through its staging and the characters' discussions. For example, they observe that the town dance is passionately discussed by the sisters long before they break into the 'strange and spontaneous' dance that marks the first act (117).[7] However, in a more nuanced analysis that soon followed, Andrews claims that dance is primarily used to signify 'a distinctively female sexual energy which eludes a patriarchal, linguistic order' (225). For the Mundy sisters specifically, it represents their 'violation' of a political order that during the 1930s and 1940s increasingly sought to stifle free will and regulate morality (223). More broadly, Andrews' lengthy analysis of the play explores the many manifestations of dance and its protean significance, especially its pagan connotations in both the Ryangans and the local Lughnasa rituals (226–28).

In his article 'Questing for Ritual' (2006), Richard Allen Cave is also interested in assessing the play's overall attitude towards dance. After summarizing the many instances that either stage or discuss dance, he seeks to explain how Friel avoids the twin risks of either a nostalgic or a romanticized attitude. In part, Cave claims that Michael's 'conservative' or 'profane' view tempers the sympathetic staging of dance (188). However, he more forcibly argues that dance's associations with the Lughnasa festival's dangers, Jack's pathetic solipsism, and Gerry's irresponsibilities allow the audience to maintain a critical attitude towards the charms of staged dances (189–90).

Helen Lojek's 1994 article 'Brian Friel's Plays and George Steiner's Linguistics' marks a significant shift from viewing dance as a social act to seeing it as a semiotic one. She notes the importance of Steiner's observation that language is also used 'to conceal' (86) and, again quoting Steiner, that 'true understanding is possible only when there is silence' (88). Thus she sees the dances between Gerry and Chris, which are repeatedly referred to as 'ceremony', as having a 'sacred, religious dimension' (89). She argues that, throughout the play, when dance begins talking ceases and real communication starts, revealing

■ Friel's central point about the true understanding of silent communication. And it clarifies the link between individual love (Chris and Gerry), family love (the aunts), communal love (Ireland, Uganda), and the sacred love which links all humans. (90) □

Corbett develops some of the potential of Lojek's insights in his 2002 book, where he charts various characters' struggles with or outright resistance to using language to articulate reality. Noting the dance between Chris and

Gerry, where she rejects conversation, as indicative of the struggle between language and music, Corbett explores the play's various competing discourses (68). He adds that each of these discourses is itself splintered against itself: English and Swahili reveal that 'a shift between words...is a shift between worlds' (135), while the traditional Irish music and the American jazz emitted by the wireless equally reveal the struggle between 'Irish discourse' and its 'alien' counterpart (136).

Lojek returns to the pervasive importance of dance to the play in a second article, '*Dancing at Lughnasa* and the Unfinished Revolution', where she seeks to broaden our knowledge of the Irish government's regulation of both public dancing and the radio broadcast of popular music in the 1930s and 1940s (82–83). However, one of her article's stated intentions is to direct our attention away from the sisters' céilí dance to Jack's awkward Ryangan 'shuffle' later in Act 1, and the 'tremendous possibilities' it suggests (84). For Lojek, though less choreographed, Jack's dance equally 'represents a breaking away from Donegal's repressive environment' and 'the same primal elements' as seen earlier in the group dance.

In a play filled with staged, remembered, and anticipated dances, the sisters' ecstatic and explosive dance in Act 1 to 'The Mason's Apron' has been seen as the play's most representative moment. In *The Art of Brian Friel*, Andrews is the first scholar to highlight it, recognizing it as important to understanding each sister's character. While briefly characterizing the insights the dance provides into Agnes and Rose, he is most interested in juxtaposing Maggie's embodiment of defiance to Kate's repression (224).

Claudia Harris's oft-quoted survey of Friel's female characters, 'The Engendered Space' (1997), explores this scene as the representative moment of the play, one that demanded the attention of every reviewer in Dublin, London, and New York (45–46). She notes that, during rehearsals for the premiere, Friel 'kept emphasizing the word "defiance"' in his advice for staging this scene, and she argues that this emerges in the reviewers' repeated comments on 'the wildness, the ferocity, the sexuality, the freedom' of the sisters (46).[8] Yet Harris asserts that by themselves Friel's stage directions possibly 'demeaned' these 'passionate women' and trapped them in the male gaze (48); but the dance 'frees the actors to develop fuller portraits' that 'makes them subjects rather than objects' (49).[9] Not only does she, perhaps insightfully, believe that 'these brief moments of daring' were the reason that *Lughnasa* won its Tony Awards but also that 'every new Friel play and...old Friel play will be judged against these exuberant, exhilarating moments in Act 1' (45).

Anna McMullan situates her reading of the five sisters' dance within Harris's general contours, though she notes that this moment needs to be contextualized within Ballybeg's pagan Lughnasa dance secretly held in the back hills by Lough Anna and, to a lesser extent, the Ryangan dance rituals reported by their uncle Jack (94). She critically points out that, once the dance ends, its promise of change or liberation evaporates, leaving the sisters as repressed as before with 'the rule of conventional order' restored (94). Likewise, by placing this explosive moment of theatre so early in the play, its force is similarly blunted because by the end 'it has become a memory even for the audience', replaced by Michael's emphasis on dance as a form of language (99).

Richard Allen Cave identifies an alternative context for this dance: 'the traditional image of the Maenad or Bacchante of classical lore' (191). Not only does he propose that Maggie's flour mask suggests that she is 'given over to bodily impulse' (192), but he argues that the sisters embody more 'than merely joy in dancing'; rather, there is something disturbingly 'frantic' and 'manic' in their dance (191). Indeed, he claims that Friel uses 'dervish' in his stage directions to suggest their desire for 'union with the divine through the medium of the dance' (192). Finally, in 2014, Russell argues that the sisters' dance, as well as many of their memories leading up to it, 'laments the lack of men in their lives' (210). In this respect, he considers Maggie the representative sister, and her various actions from streaking her face with flour to enjoying a Woodbine all point to her sexual longing (213–15).

Gerry Evans

Peacock and Devine recognize that the unexpected arrival of Gerry Evans, Michael's father, is 'the pivotal event' of the play (118). In a reading that teases out every possible association with paganism, they regard him as embodying 'the mysterious processes of Lughnasa' in his sexual connection with Michael's mother Chris and his libidinal connection to fertility for Agnes and Maggie (118–19). But when he is formally accepted by Father Jack, in the priest's elaborately staged ceremony to exchange hats, they posit that Gerry may represent 'some kind of manifestation of Lugh himself' (121), or as they later add, 'a figure in fertility myth' (123).

This interpretation of Gerry as a divine interloper who entices the sisters into a world of passion is taken further by Ron Rollins the following year in his very brief 'Friel's *Dancing at Lughnasa*' (1993). The importance of Gerry as 'dance-master' is first discussed by Rollins, who sees the Welshman as the messenger of Lugh's divine passion, using dance throughout the Celtic lands of Ireland and Wales as a way to introduce people to the pagan god (85). Andrews, however, takes a distinctly different view, observing that Gerry is associated not with the sisters' bacchanalian dance but with ballroom, the controlled and civilized antithesis of the many ecstatic dances staged and discussed by the sisters (225).[10] In this respect, he compares Gerry to Shane in Friel's *Gentle Island*

(1971), the outsider who serves as 'a catalyst for many of the tensions that exist between members of the family' (229).

While Gerry generally fades from the criticism in the new century, in his 2014 book Murray argues for the dignity of this 'irresponsible and farcical' character. Not only does Gerry occasionally make surprisingly insightful comments on other characters, but he offers an ethical argument for fighting in the Spanish Civil War (140). More importantly, Murray asserts that Michael 'protects his memory' by keeping his father's bigamy a secret from his mother and even 'identifies with his father' in the various depictions of his actions and statements (140).

Friel's Sororal Play

In his *Contemporary Irish Drama* (1994), Anthony Roche briefly notes that Friel may have been reluctant to offer *Lughnasa* to Field Day because of the company's inability to stage a play that distributes 'the dramatic weight equally among five female characters' (284). Similarly, he argues that the play marks a significant break with Irish drama since the 1960s in several ways, most importantly in the prominent roles assigned to so many women (285). In 'The Engendered Space', Harris follows Roche's observation on *Lughnasa* with one of her own: 'No matter how they might try to dance, women cannot escape their crushing responsibilities—the drudgery, the poverty, the disappointment' (62).

However, the first sustained attempt to offer a distinctly feminist interpretation of the play comes more than a decade after its premiere, by Tony Corbett in his *Brian Friel* (2002). Corbett notes that the Mundy sisters' stability is threatened by a series of men; as well as the disruptions introduced by Uncle Jack, Gerry Evans, and Danny Bradley, even the radio 'is given a male persona' and 'the knitting factory establishes a male hegemony over a traditionally female activity' (138). Moreover, Corbett assertively contextualizes the play's setting within 'the idea of rape', established by a series of male 'penetrations' (138). However, in a less pyrotechnic manner, he also explores how the new Irish Constitution of 1937 and its special attention to the 'mothers of a family' ('máithreachaibh cloinne') convey that 'the position of the unmarried mature woman was a social embarrassment' (139). Thus, he surveys the 'socially conditioned' and romantic attachment to men that each of the Mundy sisters forms or, occasionally, seeks to repress.

In her 2006 article, Lojek also observes how each of the Mundy sisters must contend with a community in which there are 'no reliable men', whether they be priests and shopkeepers or romantic interlopers. Making this argument, she gives special emphasis to their various acts of 'subversive resistance to patriarchal expectations', whether that be their bawdy humour, their devotion to the child Michael, or Chris' rejection of Gerry's proposal (86). Furthermore, Lojek is equally attentive to the play's place in the 1990s challenge by a generation of women to the 'constitutional and cultural restrictions on *their* lives', from the hostile reaction to the *Field Day Anthology of Irish Writing* (1991), which in her words 'seemed edited by, for and about men', to the election of Mary Robinson as the first female Irish president in 1990 (87).

Kate

The first intention to expand the discussion of the sisters to the eldest, Kate, comes in Andrews' 1995 book chapter, where she is central to his explication of the play's tensions between civilized stability and libidinal excitement. Like Judith in *Aristocrats* or Manus in *The Gentle Island*, Kate struggles to maintain a traditional order that is threatened by social change (222–23). In her 1999 article 'In touch with some otherness', Anna McMullan treats Kate as the most important sister because, through her employment as teacher in the town, she is the family's interface to broader Irish society. Aware of the social risks associated with Chris's illegitimate son and their apostate brother, Kate recognizes that 'the status and even the survival of the family' depends on the town's perception of the family's loyalty to the strict *mores* of 1930s Ireland (92).[11] Thus, she repeatedly scolds and insists upon her sisters' orthodoxy because she is directly aware, in particular, of the parish priest's power over the family.

Conversely, Corbett claims that Kate is 'an agent of repression' who exerts a chilling effect on her sisters (67). In his view, she does not negotiate between the family and Irish social norms; rather, she 'embodies the inward-looking Ireland of the 1930s' in all its moral inflexibility and untenable ideals of respectability (135). Cave similarly notes that Kate is portrayed as 'judgemental to a degree that verges on the cruelty of caricature' (187). However, he carefully analyses Friel's stage directions for her role in the sisters' dance to develop a more sympathetic and nuanced reading of her character. Here, he argues, the audience sees beyond her 'fiercely repressed' exterior to glimpse something both beautiful and tragic (193–94). When Higgins considers Kate in her 2010 book, she notes that she functions as the play's 'principal wife': not just the one who censors her sisters but the one who brings back to the family news of the Lughnasa festival, the town dance, the knitting trade, and her encounters with various old friends (87).

Agnes and Rose

Patrick Lonergan explores the subtle representations of Agnes and Rose, the two sisters who abandon the family in the middle of the night, as indicative of the limits of Michael's ability to remember events (40). He asserts that Agnes' 'suggestive silences' and Rose's refusal to answer the family's questions regarding Danny Bradley require the reader to interrogate the text. In Peacock and Devine's early article, they describe Agnes' characterization as 'the most subtly suggestive treatment' of desire to be found in the play (119). Moreover, they note that as a thirty-five year-old woman of remarkable dancing skill, she powerfully blends the play's connection between fertility and the physical passion inherent to Friel's vision of paganism (119–20).

In accord with their focus on paganism, Peacock and Devine also describe how Rose embodies a gradual sexual initiation that is foreshadowed early in the play by her halting shuffle to the song 'Will you come to Abyssinia?' and her 'intuitive knowledge' of Kate's infatuation with Austin Morgan (120). Moreover, they detail the manner in which her excursion to the site of the Lughnasa bonfires, ostensibly to pick berries but in actuality to rendezvous with Danny Bradley, knowingly deploys many tropes and symbols of a rite of passage, which for her becomes the initiation into sexuality (120–21). Russell further argues that Rose's innate predisposition to the spirituality of both Christianity and Celtic paganism also allows her to 'fall prey to the sexual advances' of Danny Bradley, which in Russell's view, lead to her rape (229–30).

Michael

As noted above, Andrews is the first to discuss Michael's role in the play, though he does so in the limited context of his similarity to Tom Wingfield, the narrator in *The Glass Menagerie*. However, McMullan presents the first true analysis of Michael in her 1999 article, where she briefly outlines his 'ambiguous' role in the play. While she notes that his initial speech opens the play and establishes its controlling oppositions, she nonetheless argues that his view is shown to be both limited and suspect (98). Noting that Michael alone never dances, she asserts that the play warns us 'against the distortions of memory and the partiality of individual vision' (99) through such limited admissions as Michael's ignorance of his father's other family in Wales and the representative moment when his aunt Maggie cautions him that he only gets 'one quick glimpse' of things (98). Indeed, noting his antipathy to dance, McMullan asks, 'Are we to trust Michael's narrative voice?' (99).

In the same issue of the *Irish University Review* that featured McMullan's analysis, Clutterbuck indirectly responds to her question by stating that 'Michael's act of memory frames the play in a totalitarian way' (113). She argues that Michael distorts the past, describing the 1936 of his childhood as a 'golden age', because of his guilt over 'his own abandoning of the Mundy world'. For example, she notes the dissonance between his description of the sisters' dance as that of 'excited schoolgirls' and the actual event in the play, claiming that this 'amounts to a Berlin wall between representation and reality' (109). Indeed, she adds that the sisters are only able to have 'moments of self-realisation' when he is off-stage (113). Thus, Clutterbuck posits that his narration is both his attempt at 'reparation' for having abandoned home and his inability to tell the women's story except through 'the loss of his mother's and aunts' voices and stories' (116).

Prapassaree Kramer's article, published shortly after Clutterbuck's and McMullan's similarly explores how Michael's possible biases are expressed in his memories, some of which Kramer argues must be artificial because of his absence from the original events (175). Indeed, she argues that the prominence given to such characters as Kate and Maggie can be explained by their importance to the boy following the departure of Rose and Agnes (176). Such a suspicion of Michael's memory is continued by Lojek in her 2006 article, where she explores the effects of the play's doubly 'male gaze' (80). Since the play recounts a story that is both Michael's and Friel's, Lojek argues that the male gaze is both foregrounded, through the many instances where the adult Michael takes control of the narrative with his framing monologues, and hidden, because Friel's control of these women's stories is obscured by his use of a seemingly autobiographical surrogate (80–81). Indeed, a suspicion of Michael's motives and his abilities as memorialist is perhaps the most consistent critical element. While Lonergan explores the pervasive 'contrast between representation and reality' that permeates the entire play (38), he most carefully documents Michael's apparent inability to understand the memories he narrates and his overall 'suggestive silence' concerning Agnes and Rose that, again, implies his lack of narrative authority (40).

Dancing at Lughnasa, the film

In 1998, a much-anticipated film based on the play was released. It was directed by Pat O'Connor (b. 1943), a well-known Irish director who had previously directed such well-received movies as *Cal* (1984) and *Circle of Friends* (1995). Although Friel himself had adapted his *Philadelphia, Here I Come!* for John Quested's 1975 film, in this case the playwright Frank

McGuinness (b. 1953) was chosen to write the screenplay. The film attracted public attention not merely from those who had seen or loved the play, but because Meryl Streep (b. 1949), who had previously won a BAFTA (1983) and two Oscars (1980, 1983), had been cast as Kate. The film also starred the veteran British actor Michael Gambon, as well as Rhys Ifans and Catherine McCormack. Bríd Brennan was the only actor from the Abbey production to reprise her role in the film, though Gerard McSorley, who played Michael in the Abbey production, was given the voice-over role as the narrator (with the boy Michael played by a child actor).

A full survey of the reception of the film and the criticism surrounding it is beyond the scope of this chapter; however, a brief summary is provided to point students to the important works. In 2002, Llewellyn-Jones is the first to comment on the film's relationship to the play, noting how 'bland misreadings' of the play are indicated through such decisions as replacing the play's adult narrator with an adolescent boy and, more importantly, replacing the 'grotesque and hysterical' dance in Act 1 with the 'celebratory' and sentimental one that concludes the film (35–36).

Two other articles also appeared in 2002 that offered in-depth and detailed comparisons of the play to the film: Robert Evans' '*Dancing at Lughnasa*: Play, Script, and Film' and Karen Pirnie's 'Dancing at the Movies: Critical Reception of the Film *Dancing at Lughnasa*'. Evans provides an especially concise and valuable summary of the differences between the two works. Joan Dean's book-length study of the film for the Ireland into Film series appeared in 2003, and it provides the most comprehensive companion to the film and its background. However, in part owing to disappointing reviews and lacklustre performance at the box office, the film has been ignored in Friel criticism since these initial treatments.

As Friel entered his fourth decade as a playwright, the stunning success of *Lughnasa* emboldened and rejuvenated him. Although he would never again achieve the prolificacy of the 1960s or 1970s, the 1990s would see the premieres of such significant plays as *Molly Sweeney* (1994) and *Give Me Your Answer, Do!* (1997). Moreover, by the decade's end, he would even direct his own plays for the first time in his career.

CHAPTER ELEVEN

Plays of the 1990s

Wonderful Tennessee (1993)

During its premiere engagement at the Abbey Theatre starting on 30 June 1993, *Wonderful Tennessee* seemed to promise Friel another success. Indeed, its initial run of eighty-one performances was considerably longer than the fifty-seven enjoyed by *Dancing at Lughnasa*; however, the play did not succeed abroad. The Plymouth Theatre, which staged *Lughnasa* during its award-winning American premiere, closed *Tennessee* after only nine performances in October 1993. This failure exerted a distinctly chilling effect on the play, and it was not again attempted abroad until 2000, when it was staged by the Nottingham Playhouse in England. Finally, it should be noted that the play's staging history has also elicited both defences of it as 'more than slightly under-praised' and criticisms of it as a clear failure.[1]

As the first book-length study of the author to appear after *Tennessee*, Elmer Andrews' *The Art of Brian Friel* (1995) devotes more than thirteen pages to the play and maps out many of the topics to be developed in the subsequent criticism. His summary touches upon a wide variety of topics, all of which focus on how various characters tell stories to 'express a spiritual truth' (253) and challenge 'any complacent understanding of the world' (255) for individuals 'shifting' between 'pagan mystery and their ordinary lives' (260). Richard Pine assertively associates pilgrimage with storytelling in the play, frequently referring to it as Friel's 'Canterbury Tales' because of its emphasis on the characters' use of allegorical tales to while away the time in their liminal state of waiting (*The Diviner*, 282). His analysis identifies three kinds of allegorical narratives all of which allow a dramatic space for characters to reveal their secrets (283).

Sources and Influences

In the Introduction of his *Contemporary Irish Drama* (1994), Anthony Roche is the first to mention, in passing, the play's affinity to Samuel Beckett's *Waiting for Godot* (1953); he compares the absent Carlin to Godot because, although both promise to arrive in the near future, they keep the characters waiting through-out their plays (5).[2] In her 'Space in *Wonderful Tennessee*' (2009), Helen Lojek, while similarly admitting the play's Beckettian allusions, suggests that its title might point us to the broad relevance of Tennessee Williams to understanding the play (54). In his *Theatre of Brian Friel*, Christopher Murray very usefully dis-cusses the play within the context of Hugh Leonard's *Summer* (1974), because Friel's depiction of Dublin's middle class shares many traits with this earlier study of 'the vodka-and-tonic Dublin *nouveaux riches*' (159–61).

Published barely a year after the play's premiere, Csilla Bertha's' Iona—Inishkeen—Oilean Draoichta' is the first of many articles to describe the play in relation to earlier Friel works.[3] Her focus is on Friel's two earlier plays occurring on islands: *The Enemy Within* (1962), about Columba's medi-eval monastery on Iona, and *The Gentle Island* (1971), about the last remain-ing family on Inishkeen. While she identifies some elements common to all three, such as a monastery in each island's history (96–97), her main focus is on delineating the tropes shared by *Tennessee* and *Gentle Island*, such as the tourists with whose arrival the plays open (90–91) and the use of storytelling to reveal simmering conflicts and passions (93–94).

However, *Tennessee* is fundamentally seen as the companion to *Dancing at Lughnasa*, in a pairing viewed as intentional as those linking *Philadelphia, Here I Come!* (1964) to *The Loves of Cass McGuire* (1966) and *Translations* (1980) to *The Communication Cord* (1982). While this relationship was recognized even in the earliest treatment of the play,[4] the first detailed analysis of *Tennessee* as a rewrit-ing of *Lughnasa* is offered by Martine Pelletier in her book *Le théâtre de Brian Friel* (282–86). Starting with the observation that both plays are set far from the centre of Ballybeg, bringing together groups united by both blood and affec-tion (282), she quickly focuses on their common setting in an anachronistic present which is suffused by the mythic past.[5] In his *Diviner*, Richard Pine also sees pervasive connections between the two, noting that *Tennessee* begins where *Lughansa* ends, 'with minimal sound and movement' (278). Observing that both plays incorporate ritualized dance and sacrifice, he asserts that they diagnose a society that has lost its cultural memory and that *Tennessee* portrays a much more advanced version of the cultural amnesia introduced in *Lughnasa* (284).

Religion

Andrews is the first to mention the importance of the long-established Lough Derg pilgrimage to understanding the play. Friel's friend Seamus Heaney had recently memorialized his own pilgrimage to the County Donegal site in *Station Island* (1985), and despite the characters' extravagant supply of del-icacies and whiskey, Andrews notes that 'a consciously religious sensibility persists' (257). After categorizing the various religious allusions in the characters' stories (253–55), Andrews roots his assessment of the play in its differences from *Faith Healer*, another play defined by the characters' stories (259–60). While the six lost souls of *Tennessee* can seem more 'clownish' and 'parodic' (257), their world is 'not so bleak' and, unlike the characters in *Faith Healer*, they achieve 'a kind of stately, immensely poignant devotional ritual' (260).

In his 1995 article 'Immaterial Contingencies', William Jent presents the first of many assessments of the play's exploration of religious desire through a 'juxtaposition of pagan and Christian mythologies' (30). However, his intention is to demonstrate that the play knowingly undermines the tropes of religious experience, from the pilgrimage (32–33) to epiphanic awakening (34–35). Jent further asserts that the source of the characters' spiritual failures is rooted in their materialism, their obsessions with earning, buying, and consuming, and the status associated with such acts. Thus, he argues that the play shares a socio-economic awareness with such earlier plays as *The Mundy Scheme* (1969) and *Freedom of the City* (1973).

A year later, in her article 'Island of Otherness', Csilla Bertha also explores the spiritual quest of these characters who, ultimately, 'are failures as individuals' and yet, she argues, embody a contemporary Irish mixture of 'faith and self-irony' (140). In this, she finds Joyce's *Ulysses* the most relevant antecedent for the play; indeed, she claims that Friel establishes a similar relationship to ancient Greek culture, which is revealed in the characters' references to Eleusis Mysteries and 'Dionysian celebrations' (133). Not surprisingly, the play's use of Hellenic religion to comment upon the unfulfilled spiritual desires of the contemporary Irish has similarly been touched upon by others, such as Corbett in his book (96–97) and Lojek in 'Beyond Lough Derg' (52–53). Pelletier develops these surface references in the play into a careful summary of its critique of the state of Irish Catholicism. Focusing especially on Frank's 'Ballybeg epiphany' (289–90) and the portrayals of human sacrifice (292–93), she asserts that the play seeks to articulate 'the permanence of need' ('la permanence du besoin'); not just a need for faith, but for ceremony and ritual (291). Writing in 2011, Roche similarly argues that Friel sought to attenuate the allusions to specific Christian practice to focus on the characters' spiritual contact with 'the Other', adding Friel's comment, 'What the Other is they do not know' (190).

Music

Although he devotes barely a page to *Tennessee* in his 1999 article 'Brian Friel and the Condition of Music', Harry White establishes the centrality of music to the play in an especially muscular fashion. Claiming that music 'becomes virtually an alternative to language', he points out that there are thirteen songs just in the play's first scene (12). Not only does George, who suffers from throat cancer, communicate almost entirely through the music he plays on his accordion, but, White also argues, Friel weaves musical snippets and allusions in a way that 'modifies and comments upon' the dialogue. Moreover, he suggests that this play about the characters' various midlife crises finds its thematic summation in George's earlier choice between a career playing classical or popular music (13).

By exploring some well-chosen examples, Tony Corbett consciously develops White's thesis on the use of music to allude to unspoken emotions, and he also categorizes the numerous songs to reveal the unexpected absence of Rock and Roll, which would have been the popular genre when the characters were in their teens and twenties (65–66). Later in his book, he notes that the music easily slips from the sacred to the secular in a manner that reinforces the play's broader attempt to 'sanctify the secular' and find a path to renewed spirituality (100–101). By exploring Friel's own comments upon his personal relationship to the song 'Down by the Cane-Brake', Lojek reveals the use of music to express the more general desire for happiness (53). Maria Szasz also explores song and its emotional impact on the characters (99–100); however, her work is of greater importance for providing a comprehensive guide to the songs of the play (90–99).

Molly Sweeney (1994)

Molly Sweeney was premiered at Dublin's Gate Theatre on 9 August 1994, barely a year after *Wonderful Tennessee*. After more than thirty years functioning solely as a playwright, this was the first play that Friel chose to direct himself. In his essay 'Friel and Performance History', Patrick Burke assesses Friel's choice to direct *Molly Sweeney* and subsequently *Give Me Yours Answer, Do!* (1997) as the culminating expression of Friel's longstanding desire 'to protect his "manuscript" from directorial intrusion' (118). While Burke describes Friel's direction of *Molly* as distractingly 'fussy', Roche in his *Brian Friel* (50–51) and Murray in his *Theatre of Brian Friel* (171) both consider Friel's directoral debut as relatively successful, owing to the play's minimal staging requirements. Friel continued to direct the play when it transferred to London's Almeida Theatre later that year and to Broadway in 1996, where it won the Drama Critics' Circle award for Best Foreign Play. *Molly* became the author's last widely popular play: by 2000, it had been produced in twenty countries on six continents, including Japan (1996), Argentina (1997), South Africa (1998), and South Korea (2000). Friel also published a selection of his working notes for the play, covering the period from August 1992 through April 1994, in *Essays, Diaries, Interviews* (1999). In his book on Friel, Anthony Roche uses several of these diary entries to establish parallels between Molly's character and Friel's own concern over his failing eyesight (196).

However, Friel's own experience with the fear of blindness and eye surgery has been viewed as a secondary inspiration for *Molly Sweeney*; in the years immediately following its premiere, the relevance of medical case studies to the play has received far greater attention. In one of the earliest articles on the play, 'Brian Friel's *Molly Sweeney*' (1998), Christopher Murray rigorously explores the influence of Oliver Sacks' article 'To See and Not See', published in the *New Yorker* (10 May 1993), on Molly herself. Murray demonstrates that Friel modelled her upon Sacks' patient known as Virgil, for both worked as massage therapists and suffered 'blindsight' following their successful operations (84–86).[6] In his book of the following year, F.C. McGrath explores the relationship between Virgil and Molly in greater detail (255–67); he also explores the relationship of two minor texts to the play: Berkeley's *An Essay Towards a New Theory of Vision* (1709), which Molly's husband Frank talks about in the play, and Diderot's 'Letter on the Blind' (1749), which Friel references in the play's epigram (251–52, 266–67). Finally, in his 1999 book on Friel, Richard Pine offers Stephen Kuusisto's book *Planet of the Blind* as 'a correlative text' offering additional insight on the experiences of long-term blind patients who have their sight restored (291–96).

Molly

The very first treatment of *Molly Sweeney* appeared in Martine Pelletier's *Le Théâtre de Brian Friel* (1997), where the play's similarities to Friel's *Faith Healer* are explored (297–300).[7] While she admits that Friel's reliance on monologues delivered by two men and a woman will associate these two plays, she usefully delineates the overall significance of the structural difference between them. Noting that, in *Molly*, all three characters occupy the stage together, though they never acknowledge the others' presence, Pelletier concludes that, while *Faith Healer* undermined any single Truth with multiple contradictions, *Molly Sweeney* seeks to reach a single truth through an accumulation of information (297). McGrath's discussion of Molly also expands beyond her relationship to Sacks' Virgil, and he focuses on the period that departs most from Sacks' model: her slow decline in Act 2 (272–75). During her final institutionalization, McGrath argues that Molly comes to understand the play's other characters (including her dead mother and father) with remarkable clarity and insight. Indeed, in her ability to transcend the difference between reality and illusion, he sees Molly as 'a metaphor for the artist and the artist-like appeal to illusion in ordinary experience' (277).

Aside from occasional references to Molly's defiant dance as a point of contact to the sisters' communal one in *Dancing at Lughnasa*,[8] discussions of Molly herself have centred on the struggle between Frank Sweeney and Doctor Patrick Rice for control of her. With her focus on the interplay of their monologues, Pelletier's analysis gives more sustained attention to the rivalry between Frank and Rice as each seeks to use Molly as a vehicle to fulfil selfish, personal dreams (300–304). Tony Corbett also regards Molly as 'a contested body', the site for the competition between Frank and Rice (125). However, he further claims that, in this contest, Molly possesses her own form of power and authority because of her unique, experiential knowledge of the world. In this reading, the play does not stage a binary struggle between two men over a manipulated woman, rather

> ■ the conflict of authority that takes place is between the undisciplined self-taught mind, the disciplined but disillusioned one, and the mind that is not shared with anyone else. Molly is a party to the conflict, the site of the conflict, and the prize for the victor in a contest that is ultimately lost by all three. (128) □

The view of Molly as victim is given its broadest cultural interpretation by Karen Moloney in 'Molly Astray' (2000), where she argues that Molly should be seen as 'symbol for the decolonized republic and … the still-colonized Irish woman' (292). Moloney argues that 'Molly's world imitates the "otherness" of Gaelic culture' (289); thus, Frank's view of her as 'irrational' and resistant to the benefits of the sighted world recapitulate the colonizer's patronizing views of colonized peoples (290–91).

Conversely, several commentators have argued against the victimization of Molly; as early as 1999, Nicholas Grene in 'Friel and Transparency' seeks to save Molly from being reduced to an appalling 'almost autistic figure', abandoned and hospitalized (143). To that end, he suggests that, like Frank Hardy in *Faith Healer*, she attains wisdom in her 'acceptance of death'. In his 2011 study, Anthony Roche offers the most wide-ranging and nuanced reading of Molly. He starts by explaining the significance of Friel's collaboration with Catherine Byrne, the playwright's preferred actress throughout the 1990s, for whom he wrote the part (192). Roche also explores how the play's distinctly static staging devices initially resisted a view of the blind Molly as impaired or physically inferior to the sighted men (193–94). Murray follows many of Roche's arguments in his *Theatre of Brian Friel* (2014), and he likewise mines Friel's diaries and directions to Byrne to argue that 'there is hope at the end' even if we think of Molly as dead (153). His argument rests, in part, on Murray's view of Molly as a 'mermaid figure or Ondine' who is destined to return to her privileged existence after an experimental life among mortals (151–52).[9]

Frank and Rice

While Molly is seen as the play's tragic heroine and central to understanding the play, her feckless husband Frank has attracted less critical attention. Murray regards him as 'a parody of the expert' in his 1998 article; he argues that Frank, with his jumble of personal anecdotes and confusion of scholarly research, suggests a caricature of Prof. Dodds from Friel's earlier *Freedom of the City* (1973). Nonetheless, Murray points out that Frank valuably introduces such important terms as 'engram', 'gnosis', and 'blindsight' into the play (91). However, the most critical view of Frank is constructed by Murray when he returns to reconsider the play in his 2014 book. In a wide-ranging criticism of the character, Murray enumerates Frank's flaws, dismisses the marriage as 'an obvious mistake', and even comments that he 'seems ... to lack a phallus' (152).

McGrath explores the three examples of engrams discussed by Frank to argue that Friel intends both Frank and Rice to manifest 'their own special forms of blindness', which prevent them from recognizing their responsibility for destroying Molly's life (268–72).[10] In my book's treatment of *Molly Sweeney*, I also focus on these two male characters to explore Friel's critique of Irish cosmopolitanism during the 1990s, when the Irish first became conscious of their new-found affluence as Europe's 'Celtic Tiger'. Unlike Friel's 1964 portrayal of Ballybeg as a forgotten cultural backwater in *Philadelphia, Here I Come!*, *Molly* shows how even the far northwest of Ireland 'has become integrated into the world economy and global culture' (187). In this context, Rice and Frank embody two Irishmen's failed attempts to create a cosmopolitan Irishness: Rice's belief that, as an Irishman, he can rival the best American and German surgical superstars; and Frank's intention to transform Ireland, not only through his quest to restore Molly's sight but also through the importation of foreign bees and goats (186–88).

Give Me Your Answer, Do! (1997)

Owing to Friel's success directing *Molly Sweeney*, he undertook the direction of the Abbey Theatre's premiere production of *Give Me Your Answer, Do!* as well. However, Patrick Burke has argued that Friel was not up to the demands of the play's large cast and realist setting; thus, in his opinion, Friel's production came across as amateurish', especially because of 'poor blocking and masking' (118). In his 2014 book, Murray furthers Burke's assessment by comparing the poor reviews for the Abbey production with the more positive ones that accompanied the 1998 London production under the direction of Robin Lefevre (176–77).[11]

Give Me Your Answer, Do! has never been considered one of Friel's most important plays; nevertheless, it received considerable critical attention because it premiered a mere two years before the commemorative issues of *Irish University Review* and *The Hungarian Journal of English and American Studies* marking Friel's seventieth birthday. The play's personal significance to Friel himself is also suggested by his decision to publish extracts from his working notes on the play in *Essays, Diaries, Interviews* (166–72). Incidentally, it should be noted that

Christopher Murray's 2014 book demonstrates how a careful analysis of these 'Extracts', provides valuable insight into the play's early development (169–71).

Richard Pine published 'Love' (1999), the first article devoted to *Give*, in the special issue of *Irish University Review*. As the title suggests, Pine sees this play as Friel's final major instalment on a theme that many critics have seen as giving unity to the playwright's initial creative burst from 1964 through 1968. This allows Pine to summarize how the theme has evolved through the course of Friel's career, before focusing on how the portrayal of the three couples in *Give* each explores 'D.H. Lawrence's concept of marriage as "a fight to the death"' (178).[12] In this exploration of 'the cost of love', Pine reminds us that this play is unique in Friel's canon for the prominence given to the 'self-sacrificing role' of the three women who are wives, mothers, and muses (184). However, in her book's survey of the condition of the play's wives, Geraldine Higgins outlines the various ways in which 'all the women in the play have been stunted by marriage'; indeed, more than other commentators, she emphasises that even Daisy, the wife of the supposedly 'true' artist, is subject to 'Tom's narcissistic drama of the blocked writer' (102).

Whereas Pine seeks to explain *Give* by its thematic relationship to Friel's earliest plays, my book chapter focuses on its position as last in a trio of 1990s plays set in 'the present'. This analysis notes especially that, unlike the dramas of the 1960s and 1970s,

> ■ Gone is the family's patrician pretensions, its social decline symbolized by the daughter's inappropriate marriage, and the traumatic death of the patriarch that haunts the family. (192) □

Indeed, I note that *Wonderful Tennessee, Molly Sweeney,* and *Give* lack the earlier decades' heroines of frustrated potential such as Judith of *Aristocrats* and Grace of *Faith Healer*; indeed, the plays of the 1990s depict a generation that has retreated into diverse, isolated groups with little idea of family history or social responsibility (190–93).

Writing and The Writer

In Richard Pine's programme note to the Abbey premiere, 'What is a Writer?', he establishes that *Give* is a play full of echoes, not only of the authors who influenced Friel, such as Yeats and Chekhov, but also of Friel's own plays from *Cass McGuire* and *Crystal and Fox* to *Faith Healer* and *Wonderful Tennessee*. While Higgins summarizes these same associations in her 2010 book, Roche's treatment in his 2011 *Brian Friel* uses the references to Yeats as a springboard into a discussion of the play's autobiographical elements, and especially Friel's similar temptation to sell his own archive to an American university (201–02).

Murray moves beyond the autobiographical nature of Friel's offer from 'the Emory man' to see the play as 'a modern parable', 'a protest against acquisitiveness in all walks of life' (171–72).

Maria Germanou in 'Brian Friel and the Scene of Writing' (2003) argues that *Give* is a play not just about Friel's relationship to other writers but about our very own relation to language; she seizes upon Jacques Derrida's statement that 'writing is unthinkable without repression' as her interpretive key to the play's meaning (472). Indeed, whether it be in the play's game of Scrabble (472), Tom's pornography (473–74) or his monologues to his daughter (475–76), Germanou explores the way Friel employs language to resist meaning and clarity:

■ language, being a shared system of signification and a slippery one, always already belongs to the Other from whom the self borrows the means of expressing its identity at the same time that it loses it. (474–75) □

Her analysis focuses especially on Tom because, in both his writing and dialogue, he demonstrates the play's most complex relationship between art and life.

Csilla Bertha and Donald Morse devote a large part of their 1999 article 'Singing of Human Unsuccess' to the play's artists, especially in light of Friel's earlier *Faith Healer*.[13] While they note some general similarities between Tom Connolly and Frank Hardy, as well as these two portrayals of the unreliability of inspiration (15–17), their article's main focus is on the later play's exploration of types of artists: Garrett, the popular writer of easily accessible fiction (24); Jack, the 'cocktail lounge piano player' (25); and Tom, the principled, 'true' writer (28–29). However, despite their valuation of Tom's artistic stature in the play, they assert that 'there is little sign that Tom…has found or will find his voice' (30). Indeed, even though, at the play's end, he announces to his daughter that he has felt the 'stirring' of a novel in twenty-three pages of his writing, Bertha and Morse worry that his statement belies his tendency towards escapism rather than genuine inspiration.

In her 'Brian Friel's Uncertainty Principle' (1999), José Lanters juxtaposes *Give* to Friel's early *Crystal and Fox* (1968) to explore the relationship between artistic inspiration and chaos (162–63). The play's 'sickness, madness, isolation, depression, kleptomania and alcoholism' that touch every character allow Friel to explore how 'the creative process…begins and ends in chaos' (167–68). Indeed, emphasizing the ability of language to spur regeneration, Lanters argues that Tom's creativity directly emerges from his drive 'to express the obscenity of his daughter's madness in words' (169).[14] I take a distinctly different view of Tom's pornography in my 2007 book, arguing that a father's writing hard-core pornography about his then twelve-year-old daughter must be viewed as troubling, 'a symptom that Tom's concern for his daughter suggests an inappropriate relationship that other critics have recognized as threatening his marriage' (196). Writing in 2011, Murray further notes that Daisy never visits Bridget, which for him is an additional part of the 'mystery ... which the play never fully divulges', though he notes that in an audience discussion during the New York production Friel '"disavowed" paedophilia as the answer' to Bridget's trauma (173–74).

While Lanters' analysis focuses on Tom, the principled novelist in crisis to whom renewal seems to be promised in the play's final moments, she revealingly explicates the constellation of failed, 'phoney', stifled, and trivial artists all of whom struggle in contemporary culture's 'loss of authenticity and identity' (170). Writing in his 2002 study *Brian Friel*, Tony Corbett recognizes that the characters' discussions of writing should be seen not as merely about the nature and value of art but 'the question of the validation of life' and a life spent devoted to art (88).

Bridget

Pine's 1999 article is especially important for its recognition of the centrality of Tom and Daisy's daughter Bridget, the young, institutionalized woman who briefly appears in the play's first and last moments. For Pine, she is the drama's 'ultimate enigma' and 'unexplained shadow' that is 'both symbol and symptom of "the cost of love"' (185–86). In this reading, her trauma betrays the lie of the Connollys' happy marriage. Similarly, Lanters finds Bridget a vital, albeit difficult, symbol for the play: at times representative of order and disorder (172), as well as 'a source of despair' and 'the potential source of artistic renewal' (173). My book's chapter on *Give* argues that Bridget is the more direct symbol of Ireland's generation born into, traumatized and silenced by the Troubles:

> ■ Bridget's childhood is marked by such events as the Bloody Friday bombings, the assassination of an Irish senator, and the bombing of Dublin's Central Criminal Court, which all occurred in 1974....the Shankill Butchers' murders (1975), the Cooley bombing that killed twenty soldiers (1979), and the hunger strikes in the Maze Prison (1981). (194) □

The Ending

The play's final moments present Tom back in his daughter's hospital room, which is intended to recall the opening by again having him prattle on with fantastic anecdotes concerning her grandparents and his own work in progress. However, Lanters notes that these final moments are significantly different because Daisy is now sitting in a deckchair on the side of the stage, supposedly at home while Tom visits their daughter. More importantly, Daisy stands and 'softly, urgently' calls out to Tom in the play's final lines.

Lanters argues that during his visit to his daughter, Tom excludes Daisy in a manner that is 'ominous', suggesting perhaps that Tom 'opts to end the questions by ending his life' (174). Bertha and Morse contend that 'there is no immediately obvious or coherent way of putting Tom's and Daisy's two phrases together' (31). While they also entertain the possibility that Tom contemplates suicide, they aver, rather, that 'like most of Friel's characters and all of Samuel Beckett's, Tom cannot go on but does go on' (32). In *The Theatre of Brian Friel*, Murray discusses Friel's advice to Kyle Donelly, the director of the New York production, and Maggie Cronin, the actor playing Daisy, not to resolve the play's ambiguous ending, but to explicate it:

■ Both Tom's proposal to Bridget and Daisy's panic 'must be emphasised as much as is theatrically possible'. He was ashamed to admit, he told Donnelly, that Tom's proposal to Bridget is defensible while Daisy's response remains understandable. (175) □

The 1990s are most important, perhaps, because after so many history plays— from *Translations* (1980) though *Lughnasa* (1990)—Friel had returned to consider the morals and mores of contemporary Ireland, in an imagined Ballybeg that had greatly changed in the decades since *Philadelphia, Here I Come!* (1964). Friel would turn away from Ballybeg, and Ireland entirely, in almost every play of the twenty-first century until his last original play, *The Home Place* (2005).

CHAPTER TWELVE

Last Plays

'Afterplay'

'Afterplay' is the imagined meeting in a Moscow cafe between two characters from plays by Anton Chekhov: Sonya Serabryakov from *Uncle Vanya*, translated by Friel for the Gate Theatre in 1998, and Andrey Prozorov from *Three Sisters*, translated by Friel for the Field Day Theatre Company in 1981. This one-act play was premiered at the Gate Theatre on 5 March 2002 along with Friel's translation of Chekhov's short farce 'The Bear' and was later collected with 'The Yalta Game', his one-act adaption of Chekhov's story 'The Lady with the Dog' (1899), into a single volume, *Three Plays After*.

In his broader discussion in 'Friel's Irish Russia' (2006), Pine reads both 'The Yalta Game' and 'Afterplay' as intentional experiments, blending the two authors' shared theme that 'there *is* no home, no truth, and ... the various types of delusion through which we lead our melancholy lives' (112–13). Nonetheless, Pine argues, we witness in 'Afterplay' a unique moment in theatre: 'the after-life of make-believe, when we discover that we are not characters in someone else's play, but responsible for our own thoughts and deeds' (113). Further, he asserts that the importance of 'Afterplay' is more than merely the novelty of combining two well-loved characters from separate plays; rather, he sees the play as forcing people who survive by lying to themselves to admit their past disappointments (113).

In his 2004 survey of Friel's 'late plays', George O'Brien claims that 'Afterplay'—indeed, all the plays in *Three Plays After*—abandons 'the world of historical conditions' to examine the difference between what the characters need to validate their beliefs and ideologies and 'what the world provides' (100). My treatment of 'Afterplay' in 2007 also seeks to account for the discrepancy between Friel's romanticized Moscow and the realities of 1920s Russia (199–202). While the new Soviet Union would have been in the throes of civil war and famine, 'this short play imagines a nostalgic survival of tsarist

Russia' (202). Thus, I argue that Friel's Russia should be read as a proxy for Ireland, which was also experiencing civil upheaval during the 1920s, following its own revolution and civil war.

Performances (2003)

In her 2006 essay 'Music and Words in Brian Friel's *Performances*', Csilla Bertha recognizes this play about Leoš Janáček's legacy 'as a unique theatrical act', largely because the play concludes with an actual string quartet playing two complete movements from Janáček's *Intimate Letters* (63). Indeed, not only do the four musicians on stage outnumber the two actors, but more than ten minutes of this hour-long play consist of the composer listening to music.

Bertha begins her discussion of *Performances* with an overview of Friel's conceptual evolution on the relationship of words to music from *Dancing at Lughnasa* (1990) through *Give Me Your Answer, Do!* (1997). While these earlier plays rely upon language to explain or contextualize the music, in *Performances* music takes 'centre stage, letting it occupy a huge proportion of performance time' (62). Moreover, she identifies that George Steiner, whose philosophy of language directly influenced *Translations* (1980), was again an important influence. Making reference to Steiner's 1966 essay 'Silence and the Poet', she argues that

■ music alone can fulfil the two requirements of a truly rigorous communicative or semiological system: to be unique to itself (untranslatable) yet immediately comprehensible. (66) □

And Bertha proceeds to demonstrate how these ideas are expressed by Friel's Janáček(67). Thus, though the play stages the debate between the composer, asserting the primacy of the artistic experience, and a graduate student, who insists that Janáček's letters can decipher and explain his music, Bertha argues that 'the play ends on a richly ambiguous note', with just the music itself playing without commentary (68). Anezka departs after her 'passionate appeal' for a scholarly reading of the music based on Janáček's letters, leaving the audience to watch him 'clutching the folder of his love letters', to hear his 'deep sigh' in the play's closing moments (70).

My treatment of *Performances* in *Brian Friel* considers not the evolution of the playwright's conceptualization of language and music but his more personal associations with the material:

■ The 74-year-old playwright who was suffering the longest artistic drought of his career was writing this short drama about a 74-year-old composer who was also struggling to end an unwanted period of silence. Indeed, both artists were 'tackling that complex architecture' of the full-length composition for the last time—Janáček in his *Intimate Letters* and Friel in *The Home Place*. (203) ☐

If I argue that in 'Afterplay' Russia serves as a proxy for Ireland, this story about a nationalist artist that avoids the topic of nation mirrors Friel's own disillusionment with Irishness in his last decade (202). However, the bulk of this discussion focuses on the thematic and structural similarities shared by *Performances* and 'Afterplay': both stage a discussion between a musician and woman in which the man struggles to admit that he has reinvented elements of his life, all of which ends with the woman leaving in exasperation (100–101).

Murray's discussion of the play stands as the most thorough summary of the actual platonic affair between Janáček and Kamila Stösslová and a brief history of their correspondence (183–85). This material serves as introduction to his focused explication of the play's two debates: 'language versus music and life versus art' (185).[1] In Murray's reading, the 'main' debate is the latter, Anezka's attempt to force Janáček' experience into a model in which 'great passion [serves] to create a great work of art' (187). Yet, Murray repeatedly argues that Anezka is 'not equipped' to debate the composer; ultimately, throughout the play, 'she is out of her depth', thus in need of 'a short master-class' from Janáček (187). Ultimately, while Murray concedes that 'both Anezka and Janáček equally misjudge how art establishes identity', he contends that Anezka's 'feminist viewpoint' becomes an insurmountable obstacle to her critical understanding of the *Intimate Letters*: 'She lacks the objectivity of the true critic' (189).

The Home Place (2005)

In 'Master Performances', a brief review of the premiere production, Tony Corbett notes how *The Home Place* forms a fitting capstone to Friel's career: he cites both the Chekhovian atmosphere of this study of a family in crisis, and its significance as the last of Friel's Ballybeg plays (38). Martine Pelletier's 'New Articulations of Irishness' (2009) also establishes the very strong thematic links between *Home Place* and Friel's most important Ballybeg plays *Aristocrats* (1979) and *Translations* (1980). She persuasively argues that *Home Place* should be seen as 'a companion piece to *Translations*' for several reasons, not the least of which is that the schoolmaster Hugh Mor O'Donnell must be the 'ancestor' of Clement O'Donnell, who are both characterized by their 'marked pomposity and a fondness for drink' (112).

Coming so late in his career, more than forty years after his first international hit, *The Home Place* has not yet established its place within Friel's oeuvre. However, at the time of the playwright's death, *The Home Place* seemed to have emerged as the most important play of the period after *Dancing at Lughnasa*. For example, in the 'Friel @80' supplement published in *The Irish Times* in early 2009, it is the only late-career work included as one of his 'finest dramas'.[2] Similarly, at the time of Friel's death in 2015, Peter Crawley, the chief theatre critic at *The Irish Times*, lists *The Home Place* as the only play after *Dancing at Lughnasa* to be included in his 'Seven Key Plays'. Even more recently, in her assessment entitled 'Brian Friel One Year On: A Critical Overview' (2016), Adrienne Leavy, the editor of *Reading Ireland: The Little Magazine*, dismisses such plays as *Molly Sweeney* (1994) and *Give Me Your Answer, Do!* (1997) as 'less critically or commercially successful' to concentrate her discussion of his 'Late Plays' on *Home Place*.[3]

Home

In the first scholarly treatment devoted to *The Home Place*, Alison O'Malley-Younger flatly states that 'nobody is at home in their place' (169). Her article, 'There's No "Race" Like Home' (2006), focuses on the father and son, Christopher and David Gore, claiming both have 'come to realise that their roots are not in Ireland', even though their family had lived there for generations (170). Claiming that the play is dominated by 'a Beckettian sense of "waiting"', she is especially interested in the plight of the Anglo-Irish Ascendancy as trapped 'between *heimat* (homeland) and *heimlich* (homely and strange)' in an attenuated 'dispossession' that has unsettled them for generations (172). Indeed, for O'Malley-Younger, the Gore's Lodge is an uncanny 'meconnaissance...a place that is a place, but not a home' (173).

George O'Brien's 'The Late Plays' in *The Cambridge Companion to Brian Friel*, which also appeared in 2006, briefly looks at the play to intensify this reading of Gore Lodge as 'a home which cannot be a home' (99). O'Brien refers to the play's many examples of 'a two-home syndrome'—such as David's dream of fleeing with Margaret anywhere in the world but the Lodge—all of which underscore that none of the play's characters can envision a viable place for themselves in the world, whether that be literal or ideological (98–99). O'Brien convincingly diagnoses how the Lodge, the Gore family's manor, is the house that various characters aspire to claim as their home but that throughout the course of the action the main characters find themselves alienated from. As part of her overview of the playwright's career, also in the *Cambridge Companion*, Csilla Bertha observes a similar contradiction: '"home place" (family seat, origins) and "home" (where one...feels at home) do not coincide' (160). Whereas the Lodge is 'a liminal place, a place of "exile"' for Margaret, who has abandoned her people but not found a legitimate home in the Gores' manor (160), neither Christopher nor David Gore suspect that they are 'doomed', because they have never 'penetrated into "the private core" of the natives' (161). Despite Bertha's superficial differences with O'Brien's argument, she too sees the play as primarily staging 'a paradigmatic colonial and post-colonial condition' that creates an 'unhomeliness' that pervades the events (161). Anna McMullan picks up on this theme in her brief 2009 article, where she focuses on the play's staging to expose how 'the continual displacement' of characters 'demonstrates the impossibility of any authentic home' (65).[4]

Richard Rankin Russell seeks to partially recuperate the idea of home in his 2013 article 'Home, Exile, and Unease', arguing that Christopher has sought to create 'a space of hybridity, betwixt and between Irish … and English cultural life' (218). He furthers this reading of the play by carefully comparing Christopher's childhood memories of Kent to the physical set of Ballybeg Lodge in the play's text and the premiere productions in Dublin, London, and Minneapolis (218). However, Russell charts the decreasing viability of this 'liminal place' throughout the play in the face of the challenges posed by both his English cousin and Irish tenants, until Christopher adopts 'the language of the original English planters' to reveal that his idealization of the Lodge has ended (219–20).

History and Politics

In my examination of the play in *Brian Friel*, I contextualize this, Friel's only treatment of the Protestant aristocracy, in the slow crumbling of Ascendancy authority in the late nineteenth century (204–06). Despite Christopher Gore's attempt to embody 'the good landlord'—to use the character's own words (210)—he understands the best interests of the Irish less than either Yolland of *Translations* (1980) or Mabel of *Making History* (1988). Considering him as the local representative of English authority, the political challenge posed to him by Con Doherty, the peasant Fenian leader, is complemented by a similar challenge to the patriarchy within Christopher's family. In this respect, I argue that David Gore recalls such earlier characters as Ben Butler of *Living Quarters* (1977) and Casimir O'Donnell of Aristocrats (1980); however, unlike these earlier sons, 'even though he has witnessed the collapse of Christopher's patriarchal authority, David fails to assert himself as the dynasty's rising patriarch' (209). Murray similarly suggests that David is blind to the political tensions that will engulf the house when the Land Wars erupt (118).

In his chapter 'Branding Identity' in his 2010 book *Theatre and Globalization*, Patrick Lonergan considers the play's intense engagement with the political issues and related theatre of the early 2000s. In Christopher's attempt to define 'himself as genuinely Irish', Lonergan sees the play interrogating the issues of the Irish Citizenship Referendum (190). In a decade that had seen the population of immigrants from Africa and Asia increase sixfold, Lonergan argues that the play's staging of Victorian ethnological practice makes it 'relevant to the debate' (192) and 'makes clear…that the construction of race (and other forms of identity) is directly related to the exercise of power' (193).

Whereas the previous paragraphs have considered the play's men, Margaret O'Donnell, the Irish woman who serves as the estate's housekeeping manager, has also attracted attention in some of the criticism. My discussion notes that every Irish character in the play refers to some aspect of her betrayal of her Irishness (211). Indeed, reading her portrayal against other Irish characters who fall in love with English interlopers, from Maire Chatach in *Translations* to Chris Mundy in *Dancing at Lughnasa*, I argue that the probable future for this romantic opportunist is likely to be disappointing (211–12). Murray less generously describes her as playing 'the West-Briton for most of the play' but being pulled back into her native Irishness upon hearing the siren voice of Moore's song (123).

Music

The play opens with an 'enraptured' Margaret listening to her father's choir sing Thomas Moore's 'Oft in the Stilly Night' in the village below; this and other scenes examining Moore's place in Irish society have attracted critical attention. In his 2014 book, Christopher Murray points out that when he was a young boy, Friel's father coached him to sing this song in an Omagh Feis; thus, when Clement O'Donnell praises Moore in the play, Murray declares, 'Friel's own weight lies behind the schoolmaster's moral voice' (120). In her 2010 book on Friel, Geraldine Higgins refers to the spectre of Moore as the 'symbol of lost civilization in the play' (109). Indeed, she reads Margaret's slow awakening to the emotive power of the song as creating a blend of 'rapture and pathos' key to the play's cultural message (110).

In her article 'Memory, Art, *Lieux de Mémoire*', Csilla Bertha advances this reading, and she too sees the rendition of Moore's song as having a transformative impact on Margaret: 'It lifts her out of the daily routine of…the alien culture surrounding her and helps her to join the other Irish characters in gravitating homewards' (239). Bertha argues that Margaret's sympathetic response to Moore's music reunites her with a cultural memory that is both 'personal and communal' and superior to the Gores' memory, which is merely personal and based on only a few generations in Ireland (236). Moreover, with the prominence given to the rendition of Moore's song at the play's end, Bertha suggests that 'basic realism becomes abandoned' at this moment, and 'the play moves into a more symbolic realm' signalling Margaret's return to a state of compassion for both her father and the Irish characters from whom she had previously sought to distance herself (242–43).

In her 2014 article 'Historical Legacies', McMullan assertively draws parallels between Richard Gore's ethnographic measuring and Clement O'Donnell's claim that Moore 'has our true measure' (196). Moreover, she argues that Friel uses Moore to demonstrate how someone reconciled the competing demands of Irish and English cultures; likewise, McMullan claims that Moore's song suggests ways of 'mediating between diverse identities, histories and generations' (197).[5]

CONCLUSION

In an interview with Jonathan North that appeared in *Ulster Week* in January 1965, the young Friel confessed to the ambition 'to write the great Irish play'. Surveying his career of twenty-seven full-length plays in fifty years, the vast majority of critics in Irish Studies would only argue over the number of times he accomplished his goal. Indeed, as earlier debates over Friel's masterworks make clear, *Philadelphia, Here I Come!* (1964), *Faith Healer* (1979), and *Dancing at Lughnasa* (1990) have been accepted as 'great' Irish plays: defining statements of twentieth-century Irish experience. The debate is whether *Aristocrats* (1979), *Translations* (1980), or *The Home Place* (2005) are also to be included.

Friel is certainly the dominant Irish playwright of the second half of the twentieth century, but how does his achievement compare to the other great Irish dramatists? While J.M. Synge (1871–1909) will always be considered the iconic playwright of the Abbey Theatre's founding period, his reputation rests upon *The Playboy of the Western World* (1907), a play that is deservedly considered a defining exploration of Irish identity. However, Synge's untimely death at thirty-seven ended his career with only four full-length plays, and such dramas as *The Well of the Saints* (1905) and *Deirdre of the Sorrows* (1910) are rarely produced and largely unread beyond a small circle of academics.

Sean O'Casey (1880–1964) presents us with a more comparable career to consider. Like Friel, he lived well into his eighties, but over a playwriting career of thirty-seven years, he saw only eleven full-length plays premiered during his lifetime. Moreover, O'Casey's reputation rests on what has become known as his Dublin Trilogy, written early in his career: *The Shadow of the Gunman* (1923), *Juno and the Paycock* (1924), and *The Plough and the Stars* (1926). While the trilogy's two latter plays are securely in the Irish repertoire, his plays of the 1930s, 1940s, and 1950s are rarely read, critically discussed, or professionally produced.

In other words, with far more plays produced during his lifetime—twenty-seven, in fact—than Synge and O'Casey combined, and international successes throughout his career (in the 1960s, 1970s, 1980s, and 1990s), Friel can rightly be recognized as the most important and successful Irish playwright of the twentieth-century. In both his prolificacy and international appeal, his achievement must be ranked alongside that of George Bernard Shaw (1856–1950) and Samuel Beckett (1906–89), Irish playwrights whose work became mainstays of world theatre, not just Irish theatre. However, unlike the works of Shaw and

Beckett, who effaced their Irish cultural identities to become figures of English or French theatre, Friel's plays remain rooted in the small-town Irish experience, while speaking to universal human experience. Finally, even when compared to the great English-language playwrights of the latter twentieth century—Harold Pinter (1930–2008), Wole Soyinka (b. 1934), Tom Stoppard (b. 1937), Caryl Churchill (b. 1938), and August Wilson (1945–2005)—Friel's achievement rivals theirs in popularity, creativity, and critical acclaim.

Legacy

After the international tributes and national mourning following his death in October 2015, both academics and theatre practitioners have been taking stock of Friel's career, deciding what to stage and what to write about in the future. While Andrienne Leavy's 'Brian Friel One Year On' represents one of the better-known critical attempts to assess his late career, others are exploring Friel's early career with renewed rigour. Indeed, with Kelly Matthews' work uncovering Friel's radio work for the BBC and my discovery of more than seventy articles he wrote for *The Irish Times* in the late 1950s, research into Friel's early career has revealed unexpectedly rich material for future work. Such considerations point to several peculiarities and issues in considering Friel's legacy.

Friel having so recently died, the stature of many of his late plays remains fluid. Whereas the critical treatment and staging history of his plays from the 1960s and 1970s has established a consensus that differentiates major from minor plays, the same cannot yet be asserted for the works of his last fifteen years. For example, as noted above, *Molly Sweeney* (1994) at first enjoyed remarkable theatrical success and has been the subject of more articles than any other play written in his last twenty years—aside from *Dancing at Lughnasa* (1990)—however, in recent years critical and theatrical interest in the play seems to have waned. Conversely, *The Home Place* (2005), the author's last full-length play and the only 'Ballybeg' drama premiered in the last decade of his career, has compelled such scholars as Robert Welch and Csilla Bertha to assert that it may yet be recognized as one of his great plays.

The plays selected for professional production by major companies over the next thirty years will exert considerable influence on critical and theatrical attitudes towards Friel's late career. Indeed, though the first production of *Faith Healer* in New York is widely seen as having been a failure, such subsequent productions as those starring Donal McCann (1980) and Ralph Fiennes (2006) firmly established the play's importance to both Friel's canon and Anglophone drama. In other words, whereas the stature of such minor plays as *Crystal and Fox* (1968) or even *Making History* (1988) is unlikely to change, the place of his last plays (*Molly Sweeney, Give Me Your Answer, Do!, Performances,* and *The Home Place*) within Friel's canon will be determined by the professional productions of and critical attention in these decades following the playwright's death.

A playwright's legacy is also ensured by the ability of his or her works to sustain a continued, robust, and varied critical interest. Throughout his career, Friel's work attracted an exceptionally large number of books, chapters, and articles, and within the past two decades interest in his work has expanded beyond Europe and the Anglophone world to such countries as China, Japan, and Brazil. Nonetheless, in the 200 works written in the last forty-five years, clear trends in the Friel criticism are easily identified, starting with an emphasis on the plays' oedipal or Chekhovian dynamics in the earliest criticism, followed in the scholarship of the 1980s by a focus on Friel as a playwright who incorporated language theory into his drama, on ritual and dance in the 1990s, and on his works' politics (both nationalist and postcolonial) in the most recent criticism.

Clearly, while this over-simplified classification of the criticism omits the ground-breaking interventions by such scholars as Shaun Richards and Richard Rankin Russell, my schemata does point to several important areas left largely ignored by the criticism. First, despite the work of Anna McMullan, Claudia Harris, and my work on Friel's 'sororal plays', the criticism historically demonstrates a bias for focusing on male characters. This is especially true of the early articles and chapters written about the emotionally embattled sons found in *Philadelphia, Here I Come!, The Gentle Island,* or *Living Quarters*; indeed, Friel's initial preference for writing male characters is nowhere more clearly observed than in *The Enemy Within* and *Volunteers*, two early plays with entirely male casts. However, even the discussions of plays notable for their female characters, such as *Aristocrats* and *Dancing at Lughnasa*, tend to focus on male characters, amid more generalizing discussions of groups of sisters. In other words, for an oeuvre that boasts such strong female characters as Cass McGuire, Judith O'Donnell, and Molly Sweeney, much more sustained critical work is needed to better understand Friel's staging of the Irish female experience.

Ballybeg, Friel's imagined town on the coast of County Donegal, is also a profoundly rich subject that has received only limited attention. The town itself (or its environs) is the setting for thirteen plays, premiered between 1964 and 2005, and through it Friel examined provincial Irish society from 1833 to the millennium. Moreover, eight of these plays from the 1960s to the late 1990s present Ballybeg in 'the present', thus providing an almost journalistic chronicle of the modernisation of Irish society from the end of the de Valera era into that of the Celtic Tiger. Indeed, the depth and refinement of the social analysis embodied by Friel's Ballybeg plays even surpass that of August Wilson's Pittsburgh Cycle, a decade-by-decade chronicle of the city's Hill District throughout the twentieth century. In other words, Ballybeg as a scenographic paradigm promises to provide material for diverse dramatic and sociological examinations of Ireland, from its religious and sexual *mores* to the nation's relation to its environment or its very conception of its national identity.

There also remain many areas of theatre history and practice for future scholarship to explore. While Anthony Roche has initiated a careful and informative exploration of Friel's relationship to such directors as Tyrone Guthrie and Joe Dowling, the broader topic of his relationship to theatre practitioners, from producers to designers, remains virtually unexplored. Likewise, there is almost an entire absence of research into the playwright's relationship to the actors who could be thought of as having served as his 'muse' at one time or another. For example, the influence of Catherine Byrne, the actor for whom he created roles throughout the 1990s, on Friel's characterization of Irish women has yet to be studied. While his relationship with such actors as Stephen Rea or Ray MacAnally may not have been as storied, research into the roles they played promises to reveal Friel's strategies for creating characters for specific actors.

Finally, this last topic of Friel's personal involvement with directors, actors, and other theatre practitioners points to the crucial need for a well-researched, critical biography. Friel lived during a crucial period of Irish history: born in the decade of the island's violent partitioning, he lived in Northern Ireland during World War Two, marched in Derry on Bloody Sunday, and witnessed the end of the Troubles and Ireland's economic rejuvenation. Yet unlike almost all of his peers, once fame freed him from the necessity of public engagement, Friel never publicly spoke on issues after 1964, stopped writing critical essays after 1967, and rarely allowed interviews after 1982. Thus, the scholarship lacks the material that normally forms the basis of an informed biographical criticism: statements of deeply held beliefs, the substance of close friendships, and the personal challenges faced. Despite his famous reclusiveness, critics have generally recognized the autobiographical contexts for many of Friel's plays, from the influence of Friel's father, a primary school principal, on his many dramatic schoolteachers to the modelling of the sisters in *Dancing at Lughnasa* upon his aunts, 'those five brave Glenties women'. Yet, aside from these generalized points of reference, the specifics of Friel's life and its relationship to the content and themes of his drama remains unknown.

In surveying the present condition of and the promise for future developments in Friel scholarship, one is struck by a type of critical momentum that seems to still be gathering. Rather than slowing and routinizing, interest in Friel is firmly established in the English-speaking world and spreading in Asia and Europe. Moreover, while such established critical topics as his plays' reliance on language theory, ritual, and Chekhovian psychological dynamics remain relevant, the exploration of new interpretive contexts and subjects is expanding, suggesting that the terms for discussing Friel's plays in the next generation will have markedly evolved and departed from the familiar contours of the criticism's first and second generations.

NOTES

INTRODUCTION

1 In the last twenty years, a growing body of Friel criticism has emerged in Chinese, French, German, Japanese, (Brazilian) Portuguese, and Spanish, and such articles are readily found in the annual Bibliography Bulletin published in Irish University Review. However, considerations of space and scope will largely limit my survey of works written in languages other than English to those that have entered into mainstream English-language criticism, such as Martine Pelletier's book *Le théâtre de Brian Friel*.

1 EARLY JOURNALISM AND STORIES

1 Jessica Evans' 'Friel's Short Fiction: Synopses and Critical Snapshots' is an alphabetically arranged thumbnail sketch of thirty-three stories published between 1952 and 1966, accompanied by brief comments on the scholarship.

2 In 2010, the Gallery Press also released *A Man's World*, a limited edition of three stories: 'Mr Sing My Heart's Delight', 'My Father and the Sergeant', and 'A Man's World'.

3 For comparisons of the story 'Foundry House' to *Aristocrats*, see also Ulf Dantanus (1988), pp. 163–64 and 170–71; George O'Brien (1990), pp. 25–26; Andrews (1995), pp. 39–40 and 150; and McGrath (1999), p. 156.

4 See also McGrath (1999), p. 62.

2 EARLY AND 'WITHDRAWN' PLAYS

1 Letter from the author, dated 23 July 2008.

2 Brian Friel, 'Self-Portrait', *Essays, Diaries, Interviews*, pp. 41–42.

3 Letter from Ronald Mason, Friel Papers MS 37,043/2. Kelly Matthews, 'Brian Friel, the BBC, and Ronald Mason', provides a very valuable examination of the collaboration between the young Friel and Mason, a director for BBC radio drama.

4 Brian Friel, *A Sort of Freedom*, Friel Papers, National Library of Ireland, MS 37,139, p. 4.

5 *Sort of Freedom*, p. 22.

6 Andrews (1995), pp. 48–49. Martine Pelletier, *Le Théâtre de Brian Friel*, pp. 35–36.

7 Robert Welch, *The Abbey Theatre*, p. 154.

8 Interview with Graham Morison, early 1965, in Friel's *Essays, Diaries, Interviews*, p. 8.

9 See also Dantanus's discussion of Columba's struggle against 'family and home' (1988), pp. 79–82.

10 For a similar assessment based on the radio script, see O'Brien (1990), pp. 39–40.

3   *PHILADELPHIA, HERE I COME!* (1964)

1   All dates associated with plays indicate the year of premiere production.

2   See also Dantanus, pp. 25–27.

3   In her 'Brian Friel's Sense of Place', a wide-ranging survey of the plays' many different settings, Helen Lojek adds that Lough Anna, a point of reference in three Ballybeg plays, is an actual lake near the Glenties (pp. 187–88).

4   From Lewis Funke's 1968 interview; see also that of 1980 with Ciaran Carty (p. 142) as well as Friel's 'Self-Portrait' of 1971 (p. 106) in *Brian Friel in Conversation*.

5   *Brian Friel in Conversation*, p. 210.

6   See *Essays, Diaries, Interviews*, p. 178.

7   In his review 'The "Big Five" of Irish Drama', published just a few months after the success of *Philadelphia* in Dublin, North favorably compares Friel to Stewart Love, who wrote such successful plays as *The Randy Dandy* (1960) and *The Big Long Bender* (1962); Sam Thompson, author of the sensational *Over the Bridge* (1958); Sam Cree, a prolific writer of popular farces; and John Hamilton, author of several political plays for the British theatre.

8   For a survey of the other rankings of Friel's 'Masterworks', see Richard Rankin Russell's *Modernity, Community, and Place*, pp. 4–5.

9   The same sentiment is frequently expressed; see, for example, Lionel Pilkington's 'The Abbey Theatre and the Irish State' (p. 240) and John Harrington's *The Irish Play on the New York Stage, 1874–1966* (p. 148).

10   Gar recites all or part of this quotation on pp. 36, 38, 50, 56, 67, 78, 80, 91, 92, and 94, *Selected Plays* (ed. Seamus Deane).

4   **PLAYS OF THE LATER 1960s**

1   In *Brian Friel, Ireland, and the North*, I note the marked drop in the number of interviews that Friel gave after 1975 (p. 227).

2   For example, in 2000 the RTÉ radio host Mike Murphy published a book of twelve interviews with Ireland's most established writers; however, Friel was the only writer who refused to speak with him, and the book appeared with an interview with Declan Kiberd and Fintan O'Toole about him. Similarly, in Morse, Bertha, and Kurdi's 2006 collection *Brian Friel's Dramatic Artistry*, the interview with Richard Pine noted that 'Brian Friel does not give interviews any more' (p. 324).

3   Broadcast on the show *Soundings*, 2 August 1970, and published in *Brian Friel in Conversation*, ed. Paul Delaney, p. 91.

4   Reprinted in *Essays, Diaries, Interviews*, p. 47.

5   The other two pairs are *Translations* (1980) and *The Communication Cord* (1982) and the later *Dancing at Lughnasa* (1990) and *Wonderful Tennessee* (1993).

6   Ulf Dantanus provides additional examples of the poor reviews for the premiere in his *Brian Friel* (pp. 106–07).

7   See also Robert Welch's *The Abbey Theatre 1899–1999* (pp. 182–83).

8   See Ulf Dantanus's *Brian Friel* (pp. 102–03) and George O'Brien's *Brian Friel* (pp. 56–57).

9   See also Ron Rollins and Nita Rollins, '*The Loves of Cass McGuire*: Friel's Wagnerian Music Drama'.

10   See the books by Dantanus (p. 119), Higgins (p. 22), Pelletier (pp. 63–64), Corbett (p. 112), and Boltwood (pp. 74–76).

11   See also Andrews (pp. 119–21), Dantanus (pp. 121–22), Higgins (pp. 23–24), McGrath (p. 75), McGuinness (pp. 24–25), Pelletier (pp. 62–63), and Roche (p. 106).

5 PLAYS OF THE EARLY 1970s

1 See also Michael Parker, 'Telling Tales', pp. 142–43.
2 See McGuinness, 'Faith Healer', p. 25, and Lojek, pp. 48–49.
3 See Stephen Watt's 'Friel and the Northern Ireland "Troubles" Play' for a brief survey of the genre, pp. 31–33.
4 Marc Mulholland's *Northern Ireland: A Very Short Introduction* (2002) provides a concise and useful summary of the Troubles, the peace process, and the reestablishment of local rule after the 1998 Good Friday Agreement.
5 Friel, *Essays, Diaries, Interviews*, p. 114.
6 For more on the reception of the Dublin premier and the first New York production, see Christopher Murray's *Twentieth-Century Irish Drama*, pp. 201–2.
7 See also McGrath, *Brian Friel's (Post)Colonial Drama*, pp. 108–11, and Helen Fulton, 'Hegemonic Discourses in Brian Friel's *The Freedom of the City*' (2003), pp. 72–75, for especially probing discussions of the Priest, Balladeer, and RTE newsman.
8 For general summaries of these three characters, see O'Brien (1990, pp. 80–81), Pine (1999, pp. 138–41), Andrews (pp. 130–32), McGrath (1999, pp. 102–03), Higgins (pp. 32–34), Fulton (pp. 76–79).
9 See also Parker, pp. 284–85.
10 A similar view is presented by Fulton in 'Hegemonic Discourses', pp. 77–78.
11 See also Watt, p. 38.
12 See Ruth Niel's 'Non-realistic Techniques in the Plays of Brian Friel', 353–54. Szasz also provides a careful argument focused on Prof. Dodds and the play's most affective agent of Brechtian alienation, pp. 115–17.
13 See also Ruth Niel's 'Digging into History'.
14 See also Pelletier for a detailed discussion of Lief and the play's examination of victimhood, pp. 162–63.

6 *LIVING QUARTERS* (1977) AND *ARISTOCRATS* (1979)

1 A similar, though less successful reading of Anna and Sir, is offered by Tony Corbett (p. 49).
2 For Andrews (p. 123), Casimir is this figure, while for Deane (p. 169) and Murray (p. 131) it is Eamon.
3 See for example, Pine's *Brian Friel and Ireland's Drama* (1990); Christopher Murray's 'Friel's "Emblems of Adversity" and the Yeatsian Example' (1993); and Alan Peacock's 'Translating the Past' (1993).
4 Corbett also discusses how Eamon and Willie 'are two aspects of the peasant response to the ascendancy' (pp. 78–80).
5 Friel, *Essays, Diaries, Interviews*, p. 65.

7 *FAITH HEALER* (1979)

1 See also my *Brian Friel, Ireland, and the North* (2007), pp. 127–29.
2 Friel, *Essays, Diaries, Interviews*, p. 111.
3 See also Maxwell (1984), p. 203; Andrews, p. 159; Welch (1993), p. 235; and McGrath (1999), p. 172.
4 See Deane (1985), p. 173, and Dantanus, p. 174.
5 For other references to Grace in the early criticism, see Etherton, p. 185, and Dantanus, pp. 174–75.

6   Only in the earliest brief reflections on the play—Maxwell (p. 201) and Deane (p. 19), both in 1984—do the critics express uncertainty about whom to believe.

7   Parenthetically, while the criticism has long recognized that Teddy's versions can usually be seen to partially support or contradict the other versions, McGrath provides the best summary of Teddy's accounts and their relationships to the other narratives (pp. 158–59, 164–67, 169–71).

8   See Kiberd, 'Brian Friel's *Faith Healer*' (1985), p. 220.

9   For McGrath, this principle of memory as a reflection of one's psychological needs leads into his argument that Friel does this to reveal 'the long-standing incompatible fictions England and Ireland have had of each other' (p. 174), with Frank embodying 'an insecure Sinn Fein Ireland' (p. 175), Grace as the traditional 'Anglo-Ireland', and Teddy as England (p. 176).

10   See also Pine (1999), pp. 110–11.

11   Barnett is specifically referring to the instances when Frank, Grace, and Teddy each repeat the same lines (pp. 380–81).

8   TRANSLATIONS (1980)

1   In Morash's history, the premiere of *Translations* is as important as the first stagings of J.M. Synge's *Playboy of the Western World* on 29 January 1907, Sean O'Casey's *Plough and the Stars* on 11 February 1926, and the Pike Theatre's production of Samuel Beckett's *Waiting for Godot* on 28 October 1955.

2   See Chapter 3 for a fuller explanation of the scholarly conditions that discouraged academic work on authors at the beginning of their careers.

3   For an earlier, though less rigorous, comparison of Steiner's book to Friel's play, see McGrath's 'Irish Babel' (1989).

4   Likewise, Corbett argues that 'Termon' must be derived from the Irish 'tearmann', not the Latin 'terminus', as Yolland believes (p. 29).

5   It is important to note that Andrews' criticism is leavened by considerable admiration for the play. He admits that 'I felt myself carried forward by it' (p. 120) and that, for all his historiographical complaints, it presents 'an extremely subtle blend of historical truth and—some other kind of truth' (p. 122); see Friel, Andrews, Barry, '*Translations* and *A Paper Landscape*'. Andrews later published 'Notes for a Future Edition of Brian Friel's *Translations*' (1992), in which he fully catalogued his objections to the playwright's mistakes.

6   'Making a Reply to the Criticism of *Translations* by J.H. Andrews', *Essays, Diaries, Interviews*, pp. 116–19.

7   See also Richtarik, pp. 38–43.

8   For a general overview of Boucicault's Irish plays, see my 'Dion Boucicault: From Stage Irishman to Staging Nationalism' (2010).

9   Born in Belfast in 1946 and educated at Queen's University, Rea started his acting career in the Abbey Theatre's production of Stewart Love's *Big Long Bender* (1966). His friendship with Friel dates from his appearance as Skinner in the 1973 production of *Freedom of the City* at the Royal Court Theatre. He assumed the leading male role in such Field Day plays as *The Communication Cord* (1982), *Boesman and Lena* (1983), *Pentecost* (1987), *Making History* (1988), and *Saint Oscar* (1989).

10   For a more detailed comparison of the two plays, see Thornton's 'Friel and Shaw'.

11   See also Lee, pp. 174–75.

12   See also his later discussion of Hugh in 'Brian Friel: The Name of the Game', pp. 108–09.

13   See also Pilkington, p. 213.

14 In his 1991 essay 'Staging History in Contemporary Anglo-Irish Drama', Ulrich Schneider is the first to associate the Carthage of Virgil's poem with the Ireland of Friel's play, pp. 86–87.

15 For a similar view, see Grene's *Politics of Irish Drama*, pp. 46–47.

16 See also Cullingford, pp. 54–56.

17 In a footnote to her article 'The Engendered Space', Claudia Harris provides the best summary of the powerful impact that this scene had on the initial reviewers of the Field Day production of *Translations*, p. 72.

18 On Sarah's 'protection of total silence', see Lojek, p. 87.

19 See also Roche's summary of Manus' actions in Act 3 and their implications in his 2011 book, pp. 140–41.

20 See also Russell (2014), pp. 189–90.

21 Analyses of Field Day's attempts to establish a non-partisan politics can be found in Kirkland's *Literature and Culture in Northern Ireland Since 1965: Moments of Danger* (pp. 134–46), Maguire's *Making Theatre in Northern Ireland* (pp. 80–83), both Richards' 'Throwing Theory at Ireland', and Richtarik's *Acting Between the Lines* (pp. 65–69). Field Day's use of the idea of creating a 'Fifth Province' is the subject of Kearney's 'The Fifth Province' in *Postnationalist Ireland* (pp. 99–107), Russell in *Modernity, Community, and Place* (pp. 146–50), and Richards' 'Field Day's Fifth Province'.

22 See *Essays, Diaries, Interviews*, pp. 102, 106, 112.

23 See Bardon's *A History of Ulster*, pp. 692–746.

9 PLAYS OF THE 1980s

1 See also Kathleen Hohenleiter, p. 380.

2 See McGrath's *Brian Friel's (Post) Colonial Drama*, p. 220, and Hohenleitner, p. 254.

3 Friel himself never complained of the demands made upon him; however, Friel's ideological and artistic struggles have been discussed widely; see Carvalho, pp. 251–54; Richtarik (2001), pp. 267–68; and Roche (2011), pp. 162–63.

4 For additional ways in which Friel's chronology of events departs from historical veracity, see Corbett (2002), p. 17.

5 Hohenleitner offers a supplementary reading of the play that more attentively includes a discussion of Field Day, which by this play's date had also published several pamphlets on Irish history and politics.

10 *DANCING AT LUGHNASA* (1990)

1 In his *History of Irish Theatre*, Christopher Morash usefully comments on how Friel's decision not to premiere *Lughnasa* through the Field Day Theatre Company coincides with significant changes both in the company and for such directors as Seamus Heaney and Stephen Rea (pp. 264–65).

2 See also Lonergan, '"Dancing on a One-Way Street": Irish Reactions to *Dancing at Lughnasa*' (2009).

3 See *Brian Friel in Conversation*, p. 203, where all three interviews may be found. For discussions of the play as autobiography, see, for example, McMullan (1999), p. 95; Lojek (2006), p. 79; and Murray (2014), pp. 133–34.

4 See *Brian Friel in Conversation*, pp. 214–15.

5 See also McMullan (1999), p. 92.

6 Richard Rankin Russell (2014) further explores the particularly powerful influence that the radio has upon the sisters; see pp. 203–8.

7   For a reading more focused on the sisters' sexual frustrations, see Rollins, 'Friel's *Dancing at Lughnasa*' (1993), pp. 81–83.
8   For a similar view, see Higgins *Brian Friel*, pp. 87–88.
9   For a similar view, see Lonergan, pp. 41–42.
10 See also McMullan (1999), p. 93.
11 See also Russell (2014), pp. 218–19.

11 PLAYS OF THE 1990s

1   Quote from Burke's 'The Historical Geography of Brian Friel' (18). For defenders of the play, see Burke (1994), Lojek (1995), Pelletier (1997), and Roche (2011); its harshest critics have been Krause (1997) and Mesterházi (1999).
2   In her 'Island of Otherness' (1996), Bertha also compares Friel's abandoned pier to Beckett's desolate crossroad (p. 134). For discussions of the play's various Beckettian aspects, see also Andrews (p. 253), Pine (p. 282), Higgins (p. 91), and Roche's *Brian Friel* (pp. 187–88).
3   By comparison Helen Lojek's 'Space in *Wonderful Tennessee*' (2009) presents the broadest exploration not of the island, but of the cultural significance of the pier in the West of Ireland (pp. 48–50).
4   See Andrews, p. 262.
5   'Toutes deux…operant aux limites d'un passé-présent mythique, d'un temps anachronique, celui de la mémoire et du rituel' (p. 283).
6   For a fuller history of case studies on 'blindsight', see Julia Temple, 'The Gift of Sight in *Molly Sweeney*', pp. 134–35.
7   See also Murray (p. 87), McGrath (pp. 250–51), and Kerrigan (pp. 152–54).
8   See Pelletier (p. 301) and Higgins (p. 99).
9   In his 2013 article 'Home, Exile, and Unease', Richard Rankin Russell similarly argues that, at the play's end, Molly becomes a 'word-mage', one with complete imaginative freedom at home in language itself (p. 210).
10 In his article 'Swimming in Words' (2002), Kerrigan expands this argument to reflect Frank's use of such terms as 'agnosic', 'blindsight', and 'gnosis' (pp. 155–58).
11 Geraldine Higgins also provides a brief, albeit revealing, discussion of the Dublin, London, and New York reviews, p. 105.
12 See also Murray's *The Theatre of Brian Friel* (2014), pp. 172–73.
13 While this article originally appeared in the special issue of the *Hungarian Journal of English and American Studies* 'in Honour of Brian Friel at 70', my citations refer to the more widely available *Brian Friel's Dramatic Artistry* (2006), where the article was reprinted.
14 For similar interpretations of Tom's pornographic treatment of Bridget, see Bertha and Morse, p. 134, and Germanou (2003), pp. 472 and 475.

12 LAST PLAYS

1   See also Roche's *Brian Friel*, pp. 205–06.
2   Quoted in Russell's *Modernity, Community, and Place*, p. 5.
3   Pelletier similarly identifies *Dancing at Lughnasa* and *The Home Place* as the two defining works of Friel's late career (p. 100).
4   See also her later 'Historical Legacies', pp. 197–98.
5   See also Russell (2013), 'Home, Exile, and Unease', pp. 220–21.

SELECT BIBLIOGRAPHY

A comprehensive bibliography of Friel's oeuvre is beyond the scope of this work. A complete list of his published plays and dramatic adaptations follows.

For a complete list of his seventy-six *Irish Times* articles (1957–62), see my article 'Mildly Eccentric'; for a complete list of his sixty *Irish Press* articles (1962–63), see O'Brien's article 'Meet Brian Friel'.

For a complete list of his published stories, see Evans, 'Friel's Short Fiction: Synopses and Critical Snapshots'.

Works by Brian Friel

Plays (in order of first professional production)

Editions cited are for first Irish/English publication except when the first US edition is significantly earlier.

The Enemy Within (Newark, DE: Proscenium Press, 1975).

Philadelphia, Here I Come! (London: Faber and Faber, 1965).

The Loves of Cass McGuire (New York: Farrar, Straus and Giroux, 1966).

Lovers ('Winners' and 'Losers') (New York: Farrar, Straus and Giroux, 1968).

Crystal and Fox (London: Faber and Faber, 1969).

The Mundy Scheme (with *Crystal and Fox*) (New York: Farrar, Straus and Giroux, 1970).

The Gentle Island (London: Davis-Poynter, 1973).

The Freedom of the City (London: Faber and Faber, 1974).

Living Quarters (London: Faber and Faber, 1978).

Volunteers (London: Faber and Faber, 1979).

Aristocrats (Dublin: Gallery Press, 1980).

Faith Healer (London: Faber and Faber, 1980).

Translations (London: Faber and Faber, 1981).

'American Welcome', *Best Short Plays, 1981* (ed. Stanley Richards) (Radnor, PA: Chilton Books, 1981).

The Communication Cord (London: Faber and Faber, 1983).

Making History (London: Faber and Faber, 1989).

Dancing at Lughnasa (London: Faber and Faber, 1990).

Wonderful Tennessee (London: Faber and Faber, 1993).

Molly Sweeney (London: Penguin, 1994).

Give Me Your Answer, Do! (London: Penguin, 1997).

'The Yalta Game' (Oldcastle, Co. Meath: Gallery Press, 2001).

Three Plays After ('The Yalta Game', 'The Bear', 'Afterplay') (Oldcastle, Co. Meath: Gallery Press, 2004).

Performances (Oldcastle, Co. Meath: Gallery Press, 2003).
The Home Place (London: Faber and Faber, 2005).

Translations and Adaptations

Three Sisters (Dublin: Gallery Press, 1981).
Fathers and Sons (After the Novel by Ivan Turgenev) (London: Faber and Faber, 1987).
The London Vertigo (Oldcastle, Co. Meath: Gallery Press, 1990).
A Month in the Country: After Turgenev (Oldcastle, Co. Meath: Gallery Press, 1992).
Uncle Vanya (Oldcastle, Co. Meath: Gallery Press, 1998).
Hedda Gabler (Oldcastle, Co. Meath: Gallery Press, 2008).

Play Collections

Selected Plays (London: Faber and Faber, 1984).
Collected Plays Vols 1–5 (London: Faber and Faber, 2016).

Film Adaptation

McGuinness, Frank. *Brian Friel's Dancing at Lughnasa* (London: Faber and Faber, 1998).

Short Story Collections

The Saucer of Larks (London: Victor Gollancz, 1962).
The Gold in the Sea (London: Victor Gollancz, 1966).
Selected Stories (Dublin: Gallery Press, 1979).

Interview Collections

(For a comprehensive list of his essays and interviews [print, radio, and television], news articles about Friel, and profiles, see the bibliography [pp. 244–80] in *Brian Friel in Conversation*.
Brian Friel in Conversation (ed. Paul Delaney) (Ann Arbor, MI: The University of Michigan Press, 2000).
Essays, Diaries, Interviews 1964–1999. (ed. Christopher Murray) (London: Faber and Faber, 1999).

Archive

The Brian Friel Papers, National Library of Ireland, MSS 37,041-37,806.
The Brian Friel Papers (Additional), National Library of Ireland, MSS 42,091-42,093 & 49,209-49,350.
The Field Day Papers, National Library of Ireland, MSS 42,038, 42,039, & 46,873-47,333, & MSL 168-171.

Criticism

Books devoted to Brian Friel

Andrews, Elmer. *The Art of Brian Friel: Neither Reality Nor Dreams* (London: Macmillan Press, 1995).

Boltwood, Scott. *Brian Friel, Ireland, and the North* (Cambridge: Cambridge University Press, 2007).

Corbett, Tony. *Brian Friel: Decoding the Language of the Tribe* (Dublin: The Liffey Press, 2002).

Dantanus, Ulf. *Brian Friel: A Study* (London: Faber and Faber, 1988).

Dean, Joan FitzPatrick. *Ireland into Film: Dancing at Lughnasa* (Cork: Cork University Press, 2003).

Grant, David. *Student Guide to the Stagecraft of Brian Friel* (London: Greenwich Exchange, 2004).

Higgins, Geraldine. *Brian Friel* (Tavistock: Northcote House, 2010).

Jones, Nesta. *A Faber Critical Guide: Brian Friel* (London: Faber and Faber, 2000).

Kerwin, William (ed.). *Brian Friel: A Casebook* (New York: Garland Press, 1997).

Maxwell, D(esmond) E(rnest) S(tewart). *Brian Friel* (Lewisburg, PN: Bucknell University Press, 1973).

McGrath, F(rancis) C(harles). *Brian Friel's (Post)Colonial Drama: Language, Illusion, and Politics* (Syracuse, NY: Syracuse University Press, 1999).

Morse, Donald E., Csilla Bertha, and Mária Kurdi (eds). *Brian Friel's Dramatic Artistry: 'The Work Has Value'* (Dublin: Carysfort Press, 2006).

Murray, Christopher. *The Theatre of Brian Friel: Tradition and Modernity* (London: Bloomsbury, 2014).

O'Brien, George. *Brian Friel* (Boston, MA: Twayne Publishers, 1990).

Peacock, Alan (ed.) *The Achievement of Brian Friel* (Gerrards Cross: Colin Smythe, 1993).

Pelletier, Martine. *Le théâtre de Brian Friel: Histoire et histoires* (Villeneuve d'Ascq: Presses Universitaires du Septentrion, 1997).

Pine, Richard. *Brian Friel and Ireland's Drama* (London: Routledge, 1990).

——*The Diviner: The Art of Brian Friel* (Dublin: University College Dublin Press, 1999).

Roche, Anthony. *Brian Friel: Theatre and Politics* (Houndmills: Palgrave Macmillan, 2011).

——(ed.). *The Cambridge Companion to Brian Friel* (Cambridge: Cambridge University Press, 2006).

Russell, Richard Rankin. *Modernity, Community, and Place in Brian Friel's Drama* (Syracuse, NY: Syracuse University Press, 2014).

Szasz, Maria. *Brian Friel and America* (Dublin: Glasnevin, 2013).

Journals: Special Issues on Brian Friel

Special Issue: Brian Friel, *Irish University Review* 29.1 (1999).

Special Issue in Honour of Brian Friel at 70, *Hungarian Journal of English and American Studies* 5.1 (1999).

Essays and Book Chapters

Achilles, Jochen. 'Homesick for Abroad: The Transition from National to Cultural Identity in Contemporary Irish Drama', *Modern Drama* 38.4 (1995), pp. 435–39.

Andrews, J.H. 'Notes for a Future Edition of Brian Friel's *Translations*', *Irish Review* 13 (1992), pp. 93–106.

Barnett, David. 'Staging the Indeterminate: Brian Friel's *Faith Healer* as a Postdramatic Theatre-Text', *Irish University Review* 36.2 (2006), pp. 374–88.

Bertha, Csilla. 'Brian Friel as Postcolonial Playwright', *The Cambridge Companion to Brian Friel* (ed. Anthony Roche) (Cambridge: Cambridge University Press, 2006), pp. 154–65.

——'"The Centre Cannot Hold": Postcolonial Discourse in Ireland and Brian Friel's *Home Place*', *Literatures in English: Priorities of Research, Studies in English and Comparative Literature* (eds Wolfgang Zach and Michael Kinneally) (Tübingen: Stauffenberg Verlag, 2008), pp. 217–30.

——'Iona—Inishkeen—Oilean Draoichta: Island-Existence in Brian Friel's Plays', *Worlds Visible and Invisible: Essays on Irish Literature* (eds Csilla Bertha and Donald Morse) (Debrecan: Lajos Kossuth University, 1994), pp. 87–102.

——'"Island of Otherness": Images of Irishness in Brian Friel's *Wonderful Tennessee*', *Hungarian Journal of English and American Studies* 2.2 (1996), pp. 129–42.

——'Memory, Art, *Lieux de Mémoire* in Brian Friel's *The Home Place*', *The Theatre of Brian Friel: Tradition and Modernity* (ed. Christopher Murray) (London: Bloomsbury, 2014), pp. 230–45.

——'Music and Words in Brian Friel's *Performances*', *Brian Friel's Dramatic Artistry: 'The Work Has Value'* (eds Donald E. Morse, Csilla Bertha, and Mária Kurdi) (Dublin: Carysfort Press, 2006), pp. 61–72.

——'A Reply to Márton Mesterházi on *Wonderful Tennessee*', *Hungarian Journal of English and American Studies* 2.2 (1996), pp. 155–59.

——'Tragedies of National Fate: A Comparison between Brian Friel's *Translations* and Its Hungarian Counterpart, András Sütő's *A szuzai menyegző*', *Irish University Review* 17 (1987), pp. 207–23.

Bertha, Csilla, and Donald E. Morse. '"Singing of Human Unsuccess": Brian Friel's Portraits of the Artist', *Brian Friel's Dramatic Artistry: 'The Work Has Value'* (eds Donald E. Morse, Csilla Bertha, and Mária Kurdi) (Dublin: Carysfort Press, 2006), pp. 13–34.

Birker, Klaus. 'The Relationship between the Stage and the Audience in Brian Friel's *The Freedom of the City*', *The Irish Writer and the City* (ed. Maurice Harmon) (Gerrards Cross: Colin Smythe Press, 1984), pp. 153–58.

Block, Ed. 'Brian Friel's *Faith Healer* as Post-Christian, Christian Drama', *Literature and Theology* 14.2 (2000), pp. 189–207.

Boltwood, Scott. '"Mildly Eccentric": Brian Friel's Writings for the *Irish Times* and the *New Yorker*', *Irish University Review* 44.2 (2014), pp. 305–22.

——'"More Real for Northern Catholics than Anybody Else": Brian Friel's Earliest Plays', *Irish Theater International* 2.1 (2009), pp. 4–15.

——'"Swapping Stories about Apollo and Cuchulainn": Brian Friel and the De-Gaelicizing of Ireland', *Modern Drama* 41 (1998), pp. 573–83.

Bradley, Anthony. 'About Communicating: Brian Friel's *Translations*', *An Gael* 3.1 (1985), pp. 6–9.

Burke, Patrick. 'Friel and Performance History', *The Cambridge Companion to Brian Friel* (ed. Anthony Roche) (Cambridge: Cambridge University Press, 2006), pp. 117–28.

——'The Historical Geography of Brian Friel', *Irish Literary Supplement* (Spring 1994), p. 18.

Carvalho, Paulo Eduardo. 'About Some Healthy Intersections: Brian Friel and Field Day', *Brian Friel's Dramatic Artistry: 'The Work Has Value'* (eds Donald E. Morse, Csilla Bertha, and Mária Kurdi) (Dublin: Carysfort Press, 2006), pp. 251–69.

Cave, Richard Allen. 'Questing for Ritual and Ceremony in a Godforsaken World: *Dancing at Lughnasa* and *Wonderful Tennessee'*, *Brian Friel's Dramatic Artistry: 'The Work Has Value'* (eds Donald E. Morse, Csilla Bertha, and Mária Kurdi) (Dublin: Carysfort Press, 2006), pp. 181–204.

Clutterbuck, Catriona. '*Lughnasa* after *Easter*: Treatments of Narrative Imperialism in Friel and Devlin', *Irish University Review* 29.1 (1999), pp. 101–18.

Coakley, James. 'Chekhov in Ireland: Brief Notes on Friel's Philadelphia,' *Comparative Drama* 7.3 (1973), pp. 191–97.

Connolly, Sean. 'Translating History: Brian Friel and the Irish Past', *The Achievement of Brian Friel* (ed. Alan Peacock) (Gerrards Cross: Colin Smythe, 1993), pp. 149–63.

Corbett, Tony. 'Master Performances', *The Irish Book Review* 1.1 (2005), pp. 38–39.

Corcoran, Neil. 'The Penalties of Retrospect: Continuities in Brian Friel', *The Achievement of Brian Friel* (ed. Alan Peacock) (Gerrards Cross: Colin Smythe, 1993), pp. 14–28.

Crawley, Peter. 'Brian Friel: Seven Key Plays', *The Irish Times* 3 October 2015, irishtimes.com.

Cronin, John. '"Donging the Tower"—The Past Did Have Meaning: The Short Stories of Brian Friel', *The Achievement of Brian Friel* (ed. Alan Peacock) (Gerrards Cross: Colin Smythe, 1993), pp. 1–13.

Crowley, Tom. 'Memory and Forgetting in a Time of Violence: Brian Friel's Meta-History Plays', *Estudios Irlandeses/Journal of Irish Studies* 3 (2008), pp. 72–83.

Cullingford, Elizabeth Butler. 'Decent Chaps: Gender, Sexuality, and Englishness in Twentieth-Century Irish Drama and Film', *Ireland's Others: Gender and Ethnicity in Irish Literature and Popular Culture* (Notre Dame, IN: University of Notre Dame Press, 2001), pp. 37–56.

Dantanus, Ulf. 'O'Neill's Last Tape: Self, Failure and Freedom in Friel and Beckett', *A Companion to Brian Friel* (eds Richard Harp and Robert C. Evans) (West Cornwall, CT: Locust Hill Press, 2002), pp. 107–32.

Deane, Seamus. 'Brian Friel: The Name of the Game', *The Achievement of Brian Friel* (ed. Alan Peacock) (Gerrards Cross: Colin Smythe, 1993), pp. 103–12.

————'In Search of a Story', *The Communication Cord* (Programme) (Belfast: Nicholson and Bass, 1982), n.p.

————'Introduction', *The Diviner* (Dublin: The O'Brien Press, 1979), pp. 9–18.

————'Introduction', *Selected Plays* (Washington, DC: The Catholic University, 1984), pp. 11–22.

Evans, Jessica. 'Friel's Short Fiction: Synopses and Critical Snapshots', *A Companion to Brian Friel* (eds Richard Harp and Robert C. Evans) (West Cornwall, CT: Locust Hill Press, 2002), pp. 291–310.

Evans, Robert C. '*Dancing at Lughnasa*: Play, Script, and Film', *A Companion to Brian Friel* (eds Richard Harp and Robert C. Evans) (West Cornwall, CT: Locust Hill Press, 2002), pp. 55–89.

Farrelly, James P. and Mark C. 'Ireland Facing the Void: The Emergence of Meaninglessness in the Works of Brian Friel', *The Canadian Journal of Irish Studies* 24.1 (1998), pp. 105–14.

Ferris, Kathleen. 'Brian Friel's Uses of Laughter', *Brian Friel: A Casebook* (ed. William Kerwin) (New York: Garland Press, 1997), pp. 117–34.

Foster, Roy. '*Faith Healer*', *Gate\Friel: A Celebration of the Work of Brian Friel* (programme). (Dublin: The Gate Theatre, 2009), n.p.

Friel, Brian, John Andrews, and Kevin Barry. '*Translations* and *A Paper Landscape*: Between Fiction and History', *The Crane Bag* 7.2 (1983), pp. 118–24.

Fulton, Helen. 'Hegemonic Discourses in Brian Friel's *The Freedom of the City*', *Language and Tradition in Ireland* (eds Maria Tymoczko and Colin Ireland) (Boston, MA: University of Massachusetts Press, 2003), pp. 62–83.

Fusco, Cassandra. 'The Dancer or the Dance? A Critical Analysis of Brian Friel's *Dancing at Lughnasa*', *Études Irlandaises* 21.1 (1996), pp. 109–26.

Garratt, Robert. 'Beyond Field Day: Brian Friel's *Dancing at Lughnasa*', *The State of Play: Irish Theatre in the Nineties* (ed. Eberhard Bort) (Trier: Wissenschaftlicher Verlag Trier, 1996), pp. 75–87.

Gauthier, Tim. 'Authenticity and Hybridity in the Post-Colonial Moment: Brian Friel's Field Day Plays', *A Companion to Brian Friel* (eds Richard Harp and Robert C. Evans) (West Cornwall, CT: Locust Hill Press, 2002), pp. 335–67.

Germanou, Maria. 'An American in Ireland: The Representation of the American in Brian Friel's Plays', *Comparative Drama* 38.2/3 (2004), pp. 259–76.

——'Brian Friel and the Scene of Writing: Reading *Give Me Your Answer, Do!*', *Modern Drama* 46.2 (2003), pp. 470–81.

Gleitman, Claire. 'Three Characters in Search of a Play: Brian Friel's *Faith Healer* and the Quest for Final Form', *New Hibernian Review* 13.1 (2009), pp. 95–108.

Grene, Nicholas. 'Brian Friel and the Sovereignty of Language', *Irish Theater International* 2.1 (2009), pp. 38–46.

——'Friel and Transparency', *Irish University Review* 29.1 (1999), pp. 136–44.

Harp, Richard. 'Manus and *Oedipus the King*', *A Companion to Brian Friel* (eds Richard Harp and Robert C. Evans) (West Cornwall, CT: Locust Hill Press, 2002), pp. 23–30.

Harris, Claudia. 'The Engendered Space: Performing Friel's Women from Cass McGuire to Molly Sweeney', *Brian Friel: A Casebook* (ed. William Kerwin) (New York: Garland Press, 1997), pp. 43–75.

Hawkins, Maureen. 'Schizophrenia and the Politics of Experience in Three Plays by Brian Friel', *Modern Drama* 39.3 (1996), pp. 465–74.

He, Chu. 'Brian Friel's Explorations of Trauma: *Volunteers* (1975) and *Living Quarters* (1977)', *New Hibernia Review* 18.2 (2014), pp. 121–36.

——'Brian Friel's Short Stories and Play Revisited: Orientating "The Visitation," "Foundry House," and *Aristocrats* in their Historical and Audience Contexts', *Estudios Irlandeses* 7 (2012), pp. 44–60.

——'Non-Modern Culture in Brian Friel's Plays', *ABEI Journal: The Brazilian Journal of Irish Studies* 16 (2014), pp. 97–108.

Heaney, Seamus. 'Digging Deeper', *Preoccupations: Selected Prose 1968–1978* (London: Faber and Faber, 1980), pp. 214–16.

——*Spelling It Out* (Dublin: Gallery Books, 2009).

——'*Translations* by Brian Friel', *Times Literary Supplement* 24 October 1980, p. 1199.

Hohenleitner, Kathleen. 'The Book at the Center of the Stage', *A Century of Irish Drama: Widening the Stage* (eds Stephen Watt, Eileen Morgan, and Shakir Mustafa) (Bloomington, IN: Indiana University Press, 2000), pp. 239–55.

Holstein, Suzy Clarkson. 'Carrying Across into Silence: Brian Friel's *Translations*', *Journal of the Midwest Modern Language Association* 37.2 (2004), pp. 1–10.

Imhof, Rudiger. 'Re-Writing History: A Fresh Look at Brian Friel's *Volunteers*', *The Canadian Journal of Irish Studies* 17.2 (1991), pp. 86–92.

Jent, William. 'Immaterial Contingencies: Relativizing the Rage for the Absolute in Brian Friel's *Wonderful Tennessee*', *The Canadian Journal of Irish Studies* 21.1 (1995), pp. 25–44.

——'Supranational Civics: Poverty and the Politics of Representation in Brian Friel's *The Freedom of the City*', *Modern Drama* 37.4 (1994), pp. 568–87.

Kearney, Richard. 'Language Play: Brian Friel and Ireland's Verbal Theatre', *Studies* LXXII (1983), pp. 20–55.

Kerrigan, John C. 'Swimming in Words: *Molly Sweeney*'s Dramatic Action', *A Companion to Brian Friel* (eds Richard Harp and Robert C. Evans) (West Cornwall, CT: Locust Hill Press, 2002), pp. 151–61.

Kiberd, Declan. 'Brian Friel's *Faith Healer*', *Irish Writers and Society at Large* (ed. Masaru Sekine) (Gerrards Cross: Colin Smythe, 1985), pp. 106–21.

Kimmer, Garland. '"Like Walking through Madame Tussaud's": The Catholic Ascendancy and Place in Brian Friel's *Aristocrats*', *Brian Friel: A Casebook* (ed. William Kerwin) (New York: Garland Publishing, 1997), pp. 193–210.

Kramer, Prapassaree. '*Dancing at Lughnasa*: Unexcused Absence', *Modern Drama* 43.2 (2000), pp. 171–81.

Krause, David. 'The Failed Words of Brian Friel', *Modern Drama* 40.3 (1997), pp. 359–73.

——'Friel's Ballybeggared Version of Chekhov', *Modern Drama* 42.4 (1999), pp. 634–49.

Lanters, José. 'Brian Friel's Uncertainty Principle', *Irish University Review* 29.1 (1999), pp. 162–75.

——'Gender and Identity in Brian Friel's *Faith Healer* and Thomas Murphy's *The Gigli Concert*', *Irish University Review* 22.2 (1992), pp. 278–90.

——'Violence and Sacrifice in Brian Friel's *The Gentle Island* and *Wonderful Tennessee*', *Irish University Review* 26.1 (1996), pp. 163–76.

Leavy, Adrienne. 'Brian Friel One Year On: A Critical Overview' *The Irish Times* (2 October 2016), irishtimes.com.

Lee, Josephine. 'Linguistic Imperialism, the Early Abbey Theatre, and the *Translations* of Brian Friel', *Imperialism and Theatre: Essays on World Theatre, Drama and Performance* (ed. J. Ellen Gainor) (London: Routledge, 1995), pp. 164–81.

Lin, Yu-chen. 'The *Unheimliche* in Brian Friel's *Faith Healer*: Memory, Aesthetics, Ethics', *Irish University Review* 40.2 (2010), pp. 71–85.

Lloyd, Michael. 'Brian Friel's Greek Tragedy: *Living Quarters*', *Irish University Review* 30.2 (2000), pp. 244–53.

Lojek, Helen. 'Beyond Lough Derg; *Wonderful Tennessee*'s Elusive Allusions', *The Canadian Journal of Irish Studies* 21.1 (1995), pp. 45–56.

——'Brian Friel's Gentle Island of Lamentation', *Irish University Review* 29.1 (1999), pp. 48–59.

——'Brian Friel's Plays and George Steiner's Linguistics: Translating the Irish', *Comparative Literature* 35.1 (1994), pp. 83–99.

——'Brian Friel's Sense of Place', *The Cambridge Companion to Twentieth-Century Irish Drama* (ed. Shaun Richards) (Cambridge: Cambridge University Press, 2004), pp. 177–90.

——'*Dancing at Lughnasa* and the Unfinished Revolution', *The Cambridge Companion to Brian Friel* (ed. Anthony Roche) (Cambridge: Cambridge University Press, 2006), pp. 78–90.

——'Space in *Wonderful Tennessee*', *Irish Theatre International* 2.1 (2009), pp. 48–61.

Lonergan, Patrick. '"Dancing on a One-Way Street": Irish Reactions to *Dancing at Lughnasa*', *Irish Theatre in America: Essays on Irish Theatre Diaspora* (ed. John Harrington) (Syracuse, NY: Syracuse University Press, 2009), pp. 147–62.

Lysandrou, Yvonne. 'Hugh O'Neill as "Hamlet-plus": (Post)colonialism and Dynamic Stasis in Brian Friel's *Making History*', *Irish Studies Review* 14.1 (2006), pp. 91–106.

Matthews, Kelly. 'Brian Friel, the BBC, and Ronald Mason', *Irish Studies Review* 47.3 (2017), pp. 470–85.

McGrath, F.C. 'Irish Babel: Brian Friel's *Translations* and George Steiner's *After Babel*', *Comparative Drama* 23.1 (1989), pp. 31–49.

McGuinness, Frank. '*Faith Healer*: All the Dead Voices', *Irish University Review* 29.1 (1999), pp. 60–63.

——'Surviving the 1960s: Three Plays by Brian Friel 1968–1971', *The Cambridge Companion to Brian Friel* (ed. Anthony Roche) (Cambridge: Cambridge University Press, 2006), pp. 18–29.

McMullan, Anna. 'Historical Legacies and Unhomely Cultural Memories in Brian Friel's *The Home Place*', *Nordic Irish Studies* 13.1 (2014), pp. 189–203.

——'*The Home Place*: Unhomely Inheritances', *Irish Theatre International* 2.1 (2009), pp. 62–68.

——'"In touch with some otherness": Gender, Authority and the Body in *Dancing at Lughnasa*', *Irish University Review* 29.1 (1999), pp. 90–100.

McVeagh, John. '"A Kind of *Comhar*": Charles Macklin and Brian Friel', *The Achievement of Brian Friel* (ed. Alan Peacock) (Gerrards Cross: Colin Smythe, 1993), pp. 215–28.

Mesterházi, Márton. 'A Practitioner's View of Brian Friel's *Wonderful Tennessee*', *Hungarian Journal of English and American Studies* 2.2 (1996), pp. 143–53.

Moloney, Karen. 'Molly Astray: Revisioning Ireland in Brian Friel's *Molly Sweeney*', *Twentieth-Century Literature* 46.3 (2000), pp. 285–311.

Morgan, Hiram. '*Making History*: A Criticism and a Manifesto', *Text and Context* 4 (1990), pp. 61–65.

Murray, Christopher. 'Brian Friel's *Molly Sweeney* and Its Sources: A Postmodern Case History', *Études Irlandaises* 23.2 (1998), pp. 81–98.

——'Friel's "Emblems of Adversity" and the Yeatsian Example', *The Achievement of Brian Friel* (ed. Alan Peacock) (Gerrards Cross: Colin Smythe, 1993), pp. 69–90.

——'Palimpsest: Two Languages as One in *Translations*', *Brian Friel's Dramatic Artistry: 'The Work Has Value'* (eds Donald E. Morse, Csilla Bertha, and Mária Kurdi) (Dublin: Carysfort Press, 2006), pp. 93–108.

——'"Recording Tremors": Friel's *Dancing at Lughnasa* and the Uses of Tradition', *Brian Friel: A Casebook* (ed. William Kerwin) (New York: Garland Press, 1997), pp. 23–41.

Ní Anluain, Clíodhna. (ed.) 'Brian Friel', *Reading the Future: Irish Writers in Conversation with Mike Murphy* (Dublin: The Lilliput Press, 2000), pp. 59–78.

Niel, Ruth. 'Digging into History: A Reading of Brian Friel's *Volunteers* and Seamus Heaney's "Viking Dublin: Trial Pieces"', *Irish University Review* 16.1 (1986), pp. 35–47.

——'Non-realistic Techniques in the Plays of Brian Friel: The Debt to International Drama', *Literary Interrelations: Ireland, England and the World, 2, Comparison and Impact* (eds Wolfgang Zach and Heinz Kosok) (Tübingen: Gunter Narr Verlag), pp. 349–59.

North, Jonathan. 'The "Big Five" of Irish Drama', *Ulster Week* (6 January 1965), pp. 3, 8.

O'Brien, George. 'The Late Plays', *The Cambridge Companion to Twentieth-Century Irish Drama* (ed. Shaun Richards) (Cambridge: Cambridge University Press, 2004), pp. 91–103.

——'"Meet Brian Friel": The *Irish Press* Columns', *Irish University Review* 29.1 (1999), pp. 30–41.

O'Grady, Thomas B. 'Insubstantial Father and Consubstantial Sons: A Note on Patrimony and Patricide in Friel and Leonard', *The Canadian Journal of Irish Studies* 15.1 (1989): 71–79.

O'Hanlon, Redmond. 'Brian Friel's Dialogue with Euripides: *Living Quarters*', *Theatre Stuff: Critical Essays on Contemporary Irish Theatre* (ed. Eamonn Jordan) (Dublin: Carysfort Press, 2000), pp. 107–21.

O'Malley-Younger, Alison. 'There's No "Race" Like Home: Race, Place, and Nation in Brian Friel's *Home Place*', *Nordic Irish Studies* 5.1 (2006), pp. 165–79.

O'Toole, Fintan. 'Marking Time: From *Making History* to *Dancing at Lughnasa*', *The Achievement of Brian Friel* (ed. Alan Peacock) (Gerrards Cross: Colin Smythe, 1993), pp. 202–14.

——'The Truth According to Brian Friel', *The Irish Times* 2 October 2015, p. 6.

Onkey, Lauren. 'The Woman as Nation in Brian Friel's *Translations*', *Brian Friel: A Casebook* (ed. William Kerwin) (New York: Garland Press, 1997), pp. 159–74.

Parker, Michael. 'Forms of Redress: Structure and Characterization in *The Freedom of the City*', *Brian Friel's Dramatic Artistry: 'The Work Has Value'* (eds Donald E. Morse, Csilla Bertha, and Mária Kurdi) (Dublin: Carysfort Press, 2006), pp. 271–300.

———'Telling Tales: Narratives of Politics and Sexuality in Brian Friel's *The Gentle Island*', *Hungarian Journal of English and American Studies* 2.2 (1996), pp. 59–86.

Paulin, Tom. 'Commencement', *The Communication Cord* (Programme) (Belfast: Nicholson and Bass, 1982), n.p.

Peacock, Alan. 'Translating the Past: Friel, Greece and Rome', *The Achievement of Brian Friel* (ed. Alan Peacock) (Gerrards Cross: Colin Smythe, 1993), pp. 113–33.

Peacock, Alan, and Kathleen Devine. '"In touch with some otherness": The Double Vision of Brian Friel's *Dancing at Lughnasa*', *Études Irlandaises* 17.1 (1992), pp. 113–27.

Pelletier, Martine. 'New Articulations of Irishness and Otherness on the Contemporary Irish Stage', *Irish Literature since 1990: Diverse Voices* (eds Scott Brewster and Michael Parker) (Manchester: Manchester University Press, 2009), pp. 98–117.

Pine, Richard. 'Brian Friel and Contemporary Irish Drama', *Colby Quarterly* 27.4 (1991), pp. 190–201.

———'Friel's Irish Russia', *The Cambridge Companion to Brian Friel* (ed. Anthony Roche) (Cambridge: Cambridge University Press, 2006), pp. 104–16.

———'Love: Brian Friel's *Give Me Your Answer Do!*', *Irish University Review* 29.1 (1999), pp. 176–88.

———'What Is a Writer?', *Give Me Your Answer Do!* (programme) (Dublin: The Abbey Theatre, 1997), n.p.

Pirnie, Karen. 'Dancing at the Movies: Critical Reception of the Film *Dancing at Lughnasa*', *A Companion to Brian Friel* (eds Richard Harp and Robert C. Evans) (West Cornwall, CT: Locust Hill Press, 2002), pp. 91–106

Richards, Shaun. 'Brian Friel: Seizing the Moment of Flux', *Renegotiating and Resisting Nationalism in 20th-Century Irish Drama* (ed. Scott Boltwood) (Gerrards Cross: Colin Smythe, 2009), pp. 81–96.

———'Field Day's Fifth Province: Avenue or Impasse?', *Culture and Politics in Northern Ireland 1960–1990* (ed. Eamonn Hughes) (Milton Keynes: Open University Press, 1991), pp. 139–50.

———'Placed Identities in Placeless Times: Brian Friel and Post-Colonial Criticism', *Irish University Review* 27.1 (1997), pp. 55–68.

Robinson, Paul N. 'Brian Friel's *Faith Healer*: An Irishman Comes Back Home', *Literary Interrelations: Ireland, England and the World—National Images and Stereotypes* (eds Wolfgang Zach and Heinz Kosok) (Tübingen: Gunter Narr Verlag, 1987), pp. 223–27.

Roche, Anthony. 'Family Affairs: Friel's Plays of the Late 1970s', *The Cambridge Companion to Brian Friel* (ed. Anthony Roche) (Cambridge: Cambridge University Press, 2006), pp. 41–52.

———'Friel and Synge: Towards a Theatrical Language', *Irish University Review* 29.1 (1999), pp. 145–61.

Rollins, Ron. 'Friel's *Dancing at Lughnasa*: Memory, Ritual, and Two Messengers for the Gods', *The Canadian Journal of Irish Studies* 19.2 (1993), pp. 81–86.

Rollins, Ronald. 'Friel's *Translations*: The Ritual of Naming', *The Canadian Journal of Irish Studies* 11.1 (1985), pp. 35–43.

Rollins, Ron, and Nita Rollins, '*The Loves of Cass McGuire*: Friel's Wagnerian Music Drama', *The Canadian Journal of Irish Studies* 16.1 (1990), pp. 24–32.

Russell, Richard Rankin. 'Brian Friel's Short Fiction: Place, Community, and Modernity', *Irish University Review* 42.2 (2012), pp. 298–326.

——'Home, Exile, and Unease in Brian Friel's Globalized Drama since 1990: *Molly Sweeney*, *The Home Place*, and *Hedda Gabler (after Ibsen)*', *Modern Drama* 56.2 (2013), pp. 206–31.

Salaris, Lucia Angelica. 'The Masks of Language in *Translations*', *Perspectives of Irish Drama and Theatre* (eds Jacqueline Genet and Richard Allen Cave) (Gerrards Cross: Colin Smythe, 1991), pp. 101–6.

Schneider, Ulrich. 'Staging History in Contemporary Anglo-Irish Drama: Brian Friel and Frank McGuinness', *The Crows Behind the Plow: History and Violence in Anglo-Irish Poetry and Drama* (ed. Geert Lernout) (Amsterdam: Editions Rodopi, 1991), pp. 79–98.

Schrank, Bernice. 'Politics, Language, Metatheatre: Friel's *Freedom of the City* and the Formation of an Engaged Audience', *Theatre Stuff: Critical Essays on Contemporary Irish Theatre* (ed. Eamonn Jordan) (Dublin: Carysfort Press, 2000), pp. 122–44.

Smith, Robert. 'The Hermeneutic Motion in Brian Friel's *Translations*', *Modern Drama* 34 (1991), pp. 392–408.

Strain, Margaret M. '"Renouncing Change": Salvation and the Sacred in Brian Friel's *Faith Healer*', *Renascence* 57.1 (2004), pp. 63–83.

Tallone, Giovanna. 'Restless Wanderers and Great Pretenders: Brian Friel's Fox Melarkey and Frank Hardy', *Brian Friel's Dramatic Artistry: 'The Work Has Value'* (eds Donald E. Morse, Csilla Bertha, and Mária Kurdi) (Dublin: Carysfort Press, 2006), pp. 35–60.

——'Unveiling the Vice: A Reading of *Faith Healer*', *Brian Friel's Dramatic Artistry: 'The Work Has Value'* (eds Donald E. Morse, Csilla Bertha, and Mária Kurdi) (Dublin: Carysfort Press, 2006), pp. 123–39.

Temple, Julia. 'The Gift of Sight in *Molly Sweeney*', *A Companion to Brian Friel* (eds Richard Harp and Robert C. Evans) (West Cornwall, CT: Locust Hill Press, 2002), pp. 133–49.

Thornton, R.K.R. 'Friel and Shaw: Dreams and Responsibilities', *Irish Writing: Exile and Subversion* (ed. Paul Hyland and Neil Sammells) (New York: St. Martin's Press, 1991), pp. 224–33.

Throne, Marilyn. 'The Disintegration of Authority: A Study of the Fathers in Five Plays of Brian Friel', *Colby Library Quarterly* 23.3 (1988), pp. 162–72.

Timm, Eitel F. 'Modern Mind, Myth, and History: Brian Friel's *Translations*', *Studies in Anglo-Irish Literature* (ed. Heinz Kosok) (Bonn: Bouvier, 1982), pp. 447–54.

Tompkins, Joanne. 'Breaching the Body's Boundaries: Abjected Subject Positions in Postcolonial Drama', *Modern Drama* 40.4 (1997), pp. 502–13.

Tracy, Robert. 'Brian Friel's Rituals of Memory', *Irish University Review* 37.2 (2007), pp. 395–412.

——'The Russian Connection: Friel and Chekhov', *Irish University Review* 29.1 (1999), pp. 64–77.

Tranier, Jacques. '"Foundry House" et *Aristocrats* de Brian Friel: Genèse d'un drame', *Études Irlandaises* 17.1 (1992), pp. 97–112.

Watt, Stephen. 'Friel and the Northern Ireland "Troubles" play', *The Cambridge Companion to Twentieth-Century Irish Drama* (ed. Anthony Roche) (Cambridge: Cambridge University Press, 2004), pp. 30–40.

White, Harry. 'Brian Friel and the Condition of Music', *Irish University Review* 29.1 (1999), pp. 6–15.

——'Brian Friel, Thomas Murphy and the Use of Music in Contemporary Irish Drama', *Modern Drama* 33.4 (1990), pp. 553–62.

Wiley, Catherine. 'Recreating Ballybeg: Two Translations by Brian Friel', *Journal of Dramatic Theory and Criticism* 1.2 (1987), pp. 51–61.

Winkler, Elizabeth Hale. 'Brian Friel's *The Freedom of the City*: Historical Actuality and Dramatic Imagination', *The Canadian Journal of Irish Studies* 7.1 (1980), pp. 12–31.

Worthen, W.B. 'Homeless Words: Field Day and the Politics of Translation', *Modern Drama* 38 (1995), pp. 22–41.

Wyse, Bruce. 'Traumatizing Romanticism in Brian Friel's *Faith Healer*', *Modern Drama* 47.3 (2004), pp. 446–63.

Yang, Cheng-hao. 'Irish Nationalism and Its Discontents: Brian Friel's *Communication Cord*', *Sochow Journal of Foreign Languages and Cultures* 24 (2007), pp. 35–63.

York, Richard. 'Friel's Russia', *The Achievement of Brian Friel* (ed. Alan Peacock) (Gerrards Cross: Colin Smythe, 1993), pp. 164–77.

General Criticism with Chapters on Brian Friel and General Background

Bardon, Jonathan. *A History of Ulster* (Belfast: The Blackstaff Press, 1992).

Barnes, Philip. *A Companion to Post-War British Theatre* (Totowa, NJ: Barnes and Noble, 1986).

Bell, Sam Hanna. *The Theatre in Ulster* (Dublin: Gill and Macmillan, 1972).

Billington, Michael. *The 101 Greatest Plays from Antiquity to the Present* (London: Faber & Faber, 2015).

Boltwood, Scott. 'Dion Boucicault: From Stage Irishman to Staging Nationalism', *A Companion to Irish Literature*, Vol. 1 (ed. Julia M. Wright) (Oxford: Blackwell Publishing, 2010), pp. 460–75.

Burke, Edmund. *Two Classics of the French Revolution: Reflections on the Revolution in France and The Rights of Man* (New York: Doubleday, 1989).

Cairns, David, and Shaun Richards. *Writing Ireland: Colonialism, Nationalism and Culture* (Manchester: Manchester University Press, 1988).

Deane, Seamus. *Celtic Revivals. Essays in Modern Irish Literature 1880–1980* (London: Faber and Faber, 1985).

Etherton, Michael. *Contemporary Irish Dramatists* (New York: St. Martin's Press, 1989).

Grene, Nicholas. *The Politics of Irish Drama: Plays in Context from Boucicault to Friel* (Cambridge: Cambridge University Press, 1999).

Harrington, John. *The Irish Play on the New York Stage, 1874–1966* (Lexington, KY: The University Press of Kentucky, 1997).

Hogan, Robert. *After the Irish Renaissance: A Critical History of the Irish Drama since The Plow and the Stars* (Minneapolis: The University of Minnesota Press, 1967).

——'Old Boys, Young Bucks, and New Women: The Contemporary Irish Story', *The Irish Short Story* (ed. James F. Kilroy) (Boston, MA: Twayne Publishers, 1984), pp. 169–215.

——'*Since O'Casey' and Other Essays on Irish Drama* (Gerrards Cross: Colin Smythe, 1983).

Kearney, Richard. *Postnationalist Ireland: Politics, Culture, Philosophy* (London: Routledge, 1997).

Kiberd, Declan. *Inventing Ireland: The Literature of the Modern Nation* (Cambridge, MA: Harvard University Press, 1999).

——*The Irish Writer and the World* (Cambridge: Cambridge University Press, 2005).

Kirkland, Richard. *Literature and Culture in Northern Ireland since 1965: Moments of Danger* (London: Longman, 1996).

Llewellyn-Jones, Margaret. *Contemporary Irish Drama and Cultural Identity* (Bristol: Intellect Books, 2002).

Lonergan, Patrick. *Theatre and Globalization: Irish Drama in the Celtic Tiger Era* (Houndmills: Palgrave Macmillan, 2010).

Longley, Edna. *Poetry in the Wars* (Newcastle upon Tyne: Bloodaxe Books, 1986).

MacNeill, Máire. *The Festival of Lughnasa: A Study of the Survival of the Celtic Festival of the Beginning of Harvest* (Oxford: Oxford University Press, 1962).

Maguire, Tom. *Making Theatre in Northern Ireland: Through and beyond the Troubles* (Exeter: University of Exeter Press, 2006).

Maxwell, D.E.S. *A Critical History of Modern Irish Drama, 1891–1980* (Cambridge: Cambridge University Press, 1985).

Morash, Christopher. *A History of Irish Theatre, 1601–2000* (Cambridge: Cambridge University Press, 2002).

Mulholland, Marc. *Northern Ireland: A Very Short Introduction* (Oxford: Oxford University Press, 2002).

Murray, Christopher. *Twentieth-Century Irish Drama: Mirror up to Nation* (Manchester: Manchester University Press, 1997).

Pilkington, Lionel. 'The Abbey Theatre and the Irish State', *The Cambridge Companion to Twentieth-Century Irish Drama* (ed. Anthony Roche) (Cambridge: Cambridge University Press, 2004), pp. 231–43.

——*Theatre and the State in Twentieth-Century Ireland: Cultivating the People* (London: Routledge, 2001).

Richards, Shaun. 'Throwing Theory at Ireland? The Field Day Theatre Company and Postcolonial Theatre Criticism', *Modern Drama* 47.4 (2004), pp. 607–23.

Richtarik, Marilynn J. *Acting Between the Lines: The Field Day Theatre Company and Irish Cultural Politics, 1980–1984* (Oxford: Oxford University Press, 2001).

Roche, Anthony. *Contemporary Irish Drama from Beckett to McGuinness* (Dublin: Gill and Macmillan, 1994).

Steiner, George. *After Babel: Aspects of Language and Translation* (Oxford: Oxford University Press, 1975).

Trotter, Mary. *Modern Irish Theatre* (Cambridge: Polity Press, 2008).

Welch, Robert. *The Abbey Theatre, 1899–1999: Form and Pressure* (Oxford: Oxford University Press, 1999).

——*Changing States: Transformations in Modern Irish Literature* (London: Routledge, 1993).

INDEX

Printed in Great Britain
by Amazon

61635761R00108